Pathways to Professorsh

CW01497941

People who become professors are experts in their field. But how does a new academic, aspiring to become a professor, choose a field of study and plan a career that leads to professorship? This practical book answers this question, guiding aspiring academics step by step through the areas in which they need to demonstrate excellence if they are to gain the international recognition and professional profile that lead to a professorial post.

Each chapter highlights real-life, internationally applicable examples of what successful achievements look like and what pitfalls to be aware of. Supported by an international survey of professors and their experiences working within university systems, the chapters outline key topics relevant to any aspiring professor. For example:

- Criteria for obtaining a professorship
- Carving out a specialist research niche
- Establishing an international reputation
- Advice on getting your research published
- Undertaking impactful research and winning funding
- Networking and developing a media presence
- Balancing research, teaching and your personal life

This must-have book is filled with tips and practical advice for building an academic career and is an essential read for anyone looking to better understand routes into professorship.

Marilyn Leask has been Professor at four universities and is co-chair of the international MESHGuides research knowledge mobilisation initiative (www.meshguides.org).

Pathways to Professorship

A Toolkit for Success

Marilyn Leask

Routledge
Taylor & Francis Group

LONDON AND NEW YORK

Designed cover image: © Getty Images

First published 2023
by Routledge
4 Park Square, Milton Park, Abingdon, Oxon OX14 4RN

and by Routledge
605 Third Avenue, New York, NY 10158

Routledge is an imprint of the Taylor & Francis Group, an informa business

British Library Cataloguing-in-Publication Data
A catalogue record for this book is available from the British Library

Library of Congress Cataloging-in-Publication Data
Names: Leask, Marilyn, 1950– author.
Title: Pathways to professorship : a toolkit for success / Marilyn Leask.
Description: Abingdon, Oxon ; New York, NY : Routledge, 2023. | Includes bibliographical references and index.
Identifiers: LCCN 2022058047 (print) | LCCN 2022058048 (ebook) | ISBN 9781032108919 (paperback) | ISBN 9781032076430 (hardback) | ISBN 9781003217596 (ebook)
Subjects: LCSH: College teachers—Vocational guidance. | College teachers—Tenure.
Classification: LCC LB1778 .L43 2023 (print) | LCC LB1778 (ebook) | DDC 378.1/2—dc23/eng/20230221
LC record available at https://lccn.loc.gov/2022058047
LC ebook record available at https://lccn.loc.gov/2022058048

ISBN: 978-1-032-07643-0 (hbk)
ISBN: 978-1-032-10891-9 (pbk)
ISBN: 978-1-003-21759-6 (ebk)

DOI: 10.4324/9781003217596

Typeset in Galliard
by Apex CoVantage, LLC

Access the Support Material: www.routledge.com/9781032108919

Online resources

These resources can be downloaded, printed, used to copy/paste text, and/ or manipulated to suit your individualised use. You can access the downloads by visiting this book's product page on our website: www.routledge.com/ 9781032108919 (then follow the links indicating related resources, which you can then download directly to your computer).

- Table 1.3 Checklist: your outline ten-year plan
- Table 2.5 Checklist: assessing your opportunities to meet the teaching, research and service criteria
- Table 3.2 Checklist: balancing teaching and research
- Table 4.2 Checklist: becoming recognised as an expert
- Table 5.3 Checklist: mentors and networks
- Table 6.1 Checklist: building your media presence and political impact
- Table 7.1 Analysing the pros and cons of particular digital tools
- Table 7.2 Checklist: your digital technology checklist and training plan
- Table 8.3 Checklist: for use when you are preparing a book proposal
- Table 9.1 Checklist: your publication plan for your articles
- Table 10.1 Checklist: building your strategies for applying for research funding
- Table 11.1 Checklist: looking forward to taking a leadership role in your discipline and in your university

This book is dedicated to my mother, Betty Markwell (née McVey, 1926–2018) who lobbied the Queensland Government for a secondary school to be built in our rural town in time for her children, including me, to be educated. Without her efforts and vision, I would not have been in a position to write this book.

This book is also dedicated to the professors of tomorrow. I hope you enjoy the pursuit of knowledge as much as I have. My main piece of advice is to carry a notebook or use the notes function on your phone so you can capture the ideas and insights from your research, which will come to you at the most unexpected times – such is the way the mind works. If you do this, then when you sit down to write, you will have ideas to shape into prose and will never be faced with starting your writing with a blank page.

Contents

8   Publishing books   102

MARILYN LEASK WITH CONTRIBUTIONS FROM ROUTLEDGE
COLLEAGUES

**9   Writing academic articles for publication and developing
your academic profile**   120

SARAH YOUNIE

Tables

Figures

Foreword

It gives me great pleasure to write a foreword for this very important and timely book. I have had the pleasure of collaborating with Marilyn Leask as she has led efforts to mobilise translational pedagogical content knowledge to a global scale. As someone who has held academic positions on three continents (Australia, Europe and the United States) and achieved the rank of professor at large private and public university systems in the United States, I am excited to continue to support her efforts in mobilising knowledge about the pathways to professorship. Now more than ever we need to provide guidance to the next generation of professors, as senior academics across the globe are re-evaluating their careers and lifestyles in the wake of the pandemic. Before we lose their wisdom from our institutions, our professors must provide guidance to those who seek to rise to the rank of professor. This book provides these individuals with a comprehensive playbook for achieving the milestones and recognition expected of professors across the globe.

The input of authors from different countries represents a rich source of advice to inform the career development of the next generation of professors at any institution. The international research base and benchmarks included in this text extend well beyond anecdotes of personal experience to raise awareness of the diversity of career stages and promotion pathways that exist at university campuses around the world. Common to all contexts are the needs for professors to publish quality articles, conduct internationally significant research, secure research grants, mentor PhD candidates to completion and, of course, develop an international profile as an expert in a field. Providing professorial candidates with this level of clarity early in their careers provides them with a set of design considerations as they plan their ten-year journey to professorship.

Earning recognition as an expert in a field represents one of the major challenges of professorship. The authors provide readers with advice on: creating a niche; developing a multi-year research programme; scaling up small-scale research; and networking beyond your institution to elevate the impact of your grant work. This advice is couched within the principle of balancing the competing demands teaching, research and service expectations. Readers of *Pathways to Professorship* will discover the importance of professional service opportunities, including strategic roles in national and international professional associations, for earning recognition as an expert in their field.

Marilyn Leask is an expert in the field of professorial career development. She has been a full professor or a visiting professor at four UK universities. Over a 55-year career, she has met all the benchmarks described in this book and held roles both in professional associations and within a UK government organisation. Her ongoing passion for mobilising research-informed knowledge on a global scale, positions her as the ideal author of *Pathways to Professorship*.

My pathway to professorship was a mix of enjoying success and rebounding from rejection. Having a playbook like this, for achieving the milestones and earning recognition required of a professor, would have provided me with a higher level of clarity and a more direct route to professorship. Nevertheless, this book now provides me with the ideal playbook for mentoring the next generation of professors as they shape the future of higher education across the globe.

James. G O'Meara

Professor and Dean of the College of Education,
Texas A&M International University
Immediate Past President of the International Council on
Education for Teaching
Immediate Past Co-Lead for the International Task Force on
Teachers for Education 2030 Thematic group on
Inclusion and Equity in Teacher Policies and Practices
US focal person for the Teacher Task Force for Education 2030

Preface

In this preface, I want to tell you how and why this book came into being. It may be that you will recognise what drives you to want to become a professor if you understand why I have written this book for you, with the help of my wonderful colleagues from 20 or so countries.

Are you driven to write, as I am? I write to understand clearly what I know and to document the experiences and research that underpin my knowledge.

I am curious and I think I have always been. I am an annoying person to some, as I question everything. I like to know how things work, how things are done and why. I like to learn new things. I am fortunate in finding a group of friends, principally through the professional associations I am a member of, who are like-minded and have been my professional collaborators with our research and writing partnerships, enduring for more than 30 years.

I write articles to share outcomes from research projects or to raise philosophical questions related to my discipline.

I author books to answer questions that puzzle me. Writing a book helps me to understand, explore and record what I know and to guide and structure my research into areas I want to know more about.

I co-author with others as I find that I learn this way and that the work we produce is more accurate and more deeply rooted in theory and practice.

For me, a highlight of academic life is working collaboratively with colleagues, and with higher degree students, to push the boundaries of knowledge. I love the process of the creation of new ideas and the insights into challenges that come from engagement with the minds of others across cultures and disciplines. If you are an academic or thinking of becoming an academic, I hope you get to experience this meeting of minds and the exhilaration that comes from the creation of new knowledge.

So, why did I write this book? While I have had a surprising, unpredictable and ultimately satisfying career over 55 years in the workforce, I can see how, if I had had access to different sorts of advice at key points in my life, I might have had an easier and more productive working life. Mentors at particular stages of my life opened doors for me, and this book is a way of paying forward – opening doors for others – as a thank you to those who did this for me.

By way of personal background, I grew up in rural Australia, and due to my mother's lobbying of the government, a secondary school was built in time for me to be educated. I started work at 17 and studied part-time for about 20 years. Initially I gained a diploma in radiography in Australia in 1970, after which I moved to the UK. I studied part-time with the Open University and gained an undergraduate humanities degree in 1980, when I was 30 with two children, a divorce and remarriage. A post-graduate qualification in teaching (my only full-time study) led to a career in education, a Master of Philosophy degree (and a third child) in 1997/8 and a doctorate in 2008. Careful management of my time has been essential, and I hope this book enables you to use your time wisely. Each hour is a valuable resource you cannot reclaim once it is gone.

Some of the research I have been involved in has led to long-term change and opportunities for many people. I am particularly proud of initiating in 1995, with Swedish civil servant Ulf Lundin, the European SchoolNet initiative (www.EUN. org), which is now supported by 34 ministries of education across Europe, and establishing the Learning to Teach in the Secondary School series of textbooks in 1992, which are published by Routledge. The tenth edition of the core textbook is under development as I write this. These textbooks are the main textbooks used for secondary teacher education in the UK.

I was fortunate to be a researcher just as personal computers become ubiquitous and then as the internet became widely available and usable for professional purposes. In the period from 1992 to 2010, governments put substantial funds into research into the usefulness of the new form of technology and into developing online research repositories for professional groups. However, those of us involved in these early developments, particularly development of government-funded knowledge banks for professionals, were in for a rude awakening.

The early 21st century brought a shocking destruction of academic work – including mine – when academics found that government-funded and published online resources simply disappeared from government websites when there was a change of administration and the existing work was not supported by the incoming government. In those early days of the internet, nobody imagined that an incoming government would, for ideological reasons ('it wasn't our idea'), take off-line research and teaching materials verified by experts and funded by the taxpayer to the tune of tens of millions of whatever the local currency was. But they did. The World Bank commissioned a review about what happened to these early knowledge banks (Truman and Dykes, 2017, p. 209). The review shows that the knowledge banks and accompanying services that seem to have survived were either funded through partnerships, so that the decision by one partner did not mean that everything was taken off-line, or they were transferred from government control to private or charitable ownership. These experiences across a number of countries guide the advice in the book about being careful to keep ownership of your work or to ensure that it cannot be suppressed or destroyed.

Dr Carol Hordatt Gentles and I conducted research for this book with 27 professors with experience in more than 30 countries across the five UNESCO regions. We were looking for differences in practice and factors in common across countries and institutions that smooth the pathway to professorship.

These professors contributed data about their experience in becoming a professor and on the procedures in the institutions they know about, so you will come across examples of different practices as you read the book.

I hope the advice in the book helps you plan and navigate your career pathway so that you are able to manage a balance between academic life, which is so demanding of your time, and your family and social life, and that in time you earn the privilege of being awarded professorial status.

Marilyn Leask
April 2023

Reference

Truman, M. and Dykes, G. (2017) *Building and Sustaining National Educational Technology Agencies: Lessons, Models and Case Studies from Around the World.*, Washington, DC: World Bank, https://openknowledge.worldbank.org/handle/10986/26507, Accessed on 26 October 2022.

Introduction
How to use this book

There is, of course, no guarantee that if you follow the advice in this book to map out and plan your personal pathway to professorship that you will ultimately achieve the status of professor. However, if you do not have a route map to guide your decisions, then you may find after some years that you have not developed the deep expertise, research and publication record and peer recognition that lead naturally to professorship.

To create your personal pathway to professorship, you will need to adapt the advice here to the procedures and criteria used in your institution or in an institution that you are thinking of applying to.

It is very easy in academia to have your time taken up with administration and teaching, leaving no time for research and writing; in any case, unless you win research funding, the money to fund your salary is likely to come from teaching. Professors' dedication to their subjects can mean that they spend much of their personal time researching and writing. I myself have found that working with colleagues on research and writing projects has helped accelerate the completion of articles and books, but in some countries, you will find pressure to produce sole authored work. This requirement dates from the pre-internet era, but you may have to do this if that is what is required.

Throughout the book, you are invited to assess what you might do to achieve the criteria for a professorial appointment. Photocopiable and downloadable/ checklists with questions to prompt your thinking and planning are available at the end of each chapter. These are freely available for photocopy or download via the Support Material tab on the Routledge website. The websites and references give you access to background papers.

Most professors mentioned that mentors are invaluable: experienced professors from whom they could learn and who could give advice about getting published, about bidding for research funds and so on. You will need to look for your own mentors, and in Chapter 5 Carol Hordatt Gentles provides you with a summary of advice from the professorial panel.

Meeting of the criteria for professorship depends on decisions you make about:

- the topic of your doctoral and post-doctoral research;
- where to work and where not to work;
- whether to change country or location;
- whether to join professional associations and dedicate personal time to the association as a way of providing a service to your discipline as well as building your professional network, consultancy and publication and research collaboration opportunities;
- whether you feel able to say 'no' to requests for your time that mean you have significantly less research and writing time than you would normally have.

It is very easy to find excuses for not researching (no funding), for not publishing (no time) and for having a career where you teach a wide range of general courses, which then cuts down the time you have to develop your specialist knowledge: not only are you not teaching in your specialist area, but your students also are not writing assignments in your specialist area. Reading assignments addressing questions in your field provides you automatically with up-to-date knowledge. When you set assignments, setting these to address issues in your field can easily lead to co-publishing with your students, which in turn builds your personal network of co-researchers.

I once compared my annual university teaching responsibilities with a colleague. Because I was teaching in a niche area, every lecture was unique. My colleague, however, taught four groups of students the same programme so her preparation time was a quarter of mine, plus she co-taught and co-planned with colleagues. However, the majority of the assignments that I assessed accelerated my personal and professional development as students researched and wrote about topics relevant to my research interests.

Opportunities to be mentored by experts in your field, for research funding, for time to research and for promotion within your field vary within and between universities and from year to year. You may have the advantage of being in a university with a large endowment and internally available research funding (University of Oxford, 2022; Harvard University, 2022). Alternatively, you may find yourself in a university where few staff research and publish, and there is little funding for research. You require stamina, resilience and persistence as well as the ability to work with the slivers of time available to you to build an academic career.

From the beginning of this book, you are asked to keep notes about how the advice might apply to you and your personal career path. I advise you to set yourself publication goals, and to consider this advice that I was given by a US academic. If, as a young academic, you have no research funds or chance of winning funds, consider having as one of the foundations to your research a topic following trends in your discipline that is important to society at large and about which you can gather data through a low-cost or free annual survey. The IT specialist colleague who advised me started carrying out annual surveys of first year undergraduate students' use of social media. Within a couple of years, he had a bank of data that he could use to identify trends, challenges and emerging possibilities and to advise governments and businesses, and which provided a foundation for a regular stream of articles and, in time, books. No one else had these data. His promotion was rapid.

Might you do something like this for your discipline?

Another colleague undertakes 'systematic reviews' of key topics, thus becoming more deeply expert in the field than others and producing material for seminal articles that show the state of play in research-based knowledge in a particular aspect of a discipline.

Might you do something like this for your discipline?

I hope you find this book useful. I know if I had had access to this advice at the beginning of my career, I would have made different decisions: I would have been more alert to opportunities, been more selective in what I took on, been more careful to be named appropriately on research papers, made more use of the media and kept the right to publish my research outputs if funders made research reports unavailable.

With best wishes for your career,

Marilyn Leask
April 2023

Acknowledgements

Following a 55-year-long career with only one year when I was a full-time student and about 20 years part-time study, I have many people to thank for opening gateways that led me down the paths of learning and gave me the experience and confidence to write this book.

I would like to thank those whose mentoring enabled me to have an amazing, life-changing career.

In particular, I thank those who interviewed me for jobs that enabled me to develop my knowledge and expertise and who weren't threatened by the prospect of an enthusiastic (over-enthusiastic?) employee.

I thank those who founded the Open University in the UK, which allowed me, as a working single parent, to complete my undergraduate degree.

In chronological order of their mentoring, I owe my career to: Tony Turner and Jenny Frost, my Science and Computing PGCE tutors at the Institute of Education, University of London, who gave me an introduction to university teaching when they invited me, as a newly qualified teacher, to give lectures to student teachers; Del Goddard, Chief Education Adviser in the London Borough of Enfield, UK; Professor Helen Simons, Institute of Education, University of London; and Professor David Hopkins, Cambridge Institute of Education, who all introduced me to qualitative research and provided the opportunity for me to become a researcher.

Other mentors include: Professor David Hargreaves, University of Cambridge; Professor Peter Walden, University of Bedfordshire; Chris Dee and Tim Tarrant, civil servants with whom I worked at the UK government agency the Training and Development Agency for Schools; and fellow board members of the following professional organisations: the Universities Council for the Education of Teachers, the British Educational Research Association, the UK Council for Subject Associations, the International Council on Education for Teaching, the Education Futures Collaboration charity and the authors of the MESHGuides (www.meshguides.org).

Contributors

Irma Eloff is a professor of Educational Psychology at the University of Pretoria, in South Africa, a registered educational psychologist and a member of the Academy of Science of South Africa (ASSAf). She is a former dean of education at the University of Pretoria. In 2018, she was awarded a *Förderkreis 1669 Wissenschafft Gesellschaft* professorship at the University of Innsbruck. She has authored 100+ scholarly articles and book chapters and edited six book publications. Irma is an alumnus of the Universities of Pretoria, Stellenbosch, Northwest and the GIBS Business School. She is an adjunct professor at the University of Innsbruck, Austria.

Ling Siew Eng is a professor in mathematics at Universiti Teknologi MARA (UiTM), Sarawak branch, Malaysia. She was a mathematics teacher from 1989–May 2002 before she joined UiTM in July 2002. Her area of research is on STEM education, especially blended learning. She has been actively involved in mathematics motivation camps and mathematics workshops, and as a motivator for various programmes in helping Indigenous students to learn mathematics. In addition, she was a speaker in various programmes to improve students' interest and motivation in mathematics ranging from primary school to university level. She is also actively involved in developing e-content, MOOC courses and digitised teaching and learning materials for higher learning institutions and school levels. She also collaborated with partners from the European Union and Asia in developing online courses and is actively engaged in research with partners from national and international levels. Currently, she is engaging in six Erasmus+ projects. Her publications include books, monographs and articles in journals. She is also actively involved in teaching innovation. She has won a few gold medals at national and international levels.

Jan Fazlagić is a professor in management at the the Poznan University of Economics and Business in Poland and a former Senior Fulbright Scholar, Marie Curie Research Fellow at the Centre in Vienna, European Commission Lead Expert in URBACT III programme and author of the first Polish Intellectual Capital Report in a Higher Education Institution (2004). He is an author of 15 books and over 70 research papers. Prof. Fazlagić has participated in numerous research projects and advised many Polish government agencies and ministries. He was a member of the research team that developed the framework for the new Act on Higher Education (Ustawa 2.0). Professor Fazlagić has participated in numerous international projects financed by the EC (DGP4) and under LdV, URBACT and E+ schemes. His research interests include knowledge management, school management, service design, services marketing, local governments and creative industries. He is currently the head researcher in the project Artificial Intelligence in Education conducted by the Institute of Educational Research, a research unit of the Polish Ministry of Science and Education.

Chris Harris has spent over 40 years in secondary schools in England as a teacher as well as a middle and senior manager in a variety of roles. He holds an NPQH and an MA in Media Education. Latterly, he has managed media departments in London. He has written for a variety of media magazines and on interdisciplinary and digital approaches to learning for journals in Spain and England. He is currently writing a MESHGuide for Media Education.

Elizabeth Hidson's career in education in the UK began with teaching computing, then school senior leadership and strategic secondments. After 14 years in the secondary school sector, she moved into higher education. Elizabeth has been a researcher on a range of international educational technology research projects as well as teaching on PGCE, MA and doctoral courses at Durham University and Newcastle University. In 2018 she joined the International Initial Teacher Training Team at the University of Sunderland. She is now the programme leader for the UK-based blended learning PgCert Education course and the Development of Learning module leader for the PGCE Education course, delivered via distance learning to over 500 students around the world each year. Elizabeth's research interests include digital tools for reflective practice, and she is a committee member of the Technology, Pedagogy and Education Association. Elizabeth continues to combine research and dissemination with her commitment to teacher education.

Carol Hordatt Gentles is the elected president of the International Council on Education for Teaching (www.icet4u.org), which she represents on the NGO committee of the UNESCO-supported International Teacher Task Force (https://teachertaskforce.org). She is a senior lecturer with the School of Education, University of the West Indies, Mona, Jamaica. She holds a PhD in curriculum, teaching and learning in teacher education from the Ontario Institute of educational studies, University of Toronto, a master's degree in educational psychology, a diploma in education specialising in geography and social studies from UWI, Mona, and a BA (Honours) in psychology from York University, Toronto, Canada. Dr Hordatt Gentles is a teacher education and teacher development specialist who has worked across the Caribbean region as an external examiner and consultant for the World Bank, UNESCO and

USAID. Her research has focused on the ideologies that inform the practice of teacher education with respect to pedagogical change, inclusion, critical pedagogy, ESD, preparation of teacher educators and teacher professional development.

Nabi Bux Jumani (Professor Dr) is a vice president (Administration, Finance and Planning) at the International Islamic University (IIUI), Islamabad – Pakistan. He has been a professor in the Department of Education, dean and director of the Directorate of Distance Education and head of an educational institution under the Ministry of Defence. He also has been acting president of IIUI. Previously he worked in the Federal Ministry of Education and at the Allama Iqbal Open University. In addition to master's and PhD degrees in education, he holds a post-graduate diploma in public administration. His qualifications have been gained in Australia, the Netherlands, the UK, China and Pakistan. His areas of research are teacher education, curriculum development, distance education and research and development. He has written many research papers, contributed to many books and is on the editorial board of a number of international journals.

Marilyn Leask has been a full professor or a visiting professor at four UK universities and Dean of Education, Sport and Tourism at the University of Bedfordshire, UK. Over a 55-year career she has written, co-edited and contributed chapters to more books than she can count, alongside a research career with consultancies with the OECD, UK universities and in several other countries. She has seen her research findings bring international and national changes and experienced UK governments engaging with academics as well as being seemingly fearful of engaging with academics. She has held roles in a number of professional associations and as a public servant in a UK government organisation as well as in the health service, in schools, in local authorities/municipalities and their national body. Her research is now focused on the use of digital technologies to support learning, and she is co-chair of the Education Futures Collaboration, which leads a knowledge management translational research initiative – translating research findings into practical advice for teachers. See MESHGuides: www.meshguides.org.

Larissa McLean Davies is a professor of teacher education and a deputy dean at the Melbourne Graduate School of Education, University of Melbourne, Australia. She became an academic in 2008, after completing a PhD in literary studies part-time and teaching senior English in various secondary schools. Building on her teaching career and doctoral scholarship, Larissa's research is in teacher knowledge, teacher education across the life-span and the role of literature in the (decolonising) English curriculum. Her work is committed to advancing racial justice and environmental imperatives and, to this end, she is co-founder of the Literary Education Lab: https://literaryeducationlab. org/. She has found great professional joy in building international networks and undertaking translational research – working closely with government and education departments to address pressing issues in education.

Sarah Younie, De Montfort University, UK, is a professor of educational innovation at De Montfort University, editor-in-chief of an international journal (*Technology, Pedagogy and Education*, Taylor/Francis), series book editor for Routledge, chair of an education charity (Education Futures Collaboration/ MESHGuides: www.meshguides.org), international board member of ICET (International Council on Education for Teaching: www.icet4u.org), board member of a national subject association (TPEA, Technology, Pedagogy and Education Association: www.tpea.ac.uk) and member of a school governing board for many years. Over 30 years she has researched and published extensively in the field of educational innovation, specifically including the use of technologies, knowledge mobilisation and translation of research.

Chapter 1

Developing your ten-year career plan

Marilyn Leask

Introduction

This book is intended for academics wanting to work in universities where the professorial title has high status and is awarded to academics who can demonstrate high-level achievements across a specified range of criteria. While specific criteria for professorial appointments vary between universities and countries, there are nevertheless general criteria for full professorial appointments. These are listed in Table 1.1 along with the number of the chapter that contains advice about how to achieve each criterion.

In some countries, the doctoral degree is the highest academic qualification, but in more than 20 countries (many in mainland Europe), academics have an additional assessment to satisfy before appointment to professorial status – the presentation of their 'habilitation' thesis (see Fazlagić's example from Poland in Chapter 11), which in essence demonstrates that the applicant meets the criteria in Tables 1.1 and 1.2. In contrast, in Brazil we are told that all university lecturers are called professors.

The advice given in the chapters in this book is intended to help you develop your academic profile so that you meet the general criteria for professorship within 10 or 15 years of you gaining your doctoral qualification. Meeting these criteria, of course, does not guarantee that you will actually be promoted within your own institution: you may need to change university or even country. Fifty-five percent of the professors in our survey were promoted within their institution; the remaining were appointed through external competition. Twelve percent of the professors surveyed achieved professorship within 10 years of their appointment; after 15 years, 39% were professors, and within 20 years 77% were professors. While 65% reported that the process of awarding professorial status was open and fair, 10% reported opaque appointment practices, nepotism and political favours, and some reported possible ethnicity or gender discrimination (both male/female and female/male). (Note survey numbers are small, so they just give an indication of issues.) You may find there is research on gender and ethnic background of professors in the country in which you live or in the country of

DOI: 10.4324/9781003217596-1

Table 1.1 General criteria for the award of professor cross-referenced to individual chapters of this book

- contributing to the efficient operation of the university (Chapter 2);
- extensive university teaching experience; including master's-level teaching and supervision of doctoral candidates to successful completion (Chapter 3);
- thought and research leadership in a field (Chapter 4);
- a national and international reputation with recognition from peers (Chapters 5, 6, 7);
- raising the profile of the university (Chapter 6);
- an extensive research and publication record (Chapters 8 and 9);
- winning research funding (Chapter 10);
- engagement with/impact on potential users and beneficiaries of your research (Chapter 11);

Chapter 7 outlines technology tools which will aid you in your journey to fulfil the criteria for professorship.

the universities you are applying to, and I suggest you look at the diversity of the staff represented on the university web profiles: does the university appoint people like you or not? In the UK, the Women's Higher Education Network (2022) cites the following data: there are about 22,800 professors, but only 41 at the time of writing are black women, while 28% are women. The Dutch Rathenau Institut (2022) data show that the Netherlands, Germany and Belgium have a lower than average number of female professors for the European countries in their survey, which shows that the percentage of the professoriat who are female varies between 20% and 30%.

To meet these general criteria for appointment even within a 10–15-year window requires planning and careful use of your time.

In this chapter, we suggest you analyse your personal situation and consider what personal and career decisions you may need to make if you are to achieve the goal of becoming a professor.

Objectives

By the end of this chapter, you should

- have an understanding of the criteria that appointment panels use in examining applications for professorial posts;
- have an understanding of the university roles that lead to professorship;
- understand the need to negotiate with the head of your university department to ensure you have the necessary opportunities to develop the skills and experience required to achieve professorial status;
- have an outline of your personal ten-year plan;
- be aware of pitfalls that may provide barriers to you achieving your goals.

Table 1.2 Detailed criteria for professorial appointments: a template for your professorial application

Teaching

Programme leadership, including coordination, staffing management, programme development from initiation through to validation via external peer review, including consultation with students and independent external experts.

Module leadership through development of curriculum and resources and delivery, including collaboration with others over curriculum design.

Teaching experience with undergraduate, post-graduate and doctoral students and for those in workplace settings; with preparation and delivery of online/blended modes of teaching.

Research student supervision, particularly doctoral student supervision to completion as principal supervisor: as a doctoral programme is typically three years, I suggest you look for such opportunities early in your career – usually you will be a second supervisor to some students, too.

Note: your application will be strengthened if you can demonstrate that higher degree students have sought you as a supervisor. Typically, they will find you through readings undertaken for their master's qualifications or through a web search. Social media may provide an avenue for you to publicise your research expertise, as will engagement in special interest groups in the relevant professional association.

Research

Track record of publishing in world leading and internationally recognised journals (see Chapters 8 and 9).

Evidence of national and international recognition of your research and thought leadership, demonstrated through presentations at key domestic and international conferences and universities (see Chapters 5, 6, 7).

Demonstrated ability to apply for, win and lead and manage to completion significant research grants (see Chapter 10).

A long-term research plan providing opportunities for publishing and applying for research funding.

Evidence of applications from international and national doctoral students.

Evidence of establishing and leading a research team as principal investigator and developing junior staff as researchers (see Chapters 10 and 11).

Community service and user impact

Elected leadership roles and engagement in national or international academic and professional/practitioner associations, for example being elected to be on the board running a professional association or taking a lead in organising an academic conference (see Chapter 5).

Journals, for instance acting as a referee for submitted articles, being invited to join a journal's editorial board or starting up a journal in a field that was not represented.

(Continued)

Table 1.2 (Continued)

Leadership in one's own institution across departments/faculty (see Chapter 11).

National and international engagement with government departments, industry and the wider community (see Chapter 11).

Impact of research on the non-academic community (see Chapter 11).

Examples of community/user group partnerships and/or public/private sector partnerships (see Chapter 11).

Mentoring junior staff, leading an internal research group, running internal academic conferences (see Chapter 11).

Playing a role on university committees e.g. quality assurance, student discipline and complaints, staff recruitment, student recruitment (see Chapter 11).

Effective management of staff using university guidelines.

Criteria for professorial appointments

The traditional route to a professorial role is through either recognition within your own university so that you are granted a personal chair or an appointment process with external advertising where a university department has a particular need for professorial leadership in defined areas.

Over decades, I have sat on/chaired numerous professorial panels for different universities, and I have reviewed applications for professorial roles from a number of countries, usually in the field of education and the social sciences. This book has been prompted by my experience that vacancies too often go unfilled because potentially good candidates simply cannot demonstrate that they meet enough of the criteria for the role. Reading the applications and curriculum vitae, I see applicants have missed opportunities and have gaps in experience – clear pitfalls in the applicant's career journey – that could have been avoided if the individual had planned to gain these experiences over time. The knowledge that I am putting into this book about networking, researching, publishing and building an international profile in a field is intended to prepare you to submit an irresistible application for a professorial post. While opportunities and different disciplines vary and you have to plot your own career journey, the advice should help you to make the most of the opportunities that come your way.

Case studies in Chapter 6 on mentoring and Chapter 11 on leadership provide examples of how experienced academics, now professors, built their professional and academic profile to meet the criteria for professorial appointments in their own countries.

Professors normally have to be able to demonstrate that they have made a unique contribution to knowledge in their chosen field and that their thought leadership in a specific field is recognised, at least nationally and preferably internationally.

Table 1.1 lists the *general* criteria for the award of professorial status, cross-referenced to the advice given in the different chapters in the book. Table 1.2 lists *detailed* criteria that professional candidates are generally expected to be able to demonstrate that they meet through their application. This detail is included to help you map out your pathway to professorship and pace your actions over a number of years.

While the list of criteria for professorial appointments looks daunting, a key purpose of this book is to help you plan to satisfy these criteria over time, enabling you to balance the demands of your day job and social and family life with the building of a career profile that leads to professorship.

Some professorial advertisements are brief, expecting the applicant to make the case for the contribution they can make to the university and their discipline. Other advertisements are so detailed that they can be off-putting. I suggest you look at the more detailed job descriptions when structuring any application to ensure you include everything relevant. Reviewing advertisements on recruitment websites or individual university websites will allow you to see the requirements of universities that you may wish to apply to. For example, jobs.ac.uk lists international job opportunities.

Table 1.2 lists detailed criteria for professorial appointments taken from application forms and advertisements. The criteria provide a detailed checklist to help you plan to develop your skills and experience.

The list may appear daunting, but over a number of years many of these opportunities should come your way as you become more experienced and as you take leading roles in your professional community. The detail in Table 1.2 provides you with a writing frame for an application. Be prepared to be proactive in asking your university, your line manager, your professional association and your local community to give you opportunities to develop your skills and experience so you meet the different criteria. See also the case studies in Chapter 11 from professors from different countries showing typical pathways to professorship in those countries.

At interview, your communication and lecturing skills along with personal presentation skills will be assessed. In my experience, interview panels include professors from disciplines other than your own as a measure for benchmarking and quality assurance, so when you address the appointment panel, you may want to check how many of them are deeply knowledgeable about your discipline. You may be wise to target any presentation you give at an interview to an audience of people outside your discipline as well as those knowledgeable about your discipline.

Your CV

Keeping your CV up to date over the years means that when you are ready to apply, you will have a record of skills you have developed and experiences you've had that otherwise you will forget. By the time you come to applying for professorship, your CV may be 16–20 pages long, as it lists the supporting documents and role descriptions related to the criteria in Tables 1.1 and 1.2. Those reading your CV and application papers may not be from your discipline, and I always suggest that a CV includes an introductory paragraph or two where you make the case for you meeting all the criteria for the post, perhaps outlining the positive impact your research has had and the leadership you have shown in your discipline and in your university.

Boysen's *Becoming a Professor* (2020) provides considerable detail on the writing of curriculum vitae and application letters. His downloadable material from the web is worth considering as you develop the paperwork for your own applications.

Professorial and lecturer titles

In exploring opportunities to become a professor, you'll find a whole range of terms used to describe the roles of academic staff in universities.

As far as I can ascertain, the title of professor is used universally across countries and across universities. Typically, a 'full' professor has to demonstrate competence in the criteria set out in Tables 1.1 and 1.2. Other titles that include the word 'professor' are used to indicate status approaching full professor status such as associate, adjunct, assistant or junior professor. However, even these terms seem to have different meanings in different universities. The title 'reader', which is the post before 'full' professor, appears to be less used. (The University of Oxford states on their website they no longer give this title.) A university may award the title 'honorary professor' to people who may or may not have worked in a university but have excelled in a field. Typically, this status is not linked to remuneration or teaching and research. Some universities also grant the title of professor to senior staff with decades of leadership in the university sector. This book, however, focuses on increasing your chances of achieving permanent/tenured remunerated 'full' professorial status based on your recognition as a researcher and thought leader in your field.

There appears to be very varied practice when it comes to naming the other university academic roles that form stepping stones on the pathway to professorship. The term 'lecturer' seems widely used, but universities may use titles such as senior, principal or adjunct lecturer. You may be given particular roles, such as programme/course or module leader or tutor, and you may be asked to sit on particular committees related to formal approval of new programmes, quality assurance and disciplinary committees. All this experience becomes relevant when you put in an application to be a professor, as you will be expected to take a leadership role with respect to a wide range of university operations. Formal recognition of the responsibilities you have through the job title or your contract provides evidence that you fulfil the criteria that relate to contributions to university life and operations.

Major university differences that affect working relationships

There are several major differences you may come across that do affect working relationships, working conditions and your chance of meeting the criteria for professorship. It is worth finding out how the university you want to work in operates, for example:

- Is there an internal research fund to which you can bid? This may give your research as an early career researcher a boost.
- How are workloads allocated?
- How many hours a week are you expected to be teaching students and how big are class sizes? Some UK universities have an 18-hour standard week with preparation and marking on top of that. I used to allow myself 15 minutes to mark a 2,500-word undergraduate assignment, and to save time but at the same time give detailed feedback, I had a feedback statement bank giving detailed advice about how to avoid common errors with respect to improving essay writing or research. Much of the advice on how to improve at undergraduate level is the same for everyone. However, assessing a 70–80,000-word PhD thesis as an external examiner takes me several days.
- Management roles such as faculty dean may be by election by peers for a fixed term, say three years to be followed by a year secondment to allow the staff member to restart their research programme, or may be advertised as a permanent position and filled by non-research active administrators. This difference in structure may have considerable impact on you. With the former structure, research is valued; with the latter structure, it is too easy for the managers not to be research active. Some professors in our survey reported resentment and obstruction in promotion applications from non-research active managers. Professor Fazlagić from Poland reports an interesting potential impact of the 'management by election' system:

    > In public (state-owned) universities the Rector is the key figure and has all the cards; in private universities, it is the Chancellor who usually represents the owner and the Rector is less important. . . . Rectors technically speaking have legal means at their disposal to dismiss a professor but they hardly ever do it. . . . Firing a full-time professor is a rare phenomenon, partly because Rectors have usually an eight-year tenure and after their term of office they return to the ranks and become vulnerable to retribution, if they put too hard measures on their subordinates.

- Job security: at what level can you expect 'tenure' i.e. your post to be permanent? In some countries, every full-time staff member has a permanent contract, in others, only professors. Some universities use a lot of part-time staff who just teach a specialist module. This can be mutually beneficial if the staff member works in industry the rest of the time as the students get up-to-date knowledge and the temporary staff member may find new employees, but otherwise staff are left with low earnings and no job security. However, even a permanent contract often will come with a clause that a few months' notice can be given on either side, and if student numbers go down and university income decreases, then staff are made redundant.

- Salaries: half of the respondents to the survey reported that the professorial salary scales in their university were set and public. The others reported that professorial salaries were secret and individually negotiated. In disciplines where high levels of research funding can be found, salaries can be quite high. Systems may also be in place that allow staff to keep a percentage of the research income they generate in addition to their salaries.

You are likely to find these differences between universities within any country. Private universities may have more options to be flexible over working conditions than public universities, which may be expected to implement standard national practices.

I trust this section has given you ideas of what to find out about a university before you are put in the position of being offered and accepting a job in a university where the working conditions may not meet your expectations.

Why a ten-year plan?

There are several reasons I suggest that you develop a ten-year plan: it takes years to meet important criteria for a professorial appointment such as doctoral supervisions and a research and publications profile. Plus, you need to factor in the impact of other social and family factors on your life.

- **Supervising doctoral students to completion.** If you are a newly appointed lecturer, it may take a couple of years for you to become established as a university teacher: you may not be allocated any doctoral supervision in your early years. Typically, your department will require you to undergo training to supervise doctoral students, and as part of this training, you start as a second supervisor for doctoral students for a couple of years before you lead as principal supervisor. As it typically takes three years for full-time doctoral students to complete and often a few years more for part-time students, you can see how quickly the years slip away. An important longer-term goal for you is to attract your own doctoral students or post-doctoral staff, who then pursue new knowledge in your field under your guidance. This provides a mutually beneficial natural pathway to joint publications, joint research bids and lifelong collaboration to advance your field.
- **The time it takes to build your ongoing research and publication programme that can demonstrate impact nationally and internationally.**

Once research is completed, it can take a couple of years for you to have an article published in an academic journal, so again the lead in time for starting to build your publication record is a couple of years. Books and journal articles may not be published for a year after you submit the manuscript. Later in the book, we suggest ways of accelerating the process and for choosing research topics that are 'hot topics' of ongoing interest; these are likely to be published quickly but can be undertaken with minimal requirement for external funding. The process of applying and waiting for decisions on external funding can take years, and as often as not the effort is wasted because competition for research grants means success rates might be low. We highlight ways of planning your career that increase the chance of your research being funded.

- **Balancing personal life with an academic career.** You may also be undertaking this work at a time where you are developing a family life, perhaps having children, as well as establishing yourself in a career. You can expect to have to balance competing demands and to face life challenges that can disrupt your plans, so having a long-term plan might help you get back on track when disruptions to your plans occur. Research, analysis and publication takes extensive time far beyond what can often be managed in a 9-to-5 working day, including university teaching, preparation, marking and committee work. The thought processes used to produce coherent, well-evidenced articles and books require significant extended periods where the researcher can focus on the task at hand. To manage family life with this need for extended periods for research and writing is without doubt challenging and requires the support of the family members who will be affected. Careful organisation and efficient ways of working can help with managing your work/life balance. I write as someone who had three children, worked full-time and studied part-time for 17 of the 30 years between the ages of 18 and 48, when I completed my MPhil through part-time study. I was lucky enough to have maternity leave a time when one thesis was due, so I spent the pre-birth maternity leave writing up my research findings and completing the thesis.

Your pathway to a professorial appointment

This part of the chapter is divided into three sections to help you develop an outline of what you need to do, and by when, over a ten-year period to have a good chance of meeting the criteria for a professorial appointment. The sections are:

- choosing a field to become specialist in: what is your passion, what is likely to be of interest to funders?
- your post-graduate academic qualifications and making the most of advice from your supervisor and examiners of your doctoral degree;
- analysing your personal situation: strengths and weaknesses.

Choosing a field and specialist areas within the field – then how to become expert in one or two fields

Routes to professorship are unique to each individual, as accumulating the experiences and expertise required takes years and depends on your ability to network, to seek and see through opportunities, to create opportunities and to use your personal time efficiently.

Each stage of your career journey comes with choices, and the choices you make or that are forced on you by circumstance can help or hinder the deepening of your knowledge in your field.

For example, typically universities employ staff with complementary skills and knowledge so as to be able to offer degree programmes with specialist options. This means that many university staff will be the only person in their department with a research passion for topic x, and unless you work with others outside your institution, you are not likely to be able to satisfy the professorial requirements for you to demonstrate you are a leader in a field (see Table 1.2 for the criteria for professorship). It is likely that other universities also have individual staff with a research passion for topic x with the same need that you have, to network to progress knowledge in the field. You will find your professional community by networking with these people either through making a personal approach to find out whether you have research interests in common, by meeting potential collaborators at professional conferences or by joining or forming a special interest group within the relevant professional association (or by creating a new professional association on topic x; see Chapter 6 on the structure and management of professional associations).

Do ask your doctoral tutors for advice on the professional associations and conferences relevant to your field.

Achieving the doctoral-level qualification indicates that you are making a contribution of new knowledge to a field. This is a basic stepping stone to an academic career leading to the post of professor – a thought leader, a researcher, a teacher advancing knowledge in a particular field.

So, how do you know you are making a new contribution to knowledge?

You will spot gaps in the field by knowing the field. Be patient, read, read, make notes, look up the profiles of people interested in what you are interested in, look at their publication profiles, attend professional conferences and note who is talking on topics of interest to you. At first the volume of material may appear overwhelming, but as you read what has been published, you are likely to find that there are teams of people working and publishing together in the same field. They are the ones consistently presenting at conferences and writing the latest books and journal articles. Your doctoral supervisor may also have guided you into research where new knowledge is needed. You may take on developing knowledge in a specialist field where no new work has been done for a decade or so because the leading researcher retired or died, or funding stopped as the field fell out of fashion.

Alternatively, an issue of major concern may have arisen in society that opens up a new field of study – the Covid-19 pandemic, for example, provided research opportunities for social scientists and natural scientists alike as well as research by political scientists and researchers into the operation of businesses, technology communication tools and online education pedagogies.

Some of the readers of this book will have come to an interest in teaching and researching in a university after a period of working in a particular field. Often, curiosity about an issue will have driven you to want to find out more and led you to the idea of undertaking research into the issue – through perhaps master's level study and then, as your interest has deepened and your curiosity has driven you, on to undertake further research leading to an MPhil or to PhD/professional doctorate research. If you are already in work, you may be undertaking this study part-time. Other readers may have followed a faster route to achieving a doctorate: first degree, master's and then perhaps a full-time doctoral scholarship or personally funded full-time doctorate study.

Following your doctorate, it is worth looking for a post-doctoral post that allows you to further develop your research career working with experienced researchers, who, it is reasonable to expect, will induct you into journal publishing and writing grant applications, if your doctoral supervisor has not already done so. When working within a research team, you are advised to ensure your work is recognised as a distinctive strand within a research team's work so that you can demonstrate your unique knowledge when it comes to bidding for research funds. See Chapters 8 and 9 for advice about how to publish from your doctoral and possibly master's level work and Chapter 10 on writing grant applications or bids to provide funding for research; see also the section in Chapter 9 about authorship issues for academic journal articles and the order of names in the published paper.

Maximising the outcomes of your doctoral programme

The outputs of your doctoral programme should provide you with immediate opportunities for publication. Whether you completed your PhD full-time or part-time, you will have spent many years on this project: a luxury that may be rarely repeated in the rest of your professional life as you balance research, teaching and the accompanying extensive administration. Gaining the award is a great achievement: you should now have a good grasp of the current state of knowledge in your chosen field through the literature review in your thesis, a deep understanding of research methods as you have justified your choice of method, plus the findings from your research. (Don't forget negative findings are also valuable, while they may not be exciting for you as a researcher.) These elements of your thesis give you the chance to prepare three or four academic articles, and if you do not publish from your PhD (for example because you are starting a new job or frankly you just need a long break from the topic), you will have missed a unique opportunity at an early point in your career to demonstrate your mastery of a research area in your field. I didn't publish from my MPhil or PhD thesis – I didn't put the time aside to do this – and I am sorry now that I didn't do so as these theses cover areas I have remained passionate about. I would have liked others to be able to engage with the ideas from my early research – I doubt many people would be dedicated enough to read a thesis to extract the nuggets of new knowledge.

If you have the chance to choose the panel that scrutinises your thesis, then choose carefully – undertake research to find out what their current interests are and see if you can find out if they are the editor of a journal in your field; then, once you are successful, ask if they would publish an article from your thesis. After all, what is the worst that can happen? They can refuse, in which case the experience may help you develop your professional resilience so you can deal with criticism and rejection, or they can suggest that you do indeed submit an article, which would be a very advantageous position to be in. Sending it to a journal editor when they have already expressed interest in the topic can mean that you get to publication more quickly than would be the case normally. See Chapter 9 on publishing articles.

It may be that you think the material in your doctoral thesis is of sufficient interest and value to the field and to particular audiences to warrant publication as a book. You should expect to have to rework the thesis to the different structure of a book, but this is an opportunity not to be missed given the substantial amount of work you have put in. See Chapter 8 on publishing books. In countries that require prospective professors to demonstrate impact of their work after the doctorate, through the 'habilitation' process a book may have to be produced demonstrating research impact some years after the doctorate. This is different to the thesis type publication of the UK system, which is usually not immediately publishable as a book. However, publishers do offer advice about how you might convert your thesis into a monograph. (See UCL Press in the websites at the end of the chapter.)

The system for doctoral studies does vary between countries and between universities, and individual universities offer different doctoral routes – by a straightforward research project, by publication, by professional practice. In some universities, some of these routes to a doctoral qualification are only available to internal candidates.

Those who gain a doctorate in a system where the process of achieving a doctorate requires several years of independent, self-driven research and writing are well placed for building a professorial profile by continuing and extending their research beyond their doctoral programme. This type of doctoral programme teaches you persistence, research skills, in-depth knowledge about leading edge thinking internationally in one or more fields and the ability to construct an argument, weigh up evidence and write a coherent narrative that is tens of thousands of words long – the length of a book.

University staff in disciplines that are directly linked to sectors of employment such as medicine, education, business, engineering, art and design, and law will often have decades of experience in the field, which has been recognised in their appointment as a university teacher. These staff may be undertaking a doctorate alongside teaching in the discipline, and a key message for staff in this position is not to see the doctorate as equivalent to climbing Mount Everest: the doctorate is an entry-level qualification for university staff. Achieving the doctorate demonstrates that you are capable of initiating research and carrying it through to completion over years, acknowledging weaknesses and areas for further action and thus preparing you for a career as a researcher and generator of new knowledge.

I was once in a training session for doctoral supervisors, and the staff member leading the session, who had supervised about 60 PhD students to completion, posed the question: 'What is the period of study for the full-time PhD student?' Everyone agreed three years. He posed the same question for part-time study: 'What is the period of study for the part-time PhD student?' Responses were varied and accompanied by groans – six or ten years or more. 'Wrong', he said. He made the point that the full-time PhD student stops work at 5 pm and has a social life. The part-time PhD student stops work at 5 pm, and if they replace their social life with progressing their PhD, they can be finished in three years. Such dedication of time of course requires support from those the student shares their life with; support from people who you share your life with for your writing career is essential as it generally has to be undertaken on top of teaching and administrative duties.

The following section provides you with the means of assessing aspects of your own personal situation and how that might affect your pathway to professorship

The best doctoral programmes I have come across give doctoral students experience of university teaching as part of the programme and ensure students publish from their doctoral research while they are still students. Co-publishing with the supervisor is not uncommon – both parties benefit, you are inducted into publishing and, with the supervisor's support for writing the article, you are more likely to be published more quickly.

Gaining these experiences as part of your doctoral programme means that when you are applying for a full-time university post, you already have not only the doctorate, but also teaching experience and publications. When the appointing panel has to make a choice between two candidates, both of whom could do the job but where one just has a doctorate, and the other has the doctorate plus some teaching experience and a publication or two – then the choice is obvious. Note: joint publishing is fine – it indicates that you are able to work successfully as a member of a team on research and publishing. However, as discussed in Chapter 9, the order of author surname is important and needs to be negotiated before you agree to write with somebody.

Your checklist and goals: for your ten-year plan

Using the criteria you have identified through your own search of job descriptions in the university/universities where you wish to be a professor, and the lists in Tables 1.1 and 1.2, create a list of the specific criteria you will need to satisfy to attain professorial status in your discipline and in the university of your choice. You will now have a list of areas of experience you either have or need to acquire to maximise the chance of a professorial appointment. Table 1.3 provides a pro forma to use to shape your ten-year plan.

Table 1.3 Checklist: your outline ten-year plan is freely available for download via the Support Material tab on the Routledge website.

Table 1.3 Checklist: your outline ten-year plan

Criteria for the award of professorship and ways of achieving them	Achieved	
	Yes	No
CONTRIBUTING TO THE EFFICIENT OPERATION OF THE UNIVERSITY		
What is your goal? What committees, panels, activities appeal to you? How do you get involved? Discussing possibilities with your line manager might be a first step . . .		
EXTENSIVE UNIVERSITY TEACHING EXPERIENCE: UNDERGRAD AND POST-GRAD, INCLUDING SUPERVISION OF DOCTORAL CANDIDATES TO SUCCESSFUL COMPLETION		
What is your goal? What are the steps to achieving this? Discussing possibilities with your line manager might be a first step . . .		
RAISING YOUR PROFILE AS A RESEARCHER AND THOUGHT LEADER AND THE PROFILE OF THE UNIVERSITY		
What is your goal? What engagement with the mainstream media and engagement with potential users and beneficiaries of your research do you plan? See Chapters 6 and 7 on engaging with the media. What might you do? . . . Consider having your own website where you blog regularly, have a feed from your Twitter stream and record and list your experience, research and publications. Should you move institutions, your web profile remains available.		
HAVING A NATIONAL AND INTERNATIONAL REPUTATION WITH RECOGNITION FROM PEERS		
What is your goal? See Chapter 5 on finding mentors: can you find people like you (gender, ethnicity, country, discipline) who have become professors who can provide advice? What might you do? . . .		
PUBLISHING IN ACADEMIC JOURNALS		
What is your goal? Perhaps one submission per year, at least? Or perhaps in year 1, turn your doctoral research into 2–4 publishable articles e.g. a state of the nation literature review; perhaps a methodology article; then articles about the findings . . .		

(Continued)

Table 1.3 (Continued)

Criteria for the award of professorship and ways of achieving them	Achieved	
	Yes	No
PUBLISHING IN PROFESSIONAL/PRACTITIONER JOURNALS		
What is your goal? Perhaps turn your doctoral research findings into suggestions for practice for those likely to use your research and publish in a professional journal relevant to your field? . . .		
WINNING RESEARCH FUNDING AND LEADING RESEARCH TEAMS		
What is your goal? What are the steps to achieving this? . . .		
EXTENDING THE REACH, IMPACT AND SIGNIFICANCE OF YOUR RESEARCH		
Have you a plan to improve in these three areas?		
YOUR CV		
Have you a system for recording your achievements in a 'master CV' that you can draw on when you need to provide brief bios for conferences or journal or book details? (If you have your own website, that might be a place to keep it and build it.)		
YOUR SPECIFIC GOALS: now record the goals that suit your context and your discipline . . .		

Summary: recognising success and avoiding pitfalls

At this point, the beginning of your career, success is having a clear plan with goals and actions to be undertaken to achieve these goals and a strategy for asking your line manager to allow you access to the full range of experiences to be gained in your institution. Your plan provides you with a good starting point for your pathway to professorship.

It takes years of experience and many opportunities to meet some of the criteria, such as being principal investigator on a funded research project and supervising doctoral students to completion, so you need to be patient and plan ahead while being prepared to be flexible when new opportunities come up, such as the opportunities the Covid pandemic offered to researchers across the disciplines.

Here are some pitfalls to avoid early in your career:

- **You have no plan** This is the best way to ensure you don't meet the selection criteria for a professorial status, even after decades of university teaching.
- **Falling foul of university regulations.** There are significant variations in university regulations governing post-graduate awards between institutions. One regulation that students easily fall foul of is timing – you are likely to find that if you do not submit your thesis within a set timescale, you will

be denied the chance to stay on the degree programme, and at best you have to take your research elsewhere, if you can, and start again. Another regulation that varies is the opportunity to transfer from the MPhil degree programme to the doctoral programme. My first foray into research was through a sponsored master's-level scholarship. The research was innovative and the supervisor suggested transferring to the MPhil programme and an MPhil was awarded. In fact, the research could have been continued to PhD level, but I found the regulations of the awarding university prevented me transferring the MPhil award towards the PhD programme – a colleague studying at University of Oxford at the same time had no such limitation. So for the PhD, I had to start again with a new area of research.

• **No support, not even moral support, for research at your institution.** There are university departments where the majority of staff do not engage in research, even though it is likely to be a contractual obligation. They then may have a vested interest in ensuring that research is not supported – to protect their own posts. If you feel a moral obligation as well as driving curiosity that means you can't help but engage in research, then it might be wise to move institutions as soon as possible. You are unlikely to be able to change a culture on your own. On the other hand, it may also mean that there is less competition for internal promotion to professorial status. It is probably worth asking the human resources department whether there are internal promotion rounds for different levels of lectureship and for profes-sorial status. Get copies of the criteria to be met and plan how you might meet them; look at the timescales. See the advice through the book on creat-ing a research network through your professional association, as this profes-sional support may enable you to find professional satisfaction and research partners even though you work within an environment where there is little support for or interest in research.

The next chapter leads you to consider employment choices, as these can enhance or derail your prospects from the beginning.

Websites

Rathenau Institut. (2022) www.rathenau.nl/en/science-figures/personnel/women-science/share-female-professors-netherlands-and-eu-countries, Accessed on 23 Octo-ber 2022.

UCL Press on Converting Your Thesis into a Monograph, www.uclpress.co.uk/pages/from-thesis-to-monograph, Accessed on 23 October 2022.

Women's Higher Education Network. (2022) www.whenequality.org/100, Accessed on 23 October 2022.

References

Boysen, G. (2020) *Becoming a Psychology Professor: Your Guide to Landing the Right Academic Job*, American Psychological Association, www.apa.org/pubs/books/4313054, Accessed on 23 October 2022; downloadable pro-formas are here, www.apa.org/pubs/books/4313054?tab=5, Accessed on 23 October 2022.

Harvard University. (2022) *Harvard's Endowment*, https://finance.harvard.edu/endowment, Accessed on 23 October 2022.

University of Oxford. (2022) *University of Oxford's Endowment and Investments*, www.ox.ac.uk/about/organisation/finance-and-funding/oxfords-endowment, Accessed on 23 October 2022.

Chapter 2

Which university?

Meeting the teaching, research and service criteria

Marilyn Leask

Introduction

Chapter 1 introduces the processes and criteria used for university appointments to give you an idea of what you have to achieve to become a professor. This chapter provides advice about the impact of working in particular types of universities and the accompanying teaching, research and service opportunities.

The opportunities available through the universities you work for as a lecturer and later as a professor are likely to have a profound impact on your career trajectory and, early on in your career, whether or not you will have the opportunities to acquire the skills and experience required for a professorial appointment in the future.

If you want to be able to apply for a personal chair within your own institution, i.e. a specially created, non-publicly advertised chair with professorial status based on your unique contribution to your discipline and university, then you have the chance over years to demonstrate that you are meeting the criteria: your service to the University and the quality of your teaching are likely to be well known by those on appointment panels. So, every decision you make about work and the use of your personal time may help or hinder you on this journey. If you are applying to a new university, then you have potential advantages (bringing new ideas and experience of different systems) as well as disadvantages over internal candidates who have already had an opportunity to demonstrate that they can do the job.

It is easy because of the demands of university teaching, tutoring students and administration (committee work, assessment and quality assurance) not to set aside the time to acquire the skills and experience needed to meet the criteria for professorial appointment. In Chapter 5, Carol Hordatt Gentles points at the career risk to women, who are often expected to undertake more organisational tasks than male faculty – something she calls 'cultural taxation'. If your own institution doesn't provide the opportunities you need, then you may be able to take an additional part-time role elsewhere or undertake other actions with local industry or users of your research to ensure you meet the criteria.

This chapter includes ideas about how early career support can help new academics to develop their research profile and how academic staff can satisfy the service criterion by working with alumni for the benefit of the university, the academic

DOI: 10.4324/9781003217596-2

staff, the discipline, the students and the alumni themselves. All universities, however, should be able to offer you opportunities through which you can demonstrate that you meet the teaching criteria for a professorship – but don't forget you need to teach at post-graduate level and supervise doctoral students to completion.

Objectives

This chapter covers:

- employment options: what type of university and what location;
- the impact of league tables and the type of institution on your career;
- opportunities for and benefits of post-doc/early career researcher sponsorship;
- opportunities to meet the criterion of 'service to the university community' through alumni engagement.

What type of university?

Chapter 1 mentions the differences between universities and the impact this can have on your opportunities to meet the criteria for professorship. No one can predict your career progression, as so much depends on chance and personal circumstance: being able to move, being in the right place at the right time, having the right mix of qualifications and experience when somebody in an institution you wish to apply to has decided to retire and suddenly you become the best fit for replacement.

University staff movement between countries is common, and you may find you can gain valuable experiences if you do this, which may accelerate your promotion prospects. There are, for example, expanding numbers of universities in the Middle and Far East because of the desire for education from a large young population. Many universities worldwide offer teaching in English, so for the English speaker there are many opportunities. Just as having an international student group can be beneficial for staff and students through widening the pool of insights, ideas and experiences brought to seminars and team assignments, so too universities may value having an international staff team that provides opportunities for the academic community to benchmark practices with those internationally, to draw on knowledge and staff experiences from other cultures and to forge partnerships and collaborations that might be lifelong.

As mentioned in Chapter 1, one route to a successful career leading to professorship, which might appear obvious, is to undertake your post-graduate study at an 'elite' university with a view to eventually applying for a post there or at an institution with a similar profile in the international university league tables. (If you haven't come across university league tables, then a simple internet search reveals league tables and the criteria used.) However, this route might mean that there is so much competition for posts there that your chances of getting the opportunities necessary to advance your career are more limited than if you go to a regional university that has a less strong profile in research with less access to research funds; however, this latter, university for example, might offer you the opportunity to be the only expert in your field, with the consequences that you've got a chance of becoming a 'big fish', albeit in a small pond. Regional and newly established national/international universities often seem to play a role as incubators of new talent, with staff moving to universities higher up the league tables once they have considerable experience and an established research and publication portfolio under their belt.

For many people, however, personal life factors influence their choices, and they are limited to applying for posts available near their current location. I suggest you undertake the activity suggested in Table 2.1 to weigh up the options available to you given your personal circumstances.

Opportunities to meet teaching and research criteria

Whether you like it or not and whether you consider the assessments giving rise to university league tables are valid or not, the reality is that there are league

Table 2.1 Where might you work?

Answering the questions below, step by step, might help you understand what options are available to you when it comes to applying for university positions.

Step 1. What are your preferred work locations: are you free to move to a job – nationally or internationally? Do you have to stay local? Do you have hobbies/family/friend/other connections that either tie you or attract you to particular areas?

Step 2. Make a list of universities convenient to these locations.

Step 3. Review the publicly available data about these institutions. Look at the staff profile: do they employ and promote people like you? Do they have a staff development programme? What courses are taught? What are the qualifications of those teaching those courses? What is the level of research activity (research groups/institutes are normally publicly listed). What information is there about research funders and about research degree supervision? Look also at the presence or absence of partnerships with regional, national and international employers. Make a list of those that seem to provide a working environment that suits your aspirations: use the Appendix 1 list of indicators as a guide. Does the institution you are thinking of applying to meet all these criteria? If not, which ones matter to you?

Step 4. Now look at the individual departments/faculties in these universities that might provide employment you are seeking. As you narrow your search, you may wish to contact the specialist departments of interest to you or the human resources department to gather answers to queries about the university, perhaps to ask about where they advertise posts (usually these will be on the university's website) and so on.

Step 5. Consider if there is anything you might do in the short, medium and long term to increase your chances of achieving employment with your preferred employer/s and of achieving the goal of becoming a professor, perhaps in that institution.

tables and national research assessment schemes that provide an international hierarchy of universities and specialist departments.

There are several important ways this hierarchy is likely to impact on your meeting of criteria for professorial appointments.

The perceived status of the university is likely to affect numbers of under-graduate and post-graduate students, PhD applicants, research opportunities and thus university income, and therefore jobs and job security, opportunities at the national and international levels, research income and indeed whether the university can offer internal sponsorship to jumpstart staff research.

So, depending on the university, you may have less chance of getting the experi-ence of supervising doctoral students to completion and winning research grants as a principal investigator on projects with national and international impact: however, regional universities may be able to tap into local research funds from industry or from charities.

Whatever institution you are in, you do need to ensure that you are an effec-tive teacher. Typically, UK universities expect lecturers to attend training courses in how to teach well, and UK universities normally undertake evaluations of staff teaching, perhaps via a student survey. Student surveys may also be undertaken as part of the compilation of national league tables. So, make sure you understand and can use the basic techniques of effective teaching: explaining, modelling, demonstrating, questioning, using different forms of assessment and so on. (For further details on pedagogy see, for example, my books on effective teaching e.g. Capel et al., 2022 and Meyer and Land's 2005 work on threshold concepts for university subjects.)

Shifting your research focus

If your newly acquired expertise through, say, your doctoral studies, is closely linked with a major research institute, then there is a risk that if you move institu-tions, you are less likely to be able to win funding on your own in competition with the original research institute, which already has a track record. Collabora-tion with colleagues at the original research institute may be wise. Or you may need to change the focus of your research. See Table 2.2, which has examples of how to deal with the need for a shift in focus of your research so you can man-age research and teaching together and how you can create a research niche for yourself without any funding.

I'm not saying you will be unable to meet the criteria for professorial appoint-ments if you are not at a high-status institution, just that you might need to ensure your expertise is particularly niche and world leading so as to minimise competition for funds from those institutions with a strong record in receiving and managing research grants.

In my experience, European Union processes for awarding grants seem to be more inclusive in recognising an individual academic's expertise, regard-less of the university. It is not uncommon to find regional universities with

Table 2.2 Shifting your research focus: advice from four professors

- Following a post-graduate research post at the University of X, 20 years ago, I moved to my first lecturing post at a nearby university: I had children in school, and moving location was not an option. I decided to develop a new niche research focus so as to be in a position to win research funding. I chose to specialise in an emerging but related field. The head of department at the university I moved to supported my initial research with internal funding and indeed became engaged in the research. This was a very successful strategy, leading to international consultancies as well as funded research. We won a number of research contracts, with one contract leading to another as we built the department's reputation in the new niche field.
- Work collaboratively. Try to ensure that there is a link between your teaching and your research so that you not pulled into two different directions.
- Develop a research focus that aligns with teaching assignments and institutional priorities to balance research and teaching demands.

  Step 1. Set up an annual state of the nation survey in an area of ongoing relevance to your field so you have unique research-based knowledge.
  Step 2. Research and publish.
  Step 3. Network nationally and internationally to share this new knowledge
  Step 4. Of course, teach well. (Well-established online tools such as Survey Monkey or Google forms support easy data gathering and comparisons year on year.)

significant European research fund grants. Chapter 10 provides more advice about funding.

Those sponsoring doctoral students (government departments, charities, NGOs) often restrict the choice of university to which such students can apply to those institutions with high rankings in the international league tables. So, even if you have a high profile internationally and attract students to study with you, they may not be permitted to. In such a case, it may be possible to negotiate some form of partnership with colleagues in a higher-ranking university, but university processes can be complex, and such collaboration may not be permitted by the individual university's regulations. You can yourself have qualifications from these 'elite' universities and have developed your research experience in these institutions, but this may make little difference to those sponsoring doctoral students. The number of doctoral students that apply to study at the university in turn has an impact on staff developing international networks of like-minded researchers. These contacts often lead to international consultancy, which then demonstrates that you have an international reputation, which is one of the criteria for being appointed as a professor. Many countries also have international study scholarships for post-graduate study for mid-career staff whose careers are on a trajectory leading to them becoming leaders of industry/universities or having leading political roles. See for example Fulbright scholarships, Rhodes scholarships, Erasmus scholarships, Turing scholarships and, of course, ask those in your field and perhaps your doctoral supervisor what might be available to people in your discipline and country.

The university's research environment

Appendix 1 lists criteria for assessing a university's research environment for staff and students. It sets out the criteria used by the expert panel I was on, to judge the university research environment in the 2008 UK national research assessment exercise. A review of the items there might yield more questions you could ask of a department you are thinking of working in. If your current university post is in a university that is not very supportive of research and you want to be a researcher, then you may wish to move on quickly before you lose the momentum built up through your doctoral research.

For the first few years of your academic career, you may be considered an early career researcher for the purposes of national assessment exercises and applying to funders. There are some brilliant scholarships for early career researchers (see the examples in Table 2.3). Alternatively, you might find yourself in a university where there is no support for early career researchers. So, this is another question to ask when you are considering whether to apply for a particular job or not.

Early career help

Preparing yourself to be the best candidate requires a level of planning and self-analysis. If your doctoral programme has provided you with opportunities for university teaching and academic publishing, then you have considerable advantage when it comes to applying for posts as a new lecturer.

Just as for professors, there are expectations that lecturers will undertake research, teaching and administration, but in some universities, there is specific support such as a lighter timetable or sponsorship to attend conferences for those beginning a research career: the early career researcher.

The website Early Career Researcher Central (https://ecrcentral.org/) is an international resource that lists funding opportunities and travel grants and provides forums for discussions about opportunities for early career researchers. Table 2.3 provides two examples. Winning such sponsorships usually means that you have a lot more freedom to get your research and publication record off to a good start as your salary is already covered by the sponsorship and so doesn't have to be covered by research or teaching income.

It may be that your university has a careers section that can provide you with advice about sponsored opportunities in your discipline; however, I suggest you look after your own interests and keep an eye on what is advertised on different academic websites. There is of course likely to be considerable competition for places, so you need to be as well qualified as possible, and don't forget that professional associations sometimes offer scholarships.

Research groups or centres

From each institution's website, you will be able to see what research groups exist and whether your interests fit with one of those research groups/institutes/

Table 2.3 Examples of substantial early career sponsorships

Here are two examples of grants for early career researchers, lasting several years, that provide a foundation for a research career. Some charitable foundations provide such sponsorship, but you will need to do research for those that apply to your discipline and for people of your nationality.

Example 1: Wellcome Early Career Awards: open to international applicants

This scheme provides funding for early career researchers from any discipline who are ready to develop their research identity. Through innovative projects, they will deliver shifts in understanding that could improve human life, health and wellbeing. By the end of the award, they will be ready to lead their own independent research programme . . . [open to those from the] UK, Republic of Ireland, **Low- or middle-income countries (apart from India and mainland China);** Level of funding: Your salary and up to £400,000 for research expenses; Duration of funding: Usually 5 years, but may be less for some disciplines . . .

(Wellcome Trust, 2022, p. 1)

Example 2: Sir John Plum–sponsored early career researcher and lecturer fellowship

The following was advertised for a short while on the post vacant website for Christs College University of Cambridge.

Applications are invited from suitably qualified candidates for a College Lectureship in any field of British history since 1500 or continental European history since 1800, associated with a Fellowship of Christ's College. The major part of the funding for this post was supplied by generosity of the Glenfield Trust to mark the centenary in 2011 of Sir John Plumb's birth. The Trust was established in 2002 under the terms of Sir John's will and its primary objective is to support education at Christs College.

The post is intended to provide a valuable development opportunity over [four years] for an individual at the beginning of their academic career to allow them to build teaching skills, a publication record and other academic activity with a view to obtaining a university appointment in Cambridge or elsewhere. . . .

The successful candidate . . . will be expected to undertake six hours of small-group teaching per week . . . (equivalent to 120 hours per academic year), to act whenever required as Director of Studies in History, to engage in research and publication, and to undertake other College offices or duties appropriate to an early career appointment. . . . Candidates should normally be able to teach a wide range of topics within the general fields indicated above. The Fellow . . . will be expected to sit on some College committees.

Letters of application (there are no forms) should be sent to . . . including a curriculum vitae with details of qualifications, publications and experience and the names and addresses of two persons who have agreed to act as academic referees. . . . Short-listed candidates may be asked for copies of written work . . . Further details [were] provided on the website (www.christs.cam.ac.uk/vacancies).

(Christs College, 2022, p. 1)

centres. These come and go depending on staff interests and can cease to exist if the key member of staff moves on. If not, you may need to ask whether it would be possible to set up a new research group/institute/centre.

Examples of questions it may be helpful to have answers for:

- Is there support for early career researchers through an internal process bidding for funds or through a reduced timetable?
- Does the institution have a research office supporting building for research funds, and if so, how does it operate? Typically, research offices will send you information about sources of research funding; they normally help with ensuring budgets are correct and that internal sign-off processes are completed giving approval for the project to be run within the university.
- What tools to support bid writing are there? I have worked in two institutions (one a university and one a research organisation) with absolutely brilliant research bidding support processes. Both had examples of successful bids for a range of funders that could be used by staff to model their own bids and had standard information for staff to use, for example, background information on the organisation, on successful projects, on internal processes for quality assurance, on risk assessment, on methodologies and so on. One had costing software that staff could use if working on a bid from their own home and that within ten minutes could give a costing for a research project that could then be adjusted to meet the criteria set by the potential funder. And, of course, there was training for staff in using these systems.
- How do research groups operate? In some cases, they may have research funds to support staff, they may run an international or national conference, they may run a public seminar series with invited speakers. If not, these are opportunities you may wish to offer once your teaching responsibilities are well organised. Best practices I have come across that support staff research include ensuring no meetings are held on Fridays and, if possible, no teaching happens on Fridays. This gives staff Fridays to keep up with their research, and those who want to go the extra mile may find they can use Saturdays and Sundays more effectively because of the substantial period of time they can allocate to thinking just about what they're writing, or researching, or proposing to research. It does seem to me that academic work of this type needs a considerable period beyond a few hours at a time to allow the mind to work on the material to hand and to create insights and connections leading to new knowledge.

Other issues to be aware of when it comes to research are IPR – intellectual property rights – and income splits.

Ownership of IP

A fellow professor spent 30 years of his life developing and building an internationally successful research centre in his university. The centre became self-funding as clients bought the centre's data tools year in and year out. But what happened when he retired? The university sold off the centre for millions of pounds and pocketed the profits, even though the university's internal documentation indicated that such profits would be split with the staff who generated them. The staff in question had hoped to support PhD studentships for learners from developing countries. At the time of writing, the staff involved are in dispute with the university.

Typically, universities have units that can provide support about the establishment of spinoff companies and protection to your IP. If you find yourself potentially in this position, then asking colleagues in different universities about what practices operate there may help you negotiate a satisfactory situation for your own intellectual ideas. In some cases, the trade union for academics may support staff claims.

Income splits

An interesting practice I came across with one employer was a clear process for splitting research income between the academic staff and the university, so that the academic staff benefited financially from the funding of their research based on their ideas. In return, research-active staff then had to find their own funding for attending academic conferences.

Opportunities to meet service criteria

When it comes to meeting the criterion for service to your professional community and your discipline, then the power to demonstrate this lies within your control, regardless of the university that you work in.

In Chapter 1, Table 1.2 lists a wide range of ways that you might provide a service to the university community by serving on various committees and undertaking administrative duties essential to the operation of the university. You should be able to negotiate with your line manager to gain these experiences.

You should be able to find professional organisations in your discipline that operate at the international level and potentially the national level. If not, I suggest you combine with others to set up such an organisation. National and international professional organisations usually provide newsletters, publish journals and run conferences for their members. All these activities are likely to involve the use of volunteers who are specialists in the discipline. It is up to you to get engaged at this level. It's likely to involve you in investing funds in your own professional development and your career, and in some countries, these costs are tax deductible.

Public-facing activities organised by the university and alumni events and networking provide substantial opportunities for you to demonstrate that you meet the service criteria (see Table 1.2).

A university with an active programme of public-facing activities may provide you with avenues for publicising your research, for meeting leaders in different fields and for raising your profile and that of the university. (See Appendix 1.) Such internally managed programmes generally create a positive research environment for staff where new thinking around new and existing problems is valued and where the sharing of ideas across disciplines between people at different stages of their career is supported.

The absence of any such programme should send alarm signals to you – is this a university where little research activity is happening, and where relationships with at least local and regional potential research sponsors and research users are not well developed? Perhaps you could make a contribution to developing this.

I suggest you also look at the public relations activities of the university – how is the university represented in the press? Is staff research promoted in the press? When deciding whether or not you want to work at an institution, looking at absences of key activities can give you an indication of the health of the research and teaching environment, or their problems.

Whatever type of institution you work at, alumni networking can potentially provide you with a national and international network of people in your field who hopefully have a positive feeling towards your university. This means that, with little effort on your part if you have an organised alumni department, you can be in contact with people who are likely to care about the same issues as you and may provide work placements, research data, visiting lecturers, student mentoring and so on. Table 2.4 lists ways both alumni and academics can collaborate for their mutual advantage.

Table 2.4 Opportunities through alumni networks

The university's alumni department should have ongoing relationships with alumni that you can tap into for specific long-term projects or activities. Following are examples of how engagement with alumni can be beneficial to the university, the students and the staff. Alumni may:

- sit on course/research centre advisory boards to provide insights, such as what they are looking for from new graduates, and industry access, such as placements and visits, ensuring courses stay relevant;
- provide industry connections and access for research e.g. case studies/ interviews;
- lecture students; and provide course content/enriching student experience;
- support industry tours;
- mentor students;
- provide internships or projects such as work-based learning dissertations;
- sit on university councils/strategic advisory boards;
- support student recruitment by attending open days and student recruitment fairs and speak with prospective students showing the | benefits of a course;
- recruit students and alumnus, thus improving job prospects and university rankings for student employment;
- support career development skills e.g. practice interview panels;
- attend freshers/orientation sessions and talk about the impact of courses, provide advice to incoming students etc.;
- provide academics with introductions into companies that have a charitable foundation and who may donate to research initiatives.

Many surveys used for university rankings ask for responses from alumni, and strong relationships may encourage both alumni participation in surveys and the university to provide a good experience for alumni.

The alumni department may be able to support fundraising for specific projects, with alumni who are engaged with the institution more likely to give.

Your checklist and goals: for meeting the teaching, research and service criteria

Now reflect on and make notes about what you might do to meet the criteria for professorship. See the prompts in Table 2.5.

Table 2.5 Checklist: assessing your opportunities to meet the teaching, research and service criteria is freely available for download via the Support Material tab on the Routledge website.

Table 2.5 Checklist: assessing your opportunities to meet the teaching, research and service criteria

ITEM	Achieved?	
	Yes	No
TEACHING		
Does your teaching timetable allow you blocks of time to work on research? If not, can you negotiate on this matter?		
Does the range of courses that you teach fit with your expertise? Can you negotiate to get a better fit?		
RESEARCH		
Does the university have a programme of internal research grants?		
Will you have the opportunity to work with a network of post-graduate students?		
Does the university have a research centre that supports you in the submission of bids?		
SERVICE		
Are your teaching responsibilities compatible with your research goals? If not, can you negotiate to create better alignment between your teaching and your research?		
Do you know what university committees there are that would give you opportunities to build your service profile? Have you a plan for providing service to the university?		
Does the university work with alumni in the way set out in Table 2.4? Have you a plan for how you might work with alumni?		
Have you a plan for demonstrating service to your professional community?		
YOUR SPECIFIC GOALS: now record the goals that suit your context and your discipline . . .		

Summary: recognising success and avoiding pitfalls

From the preceding information, you will have picked up that you may have more chance of continuing your research career in some institutions than in others. But even if you gain your first academic posts in institutions that support research, there are still pitfalls that can disrupt your journey to achieving professorial status. Here are some examples:

- You become immersed in teaching and put off doing research. Consequence: within a few years, you are well down the path of being a non-researching member of staff with fewer job opportunities elsewhere.

- Your research topics are so diverse that it is not evident that you are deeply knowledgeable in any areas. Consequence: you are unable to demonstrate thought leadership in a specific field.
- You are on short-term contracts. Consequence: if you do not use your personal time to focus on building your research profile, you may find it hard to get a permanent post.
- You are employed by a university that has no coherent strategy for supporting staff research, no research office supporting funding bid submission and no simple supportive strategies in place. Consequence: your research does not progress, you have nothing to publish and your academic CV has gaps that cannot be filled.

I hope you see how with careful planning you might meet the criteria for service, but that meeting the criteria for teaching across the whole range of university programmes and your success in winning research funding may be considerably dependent on the resources and status of the university that you work at.

Acknowledgements

I should like to thank Isobel Kettle Head of alumni engagement at Cranfield University for her advice on how academics might engage with alumni for mutual benefit and for the benefit of the university.

References

Capel, S., Leask, M., Younie, S., Hidson, E. and Lawrence, J. (2022) *Learning to Teach in the Secondary School a Companion to School Experience*, 9th edition, Abingdon: Routledge, www.routledge.com/Learning-to-Teach-in-the-Secondary-School-A-Companion-to-School-Experience/Capel-Leask-Younie-Hidson-Lawrence/p/book/9781032062297, Accessed on 23 October 2022.

Christs College. (2022) *The Sir John Plum Sponsored Early Career Researcher and Lecturer*, Fellowship, UK: Christs College, University of Cambridge, www.christs.cam.ac.uk/vacancies, Accessed on 23 October 2022.

Meyer, J. and Land, R. (2005) *Threshold Concepts: Undergraduate Teaching, Postgraduate Training, Professional Development and School Education: A Short Introduction and a Bibliography from 2003 to 2018*, https://www.ee.ucl.ac.uk/~mflanaga/thresholds.html, Accessed on 23 October 2022.

Welcome Trust. (2022) *Wellcome Early-Career Awards*, London: Wellcome Trust, https://wellcome.org/grant-funding/schemes/early-career-awards, Accessed on 23 October 2022.

Chapter 3

Contracts, accountability, roles *and* funding your salary

Marilyn Leask

Introduction

This chapter provides advice about how you, as a junior member of academic staff, can develop an active research profile while at the same time managing your teaching and administrative responsibilities and your social and family life.

This chapter outlines different kinds of contracts and accountability measures and provides advice on maintaining a balance between your teaching, administration and research responsibilities.

The chapter also outlines the challenges university managers can face in funding salaries as, for example, if the only source of income is student fees, then as student numbers fluctuate, so do the funds available to pay staff salaries. If your expertise is in a very niche area that is not likely to generate student fees or research income, then you may find you are dependent on a grant from the university's endowment or research income generated by colleagues to pay your salary.

Do check the examples given through this book against what is common practice and what is practical in your own context. These examples are meant for guidance only; while some countries have fairly standard procedures for staff progressing to 'full' professorship, in other countries there is no common standard, and the processes vary between universities.

Objectives

By the end of this chapter, you should:

- understand the different types of employment contract you may be offered and the impact on your research profile;
- understand the accountability measures you may encounter;
- understand sources of income that fund salaries and how this might affect you;
- have developed strategies for managing your teaching and research roles with your social and family life so as to build a research career;
- be equipped to analyse critically the working environment of any university that you may apply to.

DOI: 10.4324/9781003217596-3

Types of employment contract and the impact on your research profile

If you are unfamiliar with university staff contracts, then I suggest you read the small print of any contract carefully and take advice from those you trust. In some countries and in some universities, it is common to issue junior staff with temporary contracts, some of which do not include holiday entitlement or the working conditions that full-time staff enjoy. In some countries, tenure or a permanent position is available only to those who have achieved professorial status, and this can create instability of staffing in a department as well as considerable competition between staff who do not have tenure.

The professors responding to the survey had very varied starting points with respect to their academic posts. During their careers they experienced one or more of the following contracts:

- short-term *research* contract;
- short-term *teaching* contract;
- full-time *teaching-only* contract;
- full-time/part-time permanent/temporary *teaching and research* contract;
- full-time temporary *research* contract (often time limited to end when a research grant ends).

As mentioned in a previous chapter, there is also a less traditional route where you make a name for yourself in a field through your own endeavours and then are recognised by the academic world as being of professorial status i.e. a thought leader having made a unique contribution to knowledge.

Each of these contracts has different implications for your route to a full professorship.

Short-term research contracts

This route has the potential of providing rapid development of research skills, a solid publication record and a solid foundation for an ongoing research profile. If you are on this route, try to be part of the team presenting papers at conferences and, when at the conference, take the opportunity to meet others with similar interests who might form your international network and become collaborating authors/co-researchers over decades. (Almost all professors said that international engagement was one of the criteria they had to fulfil for their appointment.)

A word of warning: it is not unknown for lead researchers to publish articles under their own names and to exclude the junior researcher, or for the researcher to be acknowledged in a footnote. The order of names on an article or book is also significant. See advice in Chapters 8 and 9. This lack of recognition can be really damaging for the junior researcher, as they may have invested years into this work and not have much in terms of academic outputs to show on their curriculum vitae as a result. How can you avoid this? A first step is being aware of the possibility to practise your skills in negotiating what could be a difficult conversation and then to initiate the conversation. You may find advice and support from colleagues, from your head of department, your professional association, the human resources department in your university or a trade union.

Short-term teaching contracts

High-quality doctoral programmes give students the chance to teach on undergraduate and post-graduate programmes so that when the student applies for a university post they already have teaching, research and publications on their CV. To meet the criteria for an academic chair based on the criteria set out in Tables 1.1 and 1.2, you will usually need to be on the permanent staff so as to gain experience of the full range of operations of a university: admissions, programme development and validation, internal and external examining processes, plagiarism and disciplinary processes, timetabling, complaints, standards, committee management and so on. Understanding and being able to operate quality assurance processes should help you ensure that your teaching and assessment are of a high standard, and these experiences should be included in your curriculum vitae.

If you are on a research-only contract, you may be able to negotiate some teaching experience so as to broaden your curriculum vitae and maximise your chances of a full-time appointment as a university member of staff.

If your university offers mostly short-term teaching contracts, then it is worth looking elsewhere for an employer prepared to offer a more permanent commitment.

Full-time teaching-only contracts

Having a *teaching-only* contract can narrow your opportunities for career progression. Your route to appointment to chair on the basis of your contribution to knowledge is likely to be restricted unless you can squeeze time for the research from your personal time. As has been mentioned, in some countries there are high-stakes national research assessment exercises linked directly to the distribution of research funding. One way that UK universities have tried to 'game' the UK system and focus research resources on a few staff is to issue some staff with teaching-only contracts. That way the rules of the game may enable them to submit for assessment only the academic staff who are likely to score the highest grades; subsequently, the university can claim their research is of the highest quality, but of course this applies just to the small number of staff submitted.

The impact of having a teaching-only contract is that staff who have these contracts but who want to be research active have to be very dedicated as they will be doing their research probably without funding or any time allowance.

However, at least you have a university job with the experience of university operations and the core business of teaching that that brings. The experience then puts you in a position to apply for a post elsewhere where the working conditions enable you to balance research and teaching more easily.

Full-time/part-time teaching and research contracts

This kind of contract allows you to participate in all aspects of university activity and to develop your profile in the areas that ultimately provide the criteria for appointment to professorship. However, given the time it takes to undertake research analysis and writing, you are unlikely to achieve the required standard without putting in significant personal time.

Teaching responsibilities that do not include options that allow you to build your personal research profile can scupper your chances of a professorship early on in your career. You may need to have discussions and negotiate with your head of department to carve out some teaching that complements your professional and research interests. The priority of senior staff is to balance the need to ensure students are taught well with support for the aspects of your academic career that align with those of the department and the university. Each university has different aspirations for high ratings internationally for research and/or teaching, and for the student experience. Making yourself aware of the criteria that apply to your context and how you can help in the achievement of those goals will help your negotiations. It would be wise to seek advice from a union, experienced colleagues and friends about what constitutes a reasonable negotiating stance.

Accountability measures

I suggest you find out before you accept an academic post just what accountability measures are in place that you will need to conform to. If you are a member of a professional association, then you should be able to ask other members about national and university accountability systems and how they prepare for them. However passionate you might be about your research, if your salary depends on income from teaching and you do not meet the basic standards for teaching quality and the other quality assurance measures your university requires, then your job is at risk (see Chapter 2).

Formal annual performance appraisals for each staff member are required in some universities, and this may give you an opportunity to discuss workloads and to negotiate a close match between your teaching programme and your research.

In some countries, academics may have both their research and their teaching assessed by external quality assurance bodies, and you need to become familiar with the systems applying in your context. See, for example, the Australian Research Council's Excellence in Research for Australia (2022), New Zealand's Tertiary Education Commission, Performance-Based Research Fund (2022), the UK's Research Excellence Framework (REF, 2021) and so on. There are many articles critiquing these exercises. See, for example, Babelytė and Mikulskienė's (2009) review of the Lithuanian approach. The criteria vary between countries, with some countries valuing the impact of your research on users as much as the academic outputs i.e. journal articles.

You may find there are national student surveys that assess a whole range of aspects of the student university experience. Students may be surveyed about the quality of your teaching. In Europe, ENQA (2022) oversees the standards expected of universities, with each member country having an organisation accredited with overseeing in-country quality assurance processes. In England, the Quality Assurance Agency for Higher Education (QAA, 2022a) is responsible for benchmarking standards across universities, and this is usually done by a review carried out by an external expert panel. For the different forms of review, see QAA (2022b, 2022c). In universities where standards are externally moderated, part of your academic role will be to prepare documentation for scrutiny by external panels. You will be required to demonstrate that course content is up-to-date and relevant and that students on the programmes you teach on are employable. You and your colleagues can expect to be asked for documents showing the process of consultation with external bodies to arrive at a teaching programme, the teaching programme session by session, the expectations of students you issue before the programme starts, assessment processes and examples of assessed work. In England, external examiners, independent of the university, sample the assessed work of undergraduate and post-graduate students to benchmark university standards across the sector.

How is your salary funded and what does it cost to employ you?

This section is included to bring a sense of reality regarding who is likely to fund your time to undertake research. Income has to come from somewhere to cover your salary. The reality is that unless you raise research funding that can be used to pay for staff to cover some of your teaching time, or you have a post funded through a legacy or scholarship, then the source of funds for your salary is student fees or a government or altruistic grant to the university.

Accounting software enables university administrators to monitor income and expenditure to a level of detail that was not available to universities until recent decades. When I was a dean of a faculty, I was presented with a monthly spreadsheet showing current income and expenditure together with future projections. It is very easy for administrators to see which academic departments are financially sound and which aren't, as well as if staff costs are balanced by the income from students and research grants once all the other costs of universities are allowed for.

For the UK, information about how much income is needed to pay staff salaries is publicly available on the University of Exeter websites (2022a, 2022b, 2022c), which show that to pay a lecturer a salary of £40,000, the university incurs costs of £54,000. The extra £14,000 is made up of the employer's national insurance contributions, the employer's pension contributions and an apprenticeship levy levied on all payrolls in the UK. In addition, universities incur 'estates' and 'indirect' costs in providing you with a pleasant working environment and with equipment, travel expenses and so on. These costs are explained on the University College London website (2022) and include internet and other digital services, human resources, training, building maintenance and development, materials for teaching and for publicity, the publicity department, library services, water, electricity and so on.

Typically, all these additional costs are 50% to 60% of full staffing costs, so that to employ the lecturer at £40,000, the university may have to find £80,000–£90,000. This information is added here as although many universities are registered charities, only some have funds from legacies that pay for staff time for research; otherwise, funding for research time has to be found by allocating other staff more students or by winning external funding. If you are applying for external funding for research, you will normally be using actual costs rather than the actual salary you receive, and this can affect your research proposal costs quite substantially.

When you are applying for a post, particularly an international post where you may make assumptions about what is included based on the experience in your existing country, it is worth finding out what's included in the salary and conditions e.g. health insurance, travel and housing allowance, equipment, conference fees so that you are not met with unpleasant surprises once you are in post. Before you make a commitment, the human resources department in the university should be able to advise you about what is included in staff packages.

Work environment

Is the work environment designed to help staff to balance their teaching, research and administrative responsibilities?

Chapter 2 includes some details about the internal structures in universities. However, the actual day-to-day operation of the internal work environment in a university is usually hidden to outsiders. Yet, it is this environment that determines whether a university is likely to be pleasant to work in and supportive of your career development – or not.

In this section, I highlight some of the variations in working conditions that can influence your ability to carry on with research while also teaching and undertaking administrative roles. I suggest you try to find out what the situation is, on those topics most important to you, in any university that might shortlist you for a post. You might be able to talk frankly to students or staff who you already have contact with, or perhaps you have to ask some of these questions directly at interview, always being sensitive of course to the impression that asking such questions will give of you.

University and departmental structures and their potential impact on your career

Universities use different terms to describe their structures, and you are advised to find out, early on, the terms and the roles used in any university where you are taking up a post. There is usually a core management team with responsibilities across the whole university e.g. the teaching programme, student recruitment, quality assurance and so on, and then a team of heads of faculties/schools. Then, each faculty or school may be made up of a collection of departments.

As mentioned earlier, understanding university processes is essential to operating effectively in the university environment and to building your path to promotion. One professor pointed out that staff often ask how much administration/committee work is enough to advance their career, but that there is no easy answer:

> younger faculty members interested in learning more about how their promotion applications will be assessed often want to know more quantitative information such as the number of committees they must serve on, the number of grad. students they must supervise, or the number of publications they must have. They don't always appreciate that there is a subjective aspect to the process and I know this causes some frustration.

Non-research and non-teaching roles

Table 3.1 lists major non-research and non-teaching roles that have to be undertaken by somebody familiar with the work of the department. As you can see, these are extensive, and the workload needs to be shared. If you can, plan and then negotiate to gain experience across these roles over a period of years. Some roles can be undertaken by a junior staff member, while others can only be undertaken by senior staff: you may be able to shadow staff undertaking these more sensitive and complex roles. Here is advice from one of the professors responding to the survey:

> Try to avoid taking on too many management roles because these get in the way of time for research and writing. Make sure you contribute explicitly to your University's success by supporting things like interviewing, open days, sitting on committees etc. Try to schedule time for writing/research and stick to it. Try to work with collaborators. Attend conferences where you are most likely to meet collaborators.

Working conditions

As mentioned, working conditions and expectations of staff vary hugely between universities. Universities with income from foundations and large research incomes can offer more flexibility to staff than those with an income largely based on student fees. Find out what you can about the university finances. In some countries, universities receive no or little government support, so if student numbers fluctuate, staff may find they are redundant.

If you really do have free choice of where you can work, then the questions and issues raised in this chapter should help you to choose a university where your

Table 3.1 Non-research and non-teaching roles that have to be undertaken by somebody familiar with the work of the department

- university committees such as quality assurance, building and maintenance, student discipline, complaints, appointments for other departments, standard management meetings, development of new programmes, interviewing new students for those programmes that require interview prior to starting, making offers and having discussions with potential new students, awards of prizes and so on;
- student liaison;
- public relations;
- local disaster management committees;
- community liaison and representation at community events;
- managing the finances: depending on the university's processes, each faculty may need to demonstrate that income is covering expenditure;
- staff management, which includes staff performance reviews, discipline, recruitment, timetabling, induction, celebrations and staff appointments.

Recruiting new staff can be quite time consuming, requiring the writing of advertisements, job descriptions and the person specification and including consulting with staff to check what the requirements are for a new member of staff as well as the human resources department to ensure processes such as ensuring equity and avoiding bias in appointments are followed.

Then there is the process of shortlisting applications and constructing an interview panel: membership will vary depending on the post. For a lecturer appointment, this would include normally a representative from the human resources department as well as an independent outsider from another department to ensure university processes are followed and to minimise the chance of bias creeping into the selection process. An additional task is to construct the format of the interview, which typically includes the applicant demonstrating how they run a seminar or give a presentation. Then there is the constructing of interview questions, which should follow from the job description and person specification. In universities that support equal opportunities, the same question should be given to each candidate, with each candidate rated independently by the panel members.

Following the interviews, there is responsibility for negotiating terms of employment such as salary and any other agreed components of the salary package with the preferred appointee. Then a formal appointment letter has to be drafted, checked by human resources, sent and the appointment accepted. Next there is the management of the induction of the new member of staff. If there is an interim vacancy, then part-time staff need to be interviewed and appointed as well as inducted and monitored.

ongoing professional development as an academic, i.e. a teacher and researcher, is supported and not stunted. Answers to the questions that follow may be found through several different routes – websites for the university, the department staff and students, asking peers in your professional association, asking staff who work in the university, asking the human resources department for information if you are considering applying for an advertised post. Informal conversations at professional conferences may help you to gain an understanding of how individual universities work and what the working conditions are in different universities.

Clearly, you don't want to bombard the department you are applying to with questions: considerable information is likely to be in the public domain.

Working conditions in different countries can also vary hugely. For example, a colleague in one country reports that because of its remote location, staff enjoy an annual travel and conference attendance allowance sufficient to allow them to make a couple of international journeys every year to meet with peers in other countries. By contrast, colleagues from other countries report having to fund conference attendance and travel themselves. Practices in universities can vary year on year depending on the financial situation.

See Chapter 2 and Appendix 1 for advice about assessing the research environment in the university and the opportunities of working with alumni to improve the quality of the content and relevance of your courses and to support your research.

University politics

Because you have chosen to read this book, I assume that you are interested in becoming deeply knowledgeable in a field or discipline to which you feel a lasting commitment.

However, not all university academic staff are driven by a passion for research, and you may wish to bear that in mind in your interactions with staff.

If you are an enthusiastic researcher, and if you have an emerging or established reputation, then this may give rise to jealousy, even if subliminal, in your interactions with staff who have no idea how to get started in creating a research profile for themselves or whose research has run into a dead end and not yielded the hoped-for contributions to new knowledge or recognition. You may face competitiveness from staff for internal promotion. Take this example from a professor responding to the survey:

> I had significant support from the Head of the School . . . but found myself caught up in a highly political battle in which my Head of Division . . . was very unsupportive in an underhand way. Basically [they] wanted to achieve a professorial title before 'allowing' me to do so. [They] had followed a managerial route whilst I had aimed to develop my research profile. So for me it was a struggle.

One of the professors responding to the survey, when asked to give advice for aspiring professors, suggested that you avoid organisational politics. This means that in taking up a new post, you may decide to keep your own counsel and avoid being drawn into factional groups. You may find that there is an element of nepotism in professorial appointments, as was reported by some professors. A safe course if you want to be a professor is teaching your students well, developing your research and publication record and fulfilling your service obligations.

Equity issues

Are you being dealt with fairly? This is a question that may occur to you, and with respect to professorial appointments, we received a range of reports from professors on practices they observed: negative discrimination on gender grounds, both male and female, was mentioned, as was positive discrimination on ethnicity and gender grounds to create a professoriat representative of perhaps the student population. More than 50% reported that they felt the process for appointment was open and transparent, rigorous but fair. A small number reported that the process was not transparent and more than one mentioned that appointments were made where the staff did not seem to have the research and publishing profiles expected of professors. In some universities, the title is used to indicate the holder is a senior member of staff rather than a research and thought leader in their field. One reported that 'racial quotas' were considered in the appointment of professors. Universities generally make their own decisions on this matter. Adetunji (2017) and Advance HE (2022) outline arguments for positive action to create a professoriate that is diverse in a wide range of ways.

Only two professors mentioned that their university has an active programme for supporting staff development to professorship. Others pointed to well-known barriers to promotion – covert or overt discrimination on any one of a range of characteristics, as well as not being in the right networks. One professor was told after their application was turned down that they needed an advocate on the internal appointments panel who could speak up for them, even though their application met all the criteria.

If you can show you meet and exceed the criteria for a professorial appointment, then at least you have a strong case for asking for advice about how to improve your chance of a successful application if it is turned down in the first instance. However, do watch out for 'cultural taxation', which is defined in Chapter 5.

Balancing research and teaching

The professors contributing to the survey providing data for this book have experience of professorial appointment processes in more than 30 countries. They were asked what advice they would give aspiring professors about how to manage teaching and research, and the answers were similar regardless of the country:

> It is challenging to balance teaching and research: you need determination. It is also very useful when you research in the areas that you teach so the one complements the other and provides [you with] motivation to push through the rough times.
>
> My tips are 1. Always write. Even if you think you don't have the time. Don't postpone the writing. Don't say 'I'll do it in the summer . . . or on the semester break . . . etc.' Time flies during these breaks and holidays and you

won't get as much done as you planned. Writing must be progressed on a weekly basis. Once you leave the writing for a long period of time it is also extremely difficult to get back to it. Small steps are necessary. 2. Go to small conferences and find a group of international people that you feel comfortable with and that are interested in the same things as you are.

So, having a clear research focus linked to your teaching, working with peers through national and international networking and managing your time effectively are critical success factors that the professorial group identifies.

If your research area is new, then act to develop teaching programmes that will recruit students. I was in this position in the period 1984–1990 when computers were being introduced into schools and internet use was being developed. I developed a master's programme in the field that I then taught on – thus aligning my research with my teaching.

Chapter 4 includes more on time management strategies.

Allocation of teaching and administrative responsibilities

Those who are responsible for timetabling have a complicated job, and compromises are often needed. For a host of reasons, what is promised at interview may not be what is available when you are appointed: professional regulations change, which may affect you if you are teaching on programmes that meet external requirements; the required number of students to make a course financially viable may not be met; staff may have left, which then means teaching duties have to be reassigned and so on. I suggest you show sensitivity to the needs of the university and students as well as keeping an eye on the skills, knowledge and experiences that you need to meet the professorial criteria. Over time, with goodwill on both sides, you may be able to negotiate access to opportunities that allow you to develop in the areas that you need to.

Examples of questions about the teaching workload that it may be helpful to have answers for:

- **What teaching is available to you?** Post-graduate? undergraduate only? Doctoral supervision – as first or second supervisor? What type of teaching: lectures, seminars, personal tutoring? . . . Do you have repeat lectures? I mentioned earlier an instance where one member of staff taught four cohorts across the year – they taught the same content four times, and yet another staff member had not one repeat lecture. As you can imagine, the planning and preparation time both staff had to put in was vastly different.
- **How much teaching is expected for the role?** How many hours per week on average – 6? 10? 15? For each hour of teaching/lecturing, expect to spend two or three additional hours in preparing your teaching and assessment.

- **Where will you be teaching?** Will you be required to travel between locations? How much time per week might be spent travelling to teach a couple of hours in one location and a couple of hours in another location?
- **When might you be teaching?** When does the normal day start and finish? What teaching is expected in the evenings, on weekends, in what might normally be seen as university holiday times? You may find that you have classes starting at 9 am one day and another class starting at 6 and finishing at 9 pm. You may be expected to run summer schools.
- **Timetabling.** How and when is the teaching timetable decided? What opportunities will you have to teach the subjects that you are most deeply knowledgeable about, and those that are related to your research focus?
- **Student information.** How many students will you be teaching? The follow-up work from lecturing a group of 100 with 100 assignments to mark is significantly higher than that from a group tutorial where feedback on presented work is given in the tutorial. What is the academic and language background of the students? Teaching and assessing the work of students writing essays in their second language can take considerably more time than a similar group working in their first language. What support services are provided?
- **Administration.** What meetings/committees do you have to attend? How often are they, how long, what location? Are students interviewed? If yes, how many days do you need to set aside for this?
- **Research and writing time.** What support is there for this? A simple strategy costing the university little is to have no meetings, say on Fridays, and as little teaching as possible. This allows staff to start intellectual work with some assurance that they won't be pulled away to meetings. If they wish, staff have the option of continuing to write over the weekend. When can holidays be booked? This knowledge will help you plan any writing and perhaps international conference attendance.

From the items on this list and their implications for a lecturer's workload, you can see how hard it might be to stay research active while you are an early career researcher. Hence, even if you can 'buy out' part of your teaching load through university grants for early career researchers, this might have a huge impact on your ability to continue to be research active through the early part of your career. If your university has an internal budget for supporting such research time for new staff, then an early application might be advisable – if only to give you time to publish from your doctoral thesis. If you have a colleague sufficiently qualified to cover for you and free to provide cover, then it will be easier for your line manager to release you from teaching. I once applied for and was granted two months of unpaid leave to finish a book. . . . I needed the continuous uninterrupted time to make sure the book was coherent. Would you be prepared to do this? Even now, 30 years later, I wonder why I was so motivated to finish the book that I was prepared to take a cut in pay. (In case you are wondering, royalties for niche academic books can be less than the university's charge-out cost of your time.)

Your checklist and goals: for balancing teaching and research

The checklist in Table 3.2 prompts you to make a list of what matters to you and what information to gather when you are applying for jobs.

Table 3.2 Checklist: balancing teaching and research is freely available for download via the Support Material tab on the Routledge website.

Table 3.2 Checklist: balancing teaching and research

ITEM	Achieved?	
	Yes	No
RESEARCHING CONTRACTS AND WORKING CONDITIONS		
Have you made a list of what matters to you, what experiences you are after (teaching, research, administration, service), when you are looking for a university job or looking to change jobs? Have you a strategy for finding out as much as you can about a university before applying and before interview?		
BUILDING YOUR NEGOTIATION SKILLS		
Have you practised your negotiation skills so that, at the appropriate time, you can respectfully negotiate which classes you teach and any timetable changes and research support/conference attendance needs that you have?		
TEACHING EXPERTISE		
Have you a plan for undertaking teacher training or improving your teaching skills? Your students are potential co-researchers/collaborators for the rest of your career, and your relationships with them start by you being a brilliant teacher.		
YOUR SPECIFIC GOALS: now record the goals that suit your context and your discipline . . .		

Summary: recognising success and avoiding pitfalls

In this chapter, examples of different contracts are included so that you can avoid the pitfalls of signing up to a contract without understanding what it might mean for your acquisition of the skills and experience required to demonstrate that you meet the criteria for professorship. At the same time, the chapter makes the point that funds have to come from somewhere to pay your salary, and much as you might enjoy research, unless there is funding for it, or it can be subsidised from grant income or from other people in the university increasing their teaching load, then you may end up doing the research in your own time. This investment in your own career and research profile is what will pay off, perhaps a decade down the line, when you look at your CV and find that you are meeting the criteria for professorship.

References

Adetunji, J. (2017) *Can People 'Like Me' Go to College? Inequality and Dreams of Higher Ed*, https://theconversation.com/can-people-like-me-go-to-college-inequality-and-dreams-of-higher-ed-73893, Accessed on 23 October 2022.

Advance HE. (2022) *Race Equality Charter*, www.advance-he.ac.uk/equality-charters/race-equality-charter, Accessed on 23 October 2022.

Australian Research Council (ARC). (2022) *Excellence in Research for Australia*, www.arc.gov.au/evaluating-research/excellence-research-australia, Accessed on 23 October 2022.

Babelytė, K. and Mikulskienė, B. (2009) Policy impact on research excellence, *European Integration Studies* (3), 8–12.

ENQA. (2022) *Standards and Guidelines for Quality Assurance in the European Higher Education Area (ESG)*, www.enqa.eu/esg-standards-and-guidelines-for-quality-assurance-in-the-european-higher-education-area/, Accessed on 23 October 2022.

New Zealand Tertiary Education Commission. (2022) *Performance-Based Research Fund*, www.tec.govt.nz/funding/funding-and-performance/funding/fund-finder/performance-based-research-fund/, Accessed on 23 October 2022.

Quality Assurance Agency for Higher Education (QAA). (2022a) *The UK's Quality Body for Higher Education*, www.qaa.ac.uk//en/home, Accessed on 23 October 2022.

Quality Assurance Agency for Higher Education (QAA). (2022b) *Reviewing Higher Education*, www.qaa.ac.uk, Accessed on 23 October 2022.

Quality Assurance Agency for Higher Education (QAA). (2022c) *European Standards and Guidelines for Higher Education*, www.qaa.ac.uk/training-and-services/iqr/about-iqr/european-standards-and-guidelines-(esg), Accessed on 23 October 2022.

Research Excellence Framework (REF). (2021) www.ref.ac.uk, Accessed on 23 October 2022.

University College London. (2022) *Costing Your Research Project*, www.ucl.ac.uk/research-innovation-services/award-services/applying-funding/costing-principles/costing-your-research-project, Accessed on 23 October 2022.

University of Exeter. (2022a) *Payroll Office and Salary Information*, www.exeter.ac.uk/staff/employment/payandconditions/payroll/salariesandoncosts/salariesandoncosts, Accessed on 23 October 2022.

University of Exeter. (2022b) *Payscales*, www.exeter.ac.uk/media/univers, Accessed on 23 October 2022.

University of Exeter. (2022c) *Pay, Pensions and Conditions of Employment*, www.exeter.ac.uk/staff/employment/payandconditions/, Accessed on 23 October 2022.

Chapter 4

Becoming an expert and a thought leader

Marilyn Leask

Introduction

About half the professors responding to the survey underpinning this book had planned and worked systematically to become professors. The others said that they wouldn't have thought of applying for professorial status before peers and senior staff suggested this to them.

Different disciplines bring different challenges to academics wanting to pursue professorial status. There is, for example, considerable scope in the social sciences for academics with no research funding to carve out specialist niches for research and to develop the expertise and experiences that lead to the award of professorial status. However, in disciplines where access to laboratories and to expensive equipment is required, there is less flexibility for potential professors to build their own independent career pathway without funding. On the other hand, in disciplines such as law, business, social work, and education, a prerequisite for some academic posts is experience as a practitioner, so aspiring academics can find they are ten years, in career terms, behind their fellow academics in the natural sciences who have followed the route to an academic career of first degree, second degree, PhD and on, becoming published academics before the age of 30.

In this chapter, I introduce a list of indicators of the esteem in which academics are held by their peers and provide advice about building the impact, reach and significance of your research – thus building a profile of you as an expert in your field. (Chapters 6 and 7 provide advice on building your social and traditional media presence.) Time is the most precious tool you have along with your personal resilience, your ability to deal positively with feedback, criticism, disappointment and challenge and your belief in yourself. This chapter addresses these issues.

Objectives

This chapter provides advice on:

- assessing yourself against indicators of professional esteem;
- maximising the impact, reach and significance of your research;

DOI: 10.4324/9781003217596-4

- identifying time management strategies that might work for you;
- overcoming self-doubt.

Esteem indicators for academic staff

If you are new to academia, it might be hard to imagine how you become the go-to expert in a field. Table 4.1 is included to provide you with a series of stepping stones to guide your pathway to success. As a panel member of the UK 2008 national research assessment exercise, I made notes about the criteria used to assess the esteem with which academics were held. This criterion was later replaced by impact measures in the UK national research assessment system; however, I feel this list of esteem characteristics may be of use to you as it shows the range of activities that junior staff may be undertaking – the entry-level

Table 4.1 Esteem indicators for academic staff (Leask, 2010)

Very high-level indicators
- engagement (research or consultancy) with international and national organisations/committees in other countries;
- influence on national/international practice;
- leadership of international research projects;
- considerable national and international doctoral-level examining;
- influence on theory/practice in other countries;
- publications have a high level of take up in other countries;
- visiting professorships – international.

High-level indicators
- positions held through election by peers on national committees;
- engagement (research or consultancy) with regional and national organisations – govt. agencies, charities etc.;
- leadership of regional and national research projects;
- national doctoral-level examining;
- influence on theory/practice nationally;
- publications have a high level of take up nationally;
- visiting professorships – national.

Medium-level indicators
- membership of editorial boards;
- engagement (research or consultancy) with local organisations;
- engagement in significant research projects;
- publications have demonstrable levels of take up;
- doctoral-level examining.

Entry-level indicators
These indicators are expected of all academics:
- engagement in research and development with perhaps small groups of local users;
- engagement in professional networks;
- presentations at national conferences;
- engagement with users;
- contribution to the body of knowledge in a chosen field.

indicators, then the high- and very high-level indicators, which are the ones that people applying for professorship are expected to meet. In reviewing the table, you will see that, as mentioned previously in this book, engaging in professional associations and presentations at conferences as well as international collaborations is expected of academics.

Maximising the impact, reach and significance of your research

I know from my UK national roles in assessing research and subsequent consultancies to review university staff research outputs that there are many talented staff – submitting well-written academic articles – who do not understand how to ensure their research is nationally and internationally significant and has impact and extensive reach in their field. These criteria for excellence were used in the UK research assessment exercise (REF, 2021a), and you can see that they fit with the core criteria for recognition as a full professor.

One role I've had for a UK government agency was to mobilise research-based knowledge underpinning the training of teachers and to provide advisory notes for ministers from time to time about educational issues. If you want your research to have influence on government decisions, then ask yourself this question before you put any proposals forward: is the evidence for the claims your research makes strong enough for a government minister to stand up in public and say their decisions are influenced by your research? Government ministers have to be very aware of public perception about their decisions. The best example of impactful research I came across during that period was Professor Kathy Sylva and her team's (Sylva et al., 2004) research on the value of early years education. She and her team had carried out longitudinal research over a number of years, and the research findings were convincing enough for the minister of education secretary of state for education at the time to argue for resources for the sector from the Treasury. Systematic reviews, too, can provide an overview of the research of the field, which provides a good foundation for decision-making at the national level. For definitions and details about how to carry out systematic reviews, see the work of the EPPI Center (Evidence-based Policy and Practice Information Centre), Campbell Collaboration for the social sciences and Cochrane Collaboration for medicine: websites for these are listed at the end of the chapter. Engaging in the work of these organisations may provide you with the opportunities to produce impactful and significant systematic reviews of evidence in particular areas in your discipline.

Professor Keith Topping's work stands out as providing many examples of the synthesis of research in key areas of knowledge to produce significant findings, which he published in succinct articles in academic journals.

My guess is that if staff do not receive mentoring at an early stage, then they can easily make decisions that stand in the way of them becoming recognised experts and thought leaders and so professors in their field. I hope this book supports new academics in avoiding the pitfalls of focusing on only small-scale, perhaps locally relevant research so that they make research decisions that help them become recognised as leading thinking, practices and research in their chosen field.

Maximising the impact of your research

The impact of some research is very easy to identify e.g. the chemical DDT was banned because of its proven impact on the environment. But for other research, proxy measures might be needed. In several chapters in this book, you will come across references to national research assessment exercises that are used to grade the research in universities. Research funds are then distributed according to the grades and the number of staff and, to a certain extent, the discipline. Some use the journal of publication as a proxy measure for quality and international recognition. (We have come across such tables in countries as far apart as Poland, Pakistan and Australia.) However, in a niche area, the journal that is likely to reach the most users may be one that is not even included in these national tables. In some cases, print or social media or professional journals may be more appropriate than academic journals.

Citation metrics are more commonly used in some disciplines than in others, but citation metrics can be flawed: controversial work or poor work may result in higher levels of citation as the work is challenged in subsequent publications. Likewise, the number of downloads from a website is no measure of the quality of the material. For an extensive database of impact studies covering different disciplines, I suggest you look at the UK Research Excellence Framework (REF, 2021b) database.

Maximising the reach of your research

Networking and collaborating within your national and international professional community from the beginning of your career is one way of maximising the reach of your research and checking its significance with peers. If your research has relevance to the curriculum for the 0–19 age group, I invite you to submit a research summary to the mapping educational specialist know-how initiative (MESHGuides initiative, www.meshguides.org), which I set up with other educators to provide a bridge between researchers and teachers who want to underpin their lessons with the latest research. At the time of writing, there are many hundreds of thousands of users of the research summaries/MESHGuides on the site, and users come from over 200 countries i.e. most countries in the world.

One professor advises:

> Have a plan, be realistic, seek out collaborators; remember you need to be proactive in seeking out and making opportunities; stay true to yourself; you can research your teaching.

Working collaboratively with peers from other universities keeps you up to date in your field, provides you with publishing and conference keynote opportunities and doesn't involve organisational politics. Long term, such international collaborations may lead to invitations to speak at conferences internationally, international external examining of PhDs and international consultancy: all of which are expected of those applying for professorships.

Maximising the significance of your research

Will your research focus lead to you becoming deeply expert? Priorities in societies come and go and can change rapidly, so choosing a research focus that provides opportunities over many years is a goal to aim for while remaining flexible about shifting your focus to hot topics in your field, particularly those that are likely to be of interest in the long-term. If you have promising small-scale research, then scaling this up through collaborations with peers in other countries may yield substantial and significant findings. Broadening your knowledge and methodological expertise will stand you in good stead when it comes to international partnerships and your ability to respond to rapidly changing needs for knowledge in society.

Choosing your research focus is a major action within your power that can make a huge difference to you being able to claim to create new knowledge in your field and to be a thought leader (professorial qualities). If you are at an early stage in your career, then it might be that your PhD provides a foundation for the next step in your research. Certainly if you can build on your PhD it is a huge advantage because you already have in-depth knowledge of the literature in the state of the field, including potential new areas of research.

Here is advice from different professors on choosing your main focus for your research.

> The first thing is to establish your research agenda and keep focused. This will greatly assist in the process of establishing a solid profile in the particular field in which you wish to establish professorship. It is helpful to interact with persons who are already professors so that you can learn from them. . . . It is also useful to collaborate with other researchers in your field locally and internationally where possible.

> Be careful about taking on too many disparate projects – there should be some breadth to your work but your research profile should look coherent, not scattered.

> Make sure your work does not only or and visibility as this means the external assessors are unlikely to see its value.

You will have noted in Tables 1.1 and 1.2 the requirement for you to demonstrate that your expertise and research in your field are recognised through your attracting of doctoral students. Attracting post-doctoral candidates and providing opportunities for post-doctoral students to work with you is another way of improving your chances of meeting the criteria for the award of professorial status. You need to make it easy for potential students (doctoral and post-doctoral), looking for supervisors, to find you. Ways of being proactive in raising your profile with these potential students include:

- identifying undergraduate and master's students who are interested in researching in your field;
- identifying opportunities for funded studentships and applying for this funding;
- paying careful attention to promoting your work through social media;
- ensuring your university web profile is up to date and written in such a way as to invite students to apply to study with you and academics in the same field to collaborate with you;
- developing a national and international profile through your engagement in the relevant professional associations or international bodies;
- developing a national and international profile through presenting your research papers/ideas at conferences, including specifically through special interest groups.

If there are limited opportunities to supervise doctoral students at your university, then it may be possible to take a part-time tutor role with say, an open, online or distance learning university, on top of your existing university role, in order to gain the experience.

Time management: using technology, balancing family and work–life

The most precious thing you have at your disposal – apart from a brain trained in critical analysis and good written and oral communication skills – is your time. It is a rare luxury for academics to have whole days to devote to research, analysis and writing, so learning how to work effectively with the slivers of time you have is a core skill if you are going to manage your teaching as well as your research in writing and family and social life. You may need to explain to those you share your life with that the time spent writing should benefit everyone in the long run. Relationships can and do fall apart under the pressure of publishing deadlines.

You will find there are many demands on your time, and some people are less able than others to keep a focus on their core work and to say no to other demands on their time. Family responsibilities can have a huge impact on what you can do, and it's always worth remembering when making decisions, about what is most important in your life. Employers can be fickle, and it doesn't matter how good you are at your research or your teaching: if it's not the flavour of the month politically/culturally/socially, then you may find you have no job at all. (See Professor Fazlagić's account of Polish academics' experiences through regime changes in Appendix 2.) So, give careful thought to how you manage your life outside work, your family relationships and your writing workload.

I have a few techniques that save me time: on long journeys or when I am waiting for the grandchildren while they have a swimming lesson, I often make rough notes or plans, perhaps researching an area via the web and copying information into the notes function on the phone, which is then also immediately available on the computer and tablet.

I rarely sit at a desk to write, preferring instead to use a reclining chair and voice operated software. If I am out and about, I use the dictate notes function on the mobile phone so that I don't lose ideas that come when they are least expected. I separate out the kinds of jobs that need to be done to produce a manuscript and note when I do each one best and which ones I can get help on e.g. checking references, indexing, proofreading. I plan the book and chapters in detail using mind mapping, making more and more detailed notes so that once I start turning them into prose, the book or article writes itself.

I use mind maps to pull together the knowledge and the questions I have around the topic, and these provide structures for, say, a book proposal, and then for the chapters and the sections within chapters. I number the items on the mind map to give a logical sequence and then usually use voice dictation tools to get the main points down and into a draft chapter. For articles, I use the REPOSE Guidelines (Appendix 3) to provide structure when I am using the dictation software to create an article. Tidying up references is a job I keep for when I'm feeling tired or not very creative. Sometimes I pay students to help do some of the tidying up. In Chapter 7, Hinson gives you advice about allocating your time in short intervals to achieve a goal by breaking it down into small tasks and staying focused on completing a small task in that period of time.

As you build your academic career, making the most of slivers of time by perhaps linking your teaching to your research and adapting your research to multiple publication types for different audiences should help build your profile steadily – becoming a professor requires resilience and sustained focus of thought over decades: it is not a sprint.

When having to stop writing, I leave a note to myself about the next thought I was going to write about so that when I sit down again, I can easily pick up the line of thought rather than be faced with a blank page. You have no doubt developed ways of incentivising yourself to sit down and write. One colleague goes for a run and finds his mind works while he is running, and he comes back ready to sit down and carry on. Although I've written more tens of thousands of words than I could possibly count, I still probably go through ten drafts of a chapter before I am satisfied with it. I usually ask colleagues to read chapters for sense on the basis that if something doesn't feel right to them, then it won't feel right to the reader. Whether I feel like writing or not, I get some text down as it can then be shaped and refined. If you wait for your ideas to form into perfect sentences, then you might be spending quite a lot of time looking at a blank page.

So how will you find the time? You will need to work this out for yourself based on your own circumstances. Making time to write and developing the discipline of not avoiding writing will help you achieve the publication profile you need.

Chapter 7 provides you with strategies for efficient working using various technologies. Become familiar with technologies that will save you time. As a minimum, use one that can manage your annotated references, allowing you to make notes on books and articles you are reading and to pull out of your stored references those relevant to particular topics you are writing about. Take a long-term view, as you can expect to be building your annotated references for the rest of your career, and make sure you are using technology that allows you to take your work with you if you change institutions. I once lost all the work I had built up as when leaving the institution, I could no longer access the referencing software.

Consider what times of day and in what places you work well and when you can put aside slivers of time for writing. Develop a writing routine and stick to it.

The first few years of university teaching are very time intensive. In Chapter 8, on writing a book, we point out the benefits of writing a textbook to underpin your teaching – while this is initially time intensive, once it is published it will save you many hours of lesson preparation. If you work with colleagues, each of you can research an area in-depth, sharing the resulting knowledge so that the quality of everybody's teaching improves. With colleagues, I have been editing a UK market leader textbook for 30 years. We update it every three years, working with colleagues with deep expertise in about 40 different areas relevant to teacher education. Writing books is a bit like doing your PhD over and over again, but you get faster and of course know you can do it as you have completed a major work of similar length in your thesis.

Self-belief and dealing with doubt

In the early stages of your career, you are likely to doubt if the research area you choose will, in time, lead to a position where your contribution to knowledge in your discipline is substantial enough to warrant the award of full professor status and to question whether your research is worth publishing. You may identify with Michelle Obama, previously one of the USA's first ladies, who talks of the feeling of imposter syndrome: personal doubt about whether one has the right to the position they hold (Weir, 2013). Alternatively, maybe you have felt like Boris Johnson, the UK's ex-PM, that you were born to be king of the world (Cowley, 2020). So, how can you know if your work is of the appropriate standard? Eighty-seven percent of the professors providing data for this book had supportive mentoring from senior colleagues, who should be able to provide you with guidance on these matters, as should your doctoral supervisors. There is no doubt that the nature of research is such that we can't be sure what we're going to find out. Researchers are rightly tentative about research findings, as we are only too aware of the limitations of research. This can be frustrating to politicians and potential research users who are looking for certainty. Developing personal resilience and having the support of peers are ways that academics cope with this uncertainty about the impact, reach and significance of their work.

Here is some advice from the professors answering the survey:

> Think about what you will 'profess'. What are the critical social and environmental questions your work addresses? What is the new knowledge you need to pursue?

Don't compare yourself with others but do your own thing in the way suitable for your personality. That way you differentiate and better fit to some positions than others.

Your checklist and goals: for becoming recognised as an expert and thought leader

There is no guarantee that your research is going to make the difference you hope for (although the negative findings can be as useful as positive findings). But you have no doubt chosen a research focus that you consider is worth dedicating your working life to for decades, perhaps to satisfy your curiosity or for the benefit of your discipline and those interested in your area of work. Perhaps you therefore owe it to yourself to put in the extra effort to bring your research to the attention of those who may benefit from it. As mentioned previously, some academics may find they have to invest their own money into the research itself and into the dissemination of the research. The checklist in Table 4.2 provides you with the opportunity to reflect on your plans for maximising the impact of your research.

Table 4.2 Checklist: becoming recognised as an expert is freely available for download via the Support Material tab on the Routledge website.

Table 4.2 Checklist: becoming recognised as an expert

ITEM	Achieved?	
	Yes	No
ASSESSING YOURSELF AGAINST INDICATORS OF PROFESSIONAL ESTEEM		
Have you considered the esteem indicator list in Table 4.1, and have you a plan for working your way through the levels? If you need to seek help and guidance, what have you done to find people who can mentor you?		
MAXIMISING THE IMPACT, REACH AND SIGNIFICANCE OF YOUR RESEARCH		
Have you considered different ways of increasing the impact, reach and significance of your research? Have you a plan to work to, to realise your goals?		
TIME MANAGEMENT		
Have you identified how you can make time to progress your research alongside balancing teaching, administration and family/social responsibilities?		
OVERCOMING SELF-DOUBT		
Have you strategies for looking after your own mental well-being as you progress along what can be a lonely road of academic endeavour?		
YOUR SPECIFIC GOALS: now record the goals that suit your context and your discipline . . .		

Summary: recognising success and avoiding pitfalls

In writing the advice in this book, I include advice for those who are at an early stage of their career as a university lecturer or, perhaps, are wondering about a career in teaching and research in the university sector. However, the advice is also relevant to you if you are already teaching in the university sector, have an established position and a knowledge of the cycle of the academic year and the systems for teaching and supporting research in your institution.

A central theme of the book is what you can do to develop yourself as a thought leader in your field while, at the same time, managing a teaching job – a job that may require you to teach outside your specialist area and to use your time and your mind in ways that decrease the likelihood of you having time to undertake the research, publications and recognition necessary to be appointed a professor. Consequence: the consequence of not being actively engaged in your discipline, pushing the boundaries of knowledge, is that what you teach your students may not be up to date and the evaluations of your teaching may not be satisfactory – thus putting your job at risk.

Having clear goals for what you want to achieve coupled with effective management of the time you have and collaboration with a group of like-minded experts will maximise your chances of achieving professorial status. Consequence: you keep your job and may be promoted.

Web sites

Campbell Collaboration for the Social Sciences, www.campbellcollaboration.org, Accessed on 24 October 2022.
Cochrane Collaboration for Medicine, www.cochrane.org, Accessed on 24 October 2022.
EPPI Centre (Evidence Based Policy and Practice Information and Coordination Centre), https://eppi.ioe.ac.uk/cms/, Accessed on 24 October 2022.
MESHGuides, www.meshguides.org, Accessed on 24 October 2022.

References

Cowley, J. (2020) From a young age Boris Johnson longed to be World King – but the gods are mocking him, *New Statesman,* 4 November 2020, www.newstatesman.com/politics/uk-politics/2020/11/young-age-boris-johnson-longed-be-world-king-gods-are-mocking-him, Accessed on 23 October 2022.

Leask, M. (2010) *Assessing Esteem, Environment, Research Income and Organisational and Departmental Research Strategies: A Framework for Self Assessment by University Faculties in the UK,* University of Bedfordshire, October 2010. See extracts in Table 4.1 and Appendix 1.

REF. (2021a) *Research Excellence Framework 2021,* Swindon: UK Research and Innovation, www.ref.ac.uk, Accessed on 24 October 2022.

REF. (2021b) *Impact Case Study Database*, https://results2021.ref.ac.uk/impact, Accessed on 24 October 2022.

Sylva, K., Melhuish, E., Sammons, P., Siraj-Blatchford, I. and Taggart, B. (2004) *The Effective Provision of Pre-School Education (EPPE) Project: Findings from Pre-school to end of Key Stage 1*, Institute of Education, University of London, University of Oxford, Birkbeck, University of London, University of Nottingham, https://dera. ioe.ac.uk/18189/2/SSU-SF-2004-01.pdf, Accessed on 24 October 2022.

Weir, K. (2013) Feel like a fraud? [Imposter Syndrome], *American Psychological Association gradPSYCH Magazine*, 11(24–25), www.apa.org/gradpsych/2013/11/ fraud, Accessed on 23 October 2022.

Chapter 5

Mentorship and international networking

Carol Hordatt Gentles

Introduction

This chapter speaks about the role of mentorship and international networking in becoming a professor. For many junior faculty members, there is a false conception that if I just work hard and publish many papers, the path to professorship will be secured. While it is true that one's record of academic publications is a major, often the primary, consideration for promotion, universities normally assess faculty members using a range of additional criteria (see Tables 1.1 and 1.2). These criteria may include teaching performance and professional impact both locally and abroad. Others include service to your department, your institution, your profession or your country. In some cases, where you may be employed by a religious institution, your personal character and morals may also be used in determining whether you are the type of person/professional worthy of becoming a professor. Some institutions have clear, detailed, accessible documentation that outlines exactly what faculty must do to satisfy criteria for promotion. Others, unfortunately, do not. Sometimes, knowledge about the pathway to professorship is shrouded in mystery, clear only to those who evaluate the work and practice of faculty members, and to those who have been promoted. Accessing this type of experiential knowledge, learning how to play the game, is vital to your success. It is also helpful to know how to leverage opportunities for international networking to build and strengthen your international impact. This is where mentorship and international networking become important.

As we speak about the role of mentorship in strengthening your pathway to professorship, you will find useful advice, collated into one table, from the 27 professors we surveyed. Consider this as a gift of mentorship from academics across the globe. Notice the commonalities in what they suggest and consider how you can incorporate their suggestions into your planning for promotion. I will also include a few anecdotes that may be helpful to you.

DOI: 10.4324/9781003217596-5

Objectives

By the end of this chapter, you will understand:

- the concept of mentorship;
- the value of mentorship;
- how to go about getting mentorship;
- how to build local and international networks.

The concept of mentorship: formal and informal

The word *mentor* comes from Greek mythology. As the story goes, when Odysseus went to fight in the Trojan War, he asked his trusted older friend, Mentor, to look after and counsel his son Telemachus. This is where the notion of *mentor* – a teacher or counsellor who is wise and trusted – comes from (Ferreres, 2018). In the world of academia, mentoring happens in two ways: formally and informally. Formal mentorship is about new faculty members being assigned a mentor who is more senior and whose work is guided by a formal university mentoring programme. The Cornell University Faculty Mentoring Programme (2021, p. 1) defines this as

> a critical tool in faculty development and in facilitating faculty success and retention. . . . Mentors assume responsibility for facilitating the professional development of [junior faculty] through potential activities, including: providing information, advice, encouragement, and connections to other mentors, colleagues and professional networks.

It might be interesting to visit this site, to get a full idea of the range of practices associated with giving and receiving mentorship in such a programme.

Informal mentorship is less easily quantified or articulated. As McLaughlin (2010, p. 4) suggests, the notion of the volunteer mentor is one of that senior person who 'reaches out . . . because of shared interests, or by chance encounters'. She says the informal mentor can provide some or several types of support. These range from 'finding a kindred spirit' who can help the junior person navigate the system in addition to learning, or later enhancing their research skills: someone to be a friend providing socioemotional support; a career guide enhancing professional development; a source of information; and an intellectual guide, even a patron who uses his or her power in the field to help advance the other's career. It is important to recognise that you do not need to have a single mentor. Some people benefit from several mentors, each supporting them in different ways at different times in their careers. Some faculty are lucky to have many mentors all at the same time. Sometimes mentorship is offered by a group of faculty, or professional associates, who share common interests with you around a discipline, a research focus or matters concerning teaching, pedagogy and professional issues.

What does mentorship look like?

For example, I was recently elected to serve as president of the International Council on Education for Teaching (ICET, www.icet4u.org). At this point in my career, I am senior faculty, and I was eligible for the position. I knew, too, that holding such an office would help with my advancement to professorship. However, I did not feel confident enough to apply for the position. Then, to my delight, several of the members of the ICET Board started sending me messages encouraging me to fill out the application. They promised that they would support me and told me why they thought I would do a good job. This was mentorship by academics from across the globe, which helped to reassure me that I had what it takes to contribute on an international level.

The value of being mentored

Research suggests that mentoring does have an impact on one's career (Kirchmeyer, 2005; Efstathiou et al., 2018). Lunsford et al. (2017) conclude that mentoring is associated with psychosocial and career benefits for faculty members. They suggest that 'early career faculty are twice as likely to be promoted, more likely to report greater career satisfaction . . . and are more likely to stay in their jobs' (p. 326). In our survey, 88% of the 27 professors surveyed said that for aspiring professors, mentoring is very, if not critically, important. Eighty-four percent also agreed that international networking is very important for aspiring professors. Blau et al. (2010) found that junior faculty who were mentored produced more publications, were more likely to have a top-tier publication and were more successful at receiving funding for research.

Equity issues

Mentorship is critical in helping women and faculty from minority groups overcome social and cultural barriers to professional advancement. Research (Turner et al., 1999; Bland et al., 2009) to determine what these barriers may be suggest the following:

- professional isolation, if you are the only faculty from a particular demographic group;
- feeling excluded from collegial networks, whether intentional or not;
- biases from colleagues who may not value the scholarly contributions of women and underrepresented minorities;
- differences in what are perceived as acceptable social behaviours. Professional behaviours required for successful advancement may be at odds with a faculty

member's cultural norms. For example, women from many backgrounds are socialised to be compliant, modest, less competitive, to refrain from participating with men in conversations. They feel uncomfortable being outspoken or promoting themselves in the workplace;

- cultural taxation – women are more likely to be asked to provide service that benefits the institution but not their own advancement.

Mentors can help faculty to navigate these barriers by providing 'safe spaces' to discuss these concerns.

Identifying your needs

Mentors can also help new faculty to be aware of what they need to know. Many years ago, when I was starting out in academia, I was struggling to adapt to my new job and manage the demands of my family as well. I had three small sons, one of whom had learning challenges. I believed that my struggles were a sign of weakness. I saw senior faculty-women at work who appeared to have it all together. One day, a very eminent female professor stopped by my office. She gently told me she had noticed how stressed I was. She then proceeded to share her own story of struggling to balance work and family when she was younger. Hearing what she had to say, and her graciousness in sharing her personal story, was a revelation. I realised I was not weak and that what I was going through was not unusual. This was a wonderful act of mentoring that made a huge impact on my career.

The literature on best practices in faculty mentoring identify a myriad of needs all junior faculty may have and that mentors can help them address. Table 5.1 offers examples of these.

Developing social capital

A core advantage of mentorship is how it can help you build and develop your own social capital. This is a term that speaks to your ability to take advantage of 'connections among individuals – social networks and the norms of reciprocity and trustworthiness that arise from them' (Putnam, 2001, p. 19), in your department, faculty, institution and even beyond. Faculty who become professors usually have a lot of social capital, acquired through experience, professional networking and their engagement with the institution where they work. Acquiring social capital is particularly significant for young faculty who come to positions in higher education with few social or professional connections. They may be overwhelmed by the newness of everything. They struggle with how to discover and learn the functional knowledge of processes, protocols and how things are organised and managed. Some people are supremely confident with strong social skills. They find it easy to reach out and ask questions. Others, however, may feel shy and anxious – not wanting to ask for help because they will appear foolish or lacking in sophistication.

Table 5.1 Junior faculty needs and how mentors can help them address them

Issues for junior faculty members	How mentors can help
How to manage demands of work–life	Knowing how to prioritise and balance work responsibilities such as teaching, research and service
How to build professional networks	Meeting and interacting with more senior colleagues who may be influential within and outside one's university Making suggestions about which conferences to attend Figuring out the most beneficial professional associations to join
How to construct knowledge of evaluation and promotion processes and regulations	Understanding the timelines to becoming a professor
How to map out one's research activities	Figuring out what research foci will best suit one's academic progress; how to build a recognised body of scholarship
How to position oneself strategically within one's institution	Figuring out which committees one should volunteer to serve on, and how to advance into positions of academic leadership
How to teach well	Learning how to improve one's pedagogy and manage students Figuring out how to get recognition for one's teaching

Source: Adapted from the Cornell University Faculty Mentoring Programme. https://facultydevelopment.cornell.edu/mentoring-guidelines

Administrative staff as mentors

It is interesting that often the people you can turn to for mentorship at this time may not be academics. Instead, administrative and clerical staff may be the best persons to offer advice about 'how things work' at the office. For example, how does one operate the photocopy machine? Are there support staff assigned to assist with tasks like printing and copying? Do you have staff assigned to help you? In some institutions that are underfunded, under-resourced and suffer from infrastructural challenges, the office staff member who knows how to access ink for the printer or how to fix the printer is a key asset. Finding/accessing administrative support can go a long way in improving your capacity to produce papers. Administrative and clerical staff are also willing to identify colleagues who offer services you may need to conduct your research, such as copy editing and transcribing. Forging cordial relationships with administrative and clerical staff may also be useful as they are often the gatekeepers for accessing senior faculty.

Mentors as advocates and patrons

The support of mentors becomes significant in helping you to recognise and identify challenges, to advise you on how to work around them and even to advocate for you when you are up for promotion. This is evident in Table 5.2, where we highlight advice to junior faculty from the professors we surveyed. Mentors themselves also have different degrees of social capital. While some may be able to only offer advice and psychosocial support, others have real social power in their institutions and disciplines. Having such a person in your corner, as a patron, can help to open doors for you. For example, they may be able to help (teach) you how to get research funding, or invitations to conferences, or maybe even invitations to give keynote presentations. Another significant accomplishment would be for a mentor to help you sit on an editorial or a professional board. I have benefitted from such a mentor twice in my career. This was a professor who recommended me to serve on two national boards in my field of education. Each time, she had been on the boards, but upon retiring recommended me to take her place. My tenure on these two boards was very important in helping me to fulfil my university's requirements for national service.

Advice from professors across the globe on networking and mentoring

The examples of advice in Table 5.2 come from the professors around the globe who contributed to the survey undertaken for this book. The quotations are included to provide you with insights into how current professors were helped by others to develop themselves so they meet professorial criteria while at the same time managing teaching, support for students and administrative tasks. The professors reported a wide range of experiences with both informal and formal mentoring.

How to get mentorship

If you are fortunate to find a position in a university with a formal mentoring programme, take advantage of everything it has to offer. If you work in an institution without such a programme, you will need to find mentors. The importance of this is clear from what has been described earlier – that mentorship really makes a difference for one's career advancement. The challenge is, how do you get mentorship?

Articulate your specific needs

The simplest but also often the most difficult way is to approach a more senior colleague and ask for help. Be specific about your needs. Are you approaching them for advice on a psychosocial concern – your wellbeing? Or are you seeking specific advice about research planning or attending a conference? Try to be smart and notice what sort of information they may have to offer. Remember that not everyone has the skills or personality to become that wise, trusted counsellor. But they may be happy to share what they have learned from their own

Table 5.2 Advice from professors across the globe on networking and mentoring

I spent a day with a professor from the USA who illustrated how the role could be used to support others and help them find opportunities to do research – this was something I was interested in – prior to this (unreasonably) I had thought being a professor required a somewhat 'selfish' orientation. I was also actively supported and encouraged by a woman colleague professor who had recently retired. She was critical in crafting my application but had been supportive of me and other staff (women) in her leadership role.

My father was a professor, and although he acted in another research field, he influenced me with his examples, conversations, and writings. Thinking about my career and looking at the past, I also noticed how important it was to work with a group of faculty members aspiring to be professors. We all wanted to be professors and were friends. We helped each other as 'critical friends' and shared mentoring experiences. Being part of good education associations (national and international) I could have chance conversations and see the way the professors were working.

I learnt a lot from the Principal Investigator on a project I was researcher on: they asked my opinion on a book proposal they had written, rang a journal editor to ask for an article we had co-authored to be published in the next edition as the topic was the subject of international/national concern, showed me a research proposal they had put to the government based on innovative regional work by practitioners that he had observed, invited my employer to second me to the project. I had three amazing secondments to national and international research projects supported by three excellent employers. Two critical points spring to mind: when I was training to teach, a fellow student said networking was important in a career. I had never thought of this before but it has been excellent advice. When a promotion came up in my school I wasn't going to apply as there was a lot to be done in my current role to establish sound processes and teaching resources. A female friend said that was why women didn't get promoted – they were too reluctant to leave jobs unfinished. Whether this is true or not, it influenced me, and I got the promotion which led directly to the career I have had.

I have been informally mentored by a colleague who has been both Research Division Lead and responsible for our [national research assessment] submission . . . ; her feedback on my writing, grant applications and advice on career progression has been pivotal.

I also had the opportunity to undertake a Fulbright Visiting Scholarship and I think this made a big difference to my academic profile and international standing. [Editor's note: a number of the professors had been Fulbright scholars.]

Network nationally and internationally and of course teach well.

We had a very charismatic dean during my early years in academia. He drove transformation at the institutions very forcefully, including the acceleration of promotion for women and minority groups.
I also had the opportunity to spend time as an assistant professor (which is a junior position in the US context) at Yale University early on.

(Continued)

Table 5.2 (Continued)

Linkage is important. From linkage, we will have the chance to work with people from different countries. When doing research, don't be too calculative, help each other in the group to succeed in the project. Your attitude will attract others to work with us. Be patient with others who need help. Plan your time properly and only be committed to the task you have the ability to carry out.

Identify a person who inspires you and try to link up or ask to be linked up.

Go to small conferences and find a group of international people that you feel comfortable with and who are interested in the same things as you are.

Networking, collaborating, synergy, strategise, be hard working, humble, keep learning, be determined, be self-disciplined, have good time management.

Think carefully if this is the career you want. The work is immense, it goes beyond the classroom, without a set time, less valued socially than it should be. If you decide for this profession, the technical aspects, you learn on the way.

Have a plan, be realistic, seek out collaborators; remember you need to be proactive in seeking out and making opportunities; stay true to yourself; you can research your teaching.

In practical terms – [you need knowledge about] what seminars to take part and how to create your social academic profiles, where to publish, how to be competitive enough for a job, how to use language towards your advantage and how to find a job in Universities in [in your country].

[There is no recipe for gaining professorial status] . . . It depends on the institution, the organisation, and the country. But you will always have to work and study hard for it. I looked for ways to like what I was doing (even when it was hard) and fed the fire inside myself to keep me moving ahead. Being around (at work, in associations, or even in congress or events) with 'good professors' also helped me.

Be an attentive collaborator.

Teaching–research balance is important to keep in mind, but also international networking.

There were a number of more experienced faculty members who took me under their wings early on and reminded me of how important it was for me to contribute to teaching, research and service and how I would need to be able to demonstrate my contributions at the institutional, provincial, national, and international levels.

The most positive informal mentoring I got was from other colleagues/ friends who already were professors at their universities. Exchange of ideas and critical points were crucial to help me get prepared to compete in recruitment processes/calls.

I do not have any informal mentoring, as stated above. I continue to perform my task as a service to God. I am actively involved in research and publication, networking, etc., because of my interest in exploring knowledge and contributing in whatever ways I can to my university, community, and country.

(Continued)

Table 5.2 (Continued)

To become a professor was never in my [plans] before this. However, I worked hard and did whatever I could contribute to university and country. I only applied for my professorship upon encouragement from colleagues and university top management.

The process was initiated by our rector. She was convinced that I am ready to start the process of applying. If it hadn't been for her, it would have taken me a longer time to do it.

[I had] positive mentoring from an older colleague, I strongly believe that this type of academic patronage is ESSENTIAL. Her guidance, wisdom and knowledge to steer me through the system, was invaluable.

I consulted about my progress with colleagues and responsible people from the Scientific Board of the University.

experiences. Take note, at meetings, what issues different faculty seem concerned about. Are these issues you share concern for?

Your personal qualities and mentorship

Try to cultivate and demonstrate qualities that make you easy to mentor. For example, adhere to the norms for healthy, collegial relationships such as mutual respect, courtesy and the ability to be confidential. Try to be mindful of and sensitive to cultural norms that are different. Try to educate yourself about what these are. If you have obtained an academic position in a country with strong hierarchical norms, then make sure you respect and follow these. At the same time, do not allow yourself to be treated with disrespect. Prospective mentors are more likely to be drawn to a mentee who has character, is reliable and demonstrates academic integrity and a desire to become a good scholar.

Get involved – active networking

Networking is powerful and vital to your pathway to professorship. Mentors can help you to access networks that are significant for you. But networking is also the best way to find mentors. At the start of your career, it is wise to be willing to volunteer to contribute to all spheres of departmental and university life. Get involved in various committees and make solid contributions. A key area in which to participate is helping to organise conferences, workshops, symposia, webinars. These are great ways to network and meet prospective mentors. In today's post-pandemic world, it is somewhat easier to meet prospective mentors across the globe because of technology. Securing funding for travel to international conferences may be problematic for many faculty. Thankfully there are now countless opportunities to attend academic gatherings virtually. Browse the internet for conferences and events that interest you professionally. Sign up to present a paper or to attend. It is wise to target smaller, more intimate physical events where you are more likely to find yourself in small discussion groups with senior academics in your field. These are wonderful ways to meet and engage with scholars who may want to work with you. Senior faculty are often also looking for international research partners. So, indicate you are available to work collaboratively. Be bold!

In my case, being bold has worked for me, especially in my later years. I was very fortunate to meet a mentor a few years ago who has been wonderfully generous with invitations to co-write chapters with her. Although we had known each other before, we had never really interacted. One day, I saw an invitation from her, in a professional organisation's WhatsApp group chat, to participate in a research project. I took up the invitation and joined the virtual meeting. There were several people online – all well-established academics in their fields. Although I felt a bit intimidated, I boldly signed up for some of the tasks the group needed to do. This led to the launch of a wonderful international research project that has opened many doors for me, across the globe.

A useful strategy for accessing mentorship is to join professional associations. There are so many to choose from. Select associations in your discipline. These are excellent spaces to meet and build mentoring relationships, locally, regionally and internationally. It is helpful to research the websites of professional associations you are considering before making a commitment to becoming a member. Find out the organisational structure of the association. Does it allow members to assume leadership roles? If so, how, and how quickly? Is the association welcoming or is it very formal? Does the association host academic events that you will be able to attend? Are there chapters in different countries? Does membership segue into opportunities for research and publications?

Formal mentoring materials and protocols

A number of universities in different countries provide very detailed advice for faculty on formal mentoring programmes and processes, and you are advised to see whether your own university or the one you wish to apply to has a mentoring programme. See for example the University of Cambridge School of Clinical Medicine (2022) Mentoring Programme.

The University of Edinburgh and the University of Auckland have materials that are publicly available (University of Edinburgh, 2022a, 2022b; University of Auckland, 2022). These materials address benefits for the university, guidance for mentors and mentees, confidentiality and ethics, contracts and timescales e.g. agreeing a finish date, protocols for giving feedback and so on. The materials also outline different forms of mentoring: one to one, group, peer to peer, team mentoring, and the University of Auckland Appendices include checklists and proformas: mentee's expectations; mentor's expectations; mentoring agreements; a mentoring diary sheet; a mentoring progress plan; conversation starters; stages of a mentoring relationship and a formal mentor matching flowchart. It may be beneficial to explore whether other universities in your country have publicly available materials that might be more specifically relevant for your context.

Your checklist and goals: for mentoring and networking

The value of mentorship in helping faculty progress in their career is outlined above. I suggest you use the criteria for achieving professorship set out in Tables 1.1 and 1.2 to develop your plan for finding and working with mentors who have the specific skills and experiences that you need to acquire. Table 5.3 provides you with a list of prompts to help you plan. As mentioned previously, you may find that you are the only expert in your specific field in the university, so for this reason you may need to seek mentors from outside your university as well as those within your university who can help you negotiate the internal processes and with meeting the non–subject-specific criteria for professorship.

Table 5.3 Checklist: mentors and networks is freely available for download via the Support Material tab on the Routledge website.

Table 5.3 Checklist: mentors and networks

ITEM	Achieved?	
	Yes	No
IDENTIFYING MENTORS		
What kind of mentoring is appropriate for you in your context: formal or informal? More than one professor has mentioned the value of having family members who understand the criteria for selection of professors, review and advice on applications. Have you looked at the criteria for professorship in Tables 1.1 and 1.2 and identified mentors either within your own university or professional association or from elsewhere who could help you develop your skills, knowledge and expertise in the different areas?		
Have you made a note of what specifically you wish to learn from each potential mentor? Have you decided how to approach them?		
ETHICAL MENTORING		
Have you reviewed the advice on contracts and ethics, for example in the University of Edinburgh (2022b) or the University of Auckland (2022) materials, and decided how you will approach ethical issues? If you ask others to mentor you, have you considered whether the prospective mentors you approach are likely to be on your interview panels in the future and whether having confidential knowledge about your aspirations might cause a conflict of interest?		
BUILDING LOCAL AND INTERNATIONAL NETWORKS		
Have you identified professional associations nationally and internationally that fit with your interests and within which you are likely to be able to progress to leadership positions?		
YOUR SPECIFIC GOALS: now record the goals that suit your context and your discipline . . .		

Summary: recognising success and avoiding pitfalls

Unless you are in a university that has a well-established mentoring programme that fits with your personal needs and your subject specialism, you are going to have to be proactive in planning your own mentorship opportunities. As this chapter suggests, mentors can come in all shapes and sizes. What they do for you can vary widely. Accept any advice and guidance graciously. You do not have to follow it, but you should consider it. At the same time, be cautious and sensible. Many new faculty have found themselves in uncomfortable positions that become detrimental to their progress. For example, if you are the kind of person who has difficulty saying no to requests to undertake work, then you might find that you are paying the cultural tax identified above: the risk here is that your skill set becomes too diverse and not specialised enough for you to qualify for professorship. Be mindful, too, when working collaboratively on research and publications, of how you receive credit for your contribution. Sadly, there are people whose offer of mentorship may be self-serving only, and who may take advantage of your naïveté. You should never allow yourself to be in a mentoring relationship or situation that makes you feel uncomfortable or where you feel you are asked to compromise your values.

While there may be pitfalls, for many, mentorship and networking have proven invaluable in helping to advance their career. A key lesson here is that as you progress along the pathway to professorship, you too should be willing to offer the gift of mentorship to others.

Website

Cornell University Faculty Mentoring Programme, https://facultydevelopment. cornell.edu/mentoring-guidelines.

References

Bland, C.J., Taylor, A.L., Shollen, L.S., Weber-Main, A.M. and Mulcahy, P.A. (2009) *Faculty Success Through Mentoring*, Lanham, MD: Rowman & Littlefield Education.

Blau, Francine D., Currie, Janet M., Croson, Rachel T.A. and Ginther, Donna K. (2010) Can mentoring help female assistant professors? Interim results from a randomized trial, *American Economic Review*, 100(2), 348–352.

Cornell University. (2021) *Best Practices in Faculty Mentoring*, Office of Faculty Development and Diversity, https://facultydevelopment.cornell.edu/mentoring-guidelines, Accessed on 27 October 2022.

Efstathiou, J.A., Drumm, M.R., Paly, J.P., Lawton, D.M., O'Neill, R.M., Niemierko, A., Leffert, L.R., Loeffler, J.S. and Shih, H.A. (2018) Long-term impact of a faculty mentoring program in academic medicine, *PLoS One*, 29 November, 13(11), e0207634, doi: 10.1371/journal.pone.0207634. PMID: 30496199; PMCID: PMC6264475.

Ferreres, A.R. (2018) Brief history of mentorship. In: Scoggins, C., Pollock, R. and Pawlik, T. (eds.) *Surgical Mentorship and Leadership. Success in Academic Surgery*,

Cham: Springer, https://doi.org/10.1007/978-3-319-71132-4_1, Accessed on 26 October 2022.

Kirchmeyer, C. (2005) The effects of mentoring on academic careers over time: Testing performance and political perspectives, *Human Relations*, 58(5), 637–660, https://doi.org/10.1177/0018726705055966, https://psycnet.apa.org/record/2005-09023-004, Accessed on 26 October 2022.

Lunsford, L.G., Crisp, G., Dolan, E.L. and Wuetherick, B. (2017) Mentoring in higher education. In: *The SAGE Handbook of Mentoring* (Chapter 20), Kindle edition. Sage Publications, 316–334, https://dx.doi.org/10.4135/9781526402011, Accessed on 26 October 2022.

McLaughlin, C. (2010) Mentoring: What is it? How do we do it and how do we get more of it? *Health Services Research*, June, 45(3), 871–884, doi: 10.1111/j.1475-6773.2010.01090.x. Epub 2010 Mar 10. PMID: 20337731; PMCID: PMC2875765.

Putnam, R.D. (2001) *Bowling Alone: The Collapse and Revival of American Community*, Simon and Schuster, ISBN 978-0-7432-0304-3.

Turner, C.S.V., Myers Jr., S.L. and Creswell, J.W. (1999) Exploring underrepresentation: The case of faculty of color in the Midwest, *Journal of Higher Education*, 70(1), 27–59.

University of Auckland. (2022) *A Guide to Mentoring*, https://cdn.auckland.ac.nz/assets/auckland/business/current-students/PDFs/mentoring-guide-final.pdf, Accessed on 26 October 2022.

University of Cambridge School of Clinical Medicine. (2022) *Mentoring Programme*, https://mentoring.medschl.cam.ac.uk, Accessed on 26 October 2022.

University of Edinburgh. (2022a) *Mentoring Connections*, https://www.ed.ac.uk/human-resources/learning-development/other-development-options/mentoring-connections, Accessed on 26 October 2022.

University of Edinburgh. (2022b) *Mentoring Connections: Mentoring Resources*, https://www.ed.ac.uk/sites/default/files/atoms/files/mentoring_connections_toolkit.pdf, Accessed on 26 October 2022.

Chapter 6

Building your media presence and political impact

Chris Harris and Marilyn Leask

Introduction

This chapter discusses how to build your digital profile and media engagement from the beginning of your academic career as part of your plan to develop a research and publishing profile. The chapter includes setting up your personal website and your blogs and how this feeds into your developing research and publishing profile. Professors are usually expected to undertake research yielding findings relevant to the challenges faced by specific groups in society and to actively communicate those findings to those to whom they are relevant, so your social media communications plan needs to include academics and other users of your research.

Building your digital profile steadily throughout your career will mean that when you are ready to engage with the mainstream media, your digital profile will enable those interested in your field to find you and your research and to understand the breadth and depth of your experience.

Some basic media training points are included, along with suggestions for self-analysis exercises to enable you to speak to lay audiences about the research relevant to them.

A checklist is included at the end of the chapter to provide a structure for planning your personal development and recording the achievement of your goals.

Objectives

This chapter challenges you to:

- identify the different audiences for your research;
- review and develop your digital presence;
- develop your use of social media;
- review your self-presentation;
- undertake media training;
- practice answering challenging questions;
- plan to engage with mainstream media;

DOI: 10.4324/9781003217596-6

- find editors interested in your field;
- plan your political engagement.

Routes to different audiences for your research

Bassey's (2000) briefing paper for the British Educational Research Association (BERA) indicates four major types of outputs for any research that enables you to reach different audiences:

> Research output 1: the research and the research data;
> Research output 2: academic articles;
> Research output 3: articles/briefings for professional audiences; and,
> Research output 4: press releases;
> *Online tools now make a fifth output easy and cost effective:*
> Research output 5: your personal online publication tools.

With respect to Output 1, research reports and full datasets are likely to be used, owned and stored by the research funder or by the institution employing the staff who have undertaken the research. (Don't forget, BERA's Ethical Guidelines for Researchers (2018) recommends the keeping of data from research [Output 1] for five years as you may face challenges about your interpretation of data.)

With respect to Output 2, journal and book publishers and academic professional associations have publication routes giving you access to academic users of your research. These routes typically include newsletters, conferences, book launches, social media and promotions on the organisation's website.

With respect to Outputs 3 and 4, dissemination routes may be less straightforward. To reach practitioner and policy audiences, you will probably need to identify these yourself as you are closest to the research, and then you will need to initiate dissemination to policy/practitioner audiences. You may find there are practitioners' professional associations or media centres, such as those listed later in the chapter.

Your university press office should be able to give you advice about how to work with the press office to maximise the impact of your work. We suggest you work through the points in this chapter before approaching your press office so that they have all the material to hand that they need to promote your work.

Practitioners' professional associations provide an important dissemination route through their newsletters, conferences, journals and online tools. For research of general interest, social media and the mainstream media provide key routes for dissemination. For policymakers, your routes to dissemination might be through the political parties directly themselves, through think tanks, through initiating contact with civil servants, through direct mail, through networking. If policymakers are your main audiences, attending political parties' annual member conferences may provide networking and dissemination opportunities. Your local member of Parliament may be able to provide contacts. In the UK, Parliament's website outlines different ways of engaging with matters before Parliament. These include responding to consultations, making submissions to select committees, taking part in All Party Parliamentary group discussions and so on. We recommend that you research the opportunities available to you in your own setting.

With respect to Output 5, see the detail in Chapter 7 on technology tools of the trade. Having your own website and social media channels gives you the chance to promote your work and to provide a consistent and clear account of your research and your research findings as they develop.

At this point, if you have not done so already, we suggest you make a list of the audiences for your research and as part of your planning undertake the research necessary to find out how to gain access to them.

Your digital presence: what does it communicate?

Until you are an established author, most of the publishers to whom you submit book proposals and academic articles are likely to explore your digital profile so as to understand more about you and your interests and connections. The danger of having an inappropriate digital profile is discussed in the following, along with the strategies of protecting and building your digital presence. Expect potential publishers to look at your digital profile and social media activity. If you have a large number of social media followers, they can assume that there is likely to be an audience for any book that you write.

Your digital presence – first steps

One of the first activities when you are considering what form and scope your media presence will take is to google yourself and find what material is currently there and on what sites. This is what potential publishers, fellow researchers and political and media outlets will see. It is important that you review this material first to establish which information supports and which detracts from the professional profile you are developing. You need to decide whether you want to keep personal social media separate to your professional social media presence or remove it completely. You may find it is appropriate to edit any existing profiles, for example those on Instagram and Facebook. Ensure you go through existing social media profiles to check there isn't anything that will impede your desire to create a strong research-based online profile.

Your university faculty profile should always be up to date and include, for instance, your existing articles and publications, mentions in newsletters, university-related blog posts and website pages, university society newsletters and professional event listings. Any accounts you have with academic publishers (Academia, Google Scholar, ORCHID, ResearchGate, for instance) should be included.

Once you have established what will stay or be removed, it's time to consider the range of your digital presence and the best ways to establish impact and connection for interested target audiences. The following comprises suggestions as to what will assist you to make your new media presence have real traction. The first two are essential.

Create a LinkedIn profile

This is a professional 'landing page' where you can detail your educational and professional experiences in a variety of sections. You can feature your writing to date and your university blogs and connect to professionals across the world. It is a great way to build followers in your field and to gain others' approval of your skills that are listed. It is ultimately a place where you can start to create your 'brand' and how you want others to view your professional research, personal profile and impact.

Create a personal website

A personal website enables you to share your personal professional profile and research more widely and comprehensively with a range of interested audiences (students, colleagues, educationalists, publishers, media outlets) who can connect with you through the contact page. It provides you with an opportunity to link all your other forms of online presence (social media, blog accounts, for instance) in one place. It also provides space to detail the totality of your work and gives you a chance to explain your projects and work more comprehensively: utilising images of yourself teaching and videos of events you have attended, for instance. These can be embedded in the website. Additionally, it provides a way to promote upcoming public engagements and lectures that you may be undertaking. There is plenty of advice on the web on setting up your own website. See for example Tooltester (www.tooltester.com/en/how-to-set-up-my-own-website/).

Creating a website is a demanding undertaking, but the process is an excellent way of evaluating how you want your research and work to be viewed by others. As Tooltester advises, you will need to:

- Plan your content, both written and visual, and how many pages you want on the website. In writing the content, make sentences clear and concise and choose images that are free to use or that your own. Shutterstock (2022) has free images for you to use.
- Decide on a domain and title for your website. For example, the domain might be researchmantle.com and the title of the website 'The Research Mantle'.
- Pick a web host to use to create the website. There are many to choose from: Wix, Square space, WordPress and Dreamweaver, for instance. The first three are particularly user-friendly and for those without previous experience.
- Use a colour scheme for your website from the menu of choices offered by the host you have chosen.

- Place your content. Create hyperlinks to your social media and other new media.
- Preview your site and check links to your social media blog sites and other media work effectively. Then go live and share.

It is essential that you take care to ensure your website looks professional. Spend time on it. Consult your web host for assistance. This will typically be in the form of a help function online as you construct the website. Resist the temptation to create your domain quickly. Keen (2007) details the pitfalls of creating online content that looks amateurish against professional accounts. Once your website goes live, it is important that it is updated regularly to ensure that it feels current.

Using social media: the importance of participatory media

You have a choice of other media and tools to supplement your LinkedIn account and website. Through creating and promoting these you will have considered:

- what groups of people might be interested in your research;
- opportunities for them to engage with your work online;
- how to allow audiences for your research to connect with you.

It is now time to consider social media as a way to connect with these target audiences further, then to link this additional content within your website to provide a cohesive online strategy. Social media is at its best when it encourages interaction and user participation; it provides additional content to that on other media platforms (Gillmor, 2004). Carrigan (2019) and Macquarie University (2022) provide advice specifically for academics on the use of social media.

Those interested in using your research are likely to expect you to have a social media presence, and new researchers are advised to build a social media following before reaching out to mainstream media. Some people who read about your research may wish to be kept up to date, and an ideal way of doing that is through your use of social media. Publishers, too, look for academics who have a social media profile and a following, as this is an indication that there is an audience for your ideas.

Social media should be as participatory as possible – social media should be a conversation. It allows you to provide advance notice of publications, ask for responses, receive feedback on your ideas from followers, advertise webinars/ conferences where you are showcasing your research and so on.

Some choices about how you use social media are:

Create a blog account. Blogs give you an opportunity to compress your research, journal articles and thoughts to provide digests of your thinking. They are particularly good for providing a link to social media accounts stimulating timely interest in your work. Blogs are a form of social media, so it is apposite that you encourage responses and dialogue about your writing and respond to readers' responses.

Set up a Twitter account. Twitter is a very useful social media tool as it has an extensive audience (353 million monthly users, according to NIBusiness Info 2022). It allows you to post short ideas (280 characters) on key issues of your research, and you can tag relevant people or institutions who may be interested in the field. You can post images and video, too.

Set up a Facebook account. For researchers, Facebook can be a way of connecting to communities of people in your chosen field and to have an ongoing conversation with them about work in progress/ideas as 'friends', thereby delivering a more personal impact, sharing thoughts, images and videos in the process.

Set up a WhatsApp group. WhatsApp provides a cohesive way of connecting to a smaller group of people than Facebook, for instance. It's a social messaging site that is very useful in communicating with a core team who are assisting you in your research or developing your online presence.

Set up an Instagram account. The benefits of using Instagram as part of your platform is that it is visual, so that you can share ideas from your research/work as images, diagrams or cartoons in microblogs that can provide real impact. As 31.2% of users are between 25 and 34, its impact is strong with a younger target audience (Aslam, 2022).

Set up a TikTok account. TikTok is a good way of engaging your students with your work and research, for example by posting or creating short educational impactful videos for them. Ideally, you would construct these with your students. Knowledge of TikTok is helpful in understanding trends, engaging with a younger audience and growing awareness of your work.

Create a YouTube account. A YouTube account is very helpful in providing a space for you to post your lectures/presentations/webinars for others to view. You can create live-streaming opportunities for real-time presentations creating impact. This will introduce you to a wider audience who can connect and share responses to your work. You will need to be able to record videos of your performance. Experiment with recording yourself using a smartphone, computer or other devices. Video is useful for blog posts on YouTube linked to your personal website and for conference presentations when you can't attend.

Utilise Teams, Zoom, Google Meet, Skype and so on. Using video-conferencing platforms can give you further live-streaming opportunities to place lectures online or opportunities to meet in real time with colleagues across the world to share ideas, research and work. The chat facility in most video-conferencing programmes provides instant feedback and evaluation of what is being said.

Your self-presentation and media training

You may only get one chance to get your point across in any radio or television interview, and thorough preparation is essential if you are to be successful and to be asked for interviews in the future.

Ask your organisation and your professional association if they provide any support for media training. Alternatively, you may wish to fund yourself to undertake such training – it's possible such expenses may be tax deductible, but you need to check with your country's tax authorities.

Media training addresses how you present yourself:

- **Your voice:** pitch, tone, quality, audibility, clarity of diction, accent.
- **Your mannerisms with respect to language:** do you need to eliminate umms and ahs?
- **Your mannerisms with respect to non-verbal communication:** your posture, use of hands/gestures, facial expressions, eyes, use and position of arms/legs. You may need advice about your breathing technique.
- **The language you use to explain your research:** are you using language likely to understood by the audience? Are you able to be precise and meet the interests of particular audiences? Can you package your research findings to answer their questions rather than your own?
- **Your dress, jewellery, make up and shoes:** do they convey the impression you want?

During your media training, you may have the opportunity to be mentored by professionals whom you recognise from their television or radio roles: do take the opportunity to learn what you can from the experts and ask for their critical feedback.

Media interviews: preparing to answer questions

You have nothing to lose by providing the people interviewing you with questions that link your research with hot topics of the day. Don't assume that they will automatically know what the most useful questions are to ask. Your preparation includes answering the questions you want to be asked as well as the ones that you would prefer were not asked. As part of your preparation, practice responses to difficult and challenging questions.

Practice what you are going to say if asked about topics outside your research area. You may decide to say, 'I have not undertaken research in that area but as a layperson my view is . . .' or, perhaps, 'I need to check for the statistics on that issue and will get back to you in time for your next programme'.

If an interview is being pre-recorded and you have not answered as clearly as you wished, you can ask if it's possible to record a section again. Cutting and pasting voice files and moving them around to create an interesting programme is relatively simple. Similarly, deleting a section of a voice/video recording can be quick and easy.

Communicating with lay audiences

Preparation for any interview includes checking you are communicating clearly – can you get your points across clearly and succinctly to a lay audience? Ask friends, family or colleagues if they can give you honest feedback and perhaps set up a role-play – with someone pointing a microphone to you and asking you a question – so that you are used to responding to questions clearly and succinctly.

Kathryn Simpson (2022, p. 1), writing for the University Association for Contemporary European Studies website, provides academics with advice based on her personal experience:

> Engaging with the media can be a daunting experience. Yet, communicating your research to the media can be a highly effective method of increasing the impact of your research expertise, not only within your field of research but to the widest possible audience: the general public. This benefits society, informs policy, encourages accurate reporting by journalists, connects public communities, raises awareness and can inspire future generations.
>
> However, such high-profile communication is not always straightforward and can be a time-consuming challenge.
>
> My own experience of engaging with and communicating my research to the media has been a positive one – and has varied substantially, from writing op-eds and blogs to interviews on both radio and television, nationally and internationally. Interviews I have given have been wide ranging, from fact-checking exercises to explaining key issues, predicting and forecasting, audience Q&A and 'presenter's friend roles' (when you are in conversation on a given topic).
>
> Feeling comfortable and confident in the analysis you provide is absolutely crucial. I always have a key phrase and two to three keywords pre-prepared, which helps me to focus and deliver my argument in the most concise, clear and accessible way.
>
> After interviews, I always ask for feedback, which most producers will give to you verbally; this not only gives you a confidence boost but also allows you to build on your expertise as an effective communicator. I always watch or listen to interviews I deliver; as excruciatingly awkward as it can be to watch yourself in action, it is extremely important in order to improve.
>
> There have of course been disappointments. These have included a politician personally attacking me live on air and online trolling of my analysis, physical appearance and mannerisms. It can be hurtful, upsetting and confidence crushing. But this is a minority of individuals, and you should not let it deter you from engaging with the media. It's perhaps no more disheartening, distressing and maddening than an unfavourable review from an anonymous

reviewer of the journal article you have worked so hard on. You still continue to work on said journal article until it gets published – the same approach should be taken when engaging with the media.

Media centres: what they can do for you

Just as journal and book publishers need a constant supply of articles and manuscripts, news outlets need a constant supply of news. It is worth considering, therefore, how to make your research newsworthy and how to make it more public.

In the UK, two media centres that have been set up to provide a route to mainstream media for researchers and are independent of any pressure groups are the Science Media Centre (www.sciencemediacentre.org) and the Education Media Centre (www.educationmediacentre.org). The Education Media Centre was a project initiated by the group of educators and politicians giving their time voluntarily to form the Coalition for Evidence-Based Education (www.cebenet work.org). It is now a charity raising funds to support its own work. The process for creating such a centre may provide a model for other disciplines that would benefit from having a centre that coordinates communications about research both from and to the media.

We asked Fran Abrams, a trustee of the Education Media Centre, to describe what the Centre offers:

> The Education Media Centre is a charity whose purpose is to 'make evidence make news.' As part of that work it aims to help researchers bring good evidence about education to wider audiences.
>
> Often, the centre's initial contact with a researcher will come via a university press office or an academic publisher – it works closely with these to ensure press releases and pitches get to the journalists who might be interested in them.
>
> The EMC is always happy to hear from individual researchers who feel their research is worthy of media attention – though it will normally suggest the university's press office should also be involved where possible.
>
> The charity also receives and responds to queries from journalists who are looking for an academic to contribute or respond to their stories, so it is happy to hear from academics who may wish to be contacted in this way about a particular area of expertise.
>
> If you have a forthcoming research publication on education or children and young people and you think it may be of interest to the media, please get in touch with them. EMC also offers a range of training and mentoring services to academic researchers – the contact address is info@educationme diacentre.org. Do you want a free weekly round-up of the evidence behind the news on education? Sign up for our free weekly newsletter: https:// tinyurl.com/9hkbrm4n. Follow on Twitter @EMCUK.

Engaging with mainstream media: newspapers, radio, TV

Having established an online presence that reaches your core audiences, you will be developing connections and awareness of your work. This, in itself, may gain you the contacts you need for publishing your work and findings in the traditional mainstream media or alternative outlets. You should be able to gain access to data collected by the website software, which can tell you which countries and towns your users are coming from.

Choosing the media

It is important to consider carefully which media will enable you to reach out to the audiences you have identified. An article published with the backing of a high-profile institution is more likely to initiate a follow-up radio or TV invitation on mainstream media than one without such support. However, it is important also to consider local radio and TV broadcasting and other alternative platforms like web radio, online TV and podcasts as vehicles to expose your work to a wider audience.

Another element of your choice is knowing the media institution you are pitching to. Are their brand values, house style and political positions ones that might reflect your work effectively? Is the outlet likely to be interested in publishing your work? For example, research on the effect on the environment with issues like fracking and fossil fuels might be less appealing to libertarian right-wing outlets such as, in the UK, the *Daily Express* and *Daily Mail* than to the *Guardian* or *Mirror*. Conversely, in England, research on the impact on grammar schools in Kent on the life chances of those who go to secondary modern schools in that area would be better pitched to the left-of-centre *New Statesman* than the conservative leaning *Spectator*.

Finding editors: preparing the pitch

Newspapers

Whatever outlets you decide to pitch to, it is important that you find the name and contact details of the commissioning editor of the subject area you are considering writing about. These can be found online at the newspaper or magazine website. A first email introducing yourself and explaining what you would like to pitch about is a good idea. It gives the commissioning editor a chance to co-construct a potential pitch with you based on their knowledge of their readership and existing articles and writing they have already placed. It is possible you will receive nothing back at first. Editors receive many pitches from freelancers and are very busy. Be patient! It is very important to keep communicating. A follow-up email whether you have received a green light to your offer, potential amendments to the subject matter or no response will be to send a basic pitch. It is very important you streamline this. Avoid writing too much and consider the house style of the publication you are attempting to be published in. Create an angle from your research for the publication that engages readers so it doesn't appear overly academic and dry.

Describe your argument from start to finish in a few clear, concise bullet points, sort out the formatting and use ordinary parentheses (like this) rather than square brackets (which are really confusing because in newspaper convention they are used within quotes to denote words understood but not stated). Remember to do a spelling, grammar, punctuation and repetition check. If you haven't written for an editor before, sloppiness in your initial email won't inspire confidence. Often if your pitch is accepted there will be further tweaks and changes made by the commissioning editor, so be prepared for some dilution of your key ideas to make the article accessible to audiences. However, the benefits of publication are that you have traction in pitching to broadcast media.

Television/radio

The process is similar here. Decide the broadcast media you wish to appear on and email or contact the editor of the programme. Choose the programme carefully – will it be suitable for you discussing your work? Don't discount popular radio and TV stations. In the UK, Radio 2's Jeremy Vine show, Radio 1's Newsbeat and ITV's Good Morning Britain are good examples of where current ideas and concerns are presented depending on the topic covered. An initial pitch with a link to the publishing article and an offer to appear or speak on a programme can be made. You may attach a showreel (clips of you speaking or presenting in different formats). Try to personalise your broadcast offer by contacting the editor by text or phone to explain you have sent a pitch to them. If you are appearing on broadcast media you will speak and be heard or seen, so it is important to show you can communicate effectively.

Overall, it is important in this communication to plug away professionally and ask for advice as to how you can tweak your offer so that it fits the broadcasting media you have chosen to pitch to. You may have your work published online first.

Other avenues

There are other ways to get your work published. A good example for academics internationally is *The Conversation*, an online 'newspaper'. To be published in *The Conversation*, you must be currently employed as a researcher or academic with a university or research institution. PhD candidates under supervision by an academic can write for them. Try researching other alternative modes and outlets of broadcasting (The Good Web Guide, 2022). Another proactive approach is to engage in creating, filming and recording your own content ('citizen journalism'), which can be placed and pitched to mainstream providers.

A quick and instant way of creating impact and knowledge of your work is producing a generic press release. Mowbray (2022) provides the following advice for academics: 'Keep it short . . . (250 to 400 words), get rid of the academic jargon . . . , target the right journalists . . . , don't make it too salesy . . . , nail the headline'. See also Dragilev (2022).

Although a press release has to focus on something that is newsworthy and exclusive, it is a way of customising your work to provide an accessible angle that gets journalists and editors talking. It can create contacts and communication with providers that will assist you in getting your work and research published and promoted across a range of media in the future.

Political engagement and communicating with policymakers

Is your work relevant to policymakers i.e. civil servants and politicians? If so, try putting yourself in their shoes and communicate your work in ways that relate to their needs and agenda. It is to be expected that they will wish to stay in power so that they can implement ideas they think will ensure the country runs in the way they want it to – so how does your research help them with their goals? Can you translate your research from theory to practice? Your impact is likely to be significantly lessened if you expect civil servants and politicians to put in the effort to interpret your research findings and draw out the relevance to their practice.

In the same way you are advised to prepare for interviews, you need to prepare your interactions with civil servants and policymakers. It makes sense when you are dealing with very busy people to have to hand your 'elevator pitch': you have three minutes in an elevator with the person who has the means to implement the changes you want following your research – can you convince them to give you time to hear your ideas at a further meeting in the time available?

Oliver and Cairney (2019, p. 1) have undertaken a systematic review of articles addressing the issue of how research can be made useful to policymakers. In brief, they propose the following:

(1) Do high quality research; (2) make your research relevant and readable; (3) understand policy processes; (4) be accessible to policymakers: engage routinely, flexible, and humbly; (5) decide if you want to be an issue advocate or honest broker; (6) build relationships (and ground rules) with policymakers; (7) be 'entrepreneurial' or find someone who is; and (8) reflect continuously: should you engage do you want to, and is it working?

It is worth reading their report in full and reflecting on what approach works for your topic and the civil servants and politicians responsible for the area. The report is freely available.

We suggest you decide whether you are happy to be publicly aligned with particular political groups or if you would prefer to maintain neutrality. Is your position clear on your web profiles? Have you identified, researched and contacted think tanks likely to be interested in the topics that you are deeply knowledgeable about? When your research outputs and findings are of a quality appropriate for presentation to civil servants and politicians, then we suggest you write to the relevant government departments and/or politicians, asking for a meeting to discuss the issues that your research is raising. We ourselves have had considerable success in this respect with some administrations in the UK.

Your checklist and goals: for engaging with traditional and social media

References at the end of this chapter include advice for academics from universities in various countries on engaging with the media. We suggest you read these publications and make notes for yourself using the prompts in Table 6.1, about the areas of development you may need to work on and the preparation you may need to do. The following checklist provides you with a starting point.

Table 6.1 Checklist: building your media presence and political impact is freely available for download via the Support Material tab on the Routledge website.

Table 6.1 Checklist: building your media presence and political impact

ITEM	Achieved?	
	Yes	No
AUDIENCES		
Have you a list of the audiences for your research and the routes to dissemination to them? Have you a dissemination plan?		
YOUR DIGITAL PRESENCE		
Have you reviewed your digital footprint, and is it presenting you in the way that you want?		
Is it relevant for you to have a YouTube channel and a personal website explaining your research to practitioners, policymakers and other academics? If so, have you got a long-term plan and the accompanying time resources for developing and updating these digital resources so they do not go out of date? Otherwise, you might just rely on your institution's website.		
SOCIAL MEDIA		
Have you made a plan for engaging with social media?		
Have you based your plan on advice in the literature (see following references) and on your analysis of the performance of others whom you have seen successfully engage with social media?		
YOUR SELF-PRESENTATION AND PERSONAL COMMUNICATION SKILLS		
Self-presentation: have you reviewed the way you present yourself, and are you acting to improve on weaknesses?		
Oral communication: have you reviewed your performance, and are you acting to improve on weaknesses?		
Non-verbal communication: have you reviewed your performance, and are you acting to improve on weaknesses?		
INTERVIEW PREPARATION		
Have you made a list of the questions you would like to answer in a radio/television interview and answers to the difficult questions that might be asked about your research?		

(Continued)

Table 6.1 (Continued)

ITEM	Achieved?	
	Yes	No
Have you video recorded yourself answering these questions and analysed your performance? Smartphones allow you to do this on your own, but we recommend that you undertake mock interviews with a friend or a colleague asking you the questions in an order that suits them so that you experience being caught unprepared and having to answer on the spot.		
Have you undertaken media training to test out your preparation and to refine your communication skills?		
Have you identified and contacted, as a first step, local radio and TV channels that may be interested in your expertise?		
POLITICAL AND MAINSTREAM MEDIA CONNECTIONS		
Have you decided whether you are aligning with particular political groups or if you are maintaining neutrality? Is this clear on your web profiles?		
Have you identified, researched and contacted think tanks likely to be interested in the topics that you are deeply knowledgeable about?		
YOUR SPECIFIC GOALS: now record the goals that suit your context and your discipline . . .		

Summary: recognising success and avoiding pitfalls

In becoming a professor, you are making a claim to have deep knowledge in an academic field. Colleagues in that field as well as the public with an interest in the area will expect you to be able to speak with authority. Developing communication skills that enable you to communicate your research to lay and policymaking audiences requires practice and dedicated work. Being able to take critical feedback is essential if you are to improve your performance and do your work justice in the public arena.

So, developing resilience as your work is scrutinised is something you will need to do, and we suggest that working with a network of trusted colleagues – perhaps through your professional association – who will give constructive feedback on ideas and the way you express them may help develop your resilience.

The consequence of not working on your media interview skills and your digital presence is that opportunities to be recognised as an expert will pass you by and you may not even have known they were there. On LinkedIn, you can pay to see who has viewed your profile, so if for example you reach out to various media outlets or parties interested in your work, you may then see that they have looked you up.

Chapter 7 provides more examples of using digital technology tools to build your profile.

References

Aslam, S. (2022) *Instagram by the Numbers: Stats, Demographics and Fun Facts*, Omnicoreagency, www.omnicoreagency.com/instagram-statistics/, Accessed on 19 September 2022.

Bassey, M. (2000) *Good Practice in Research Writing*, British Educational Research Association, www.docs.hss.ed.ac.uk/iad/Learning_teaching/Academic_teaching/Resources/BERA_guide_educational_research_writing.pdf, Accessed on 19 September 2022.

BERA. (2018) *Ethical Guidelines for Educational Research*, 4th edition, www.bera.ac.uk/publication/ethical-guidelines-for-educational-research-2018, Accessed on 19 September 2022.

Carrigan, M. (2019) *Social Media for Academics*, 2nd edition, Sage, https://uk.sagepub.com/en-gb/eur/social-media-for-academics/book261904#contents, Accessed on 19 September 2022.

Dragilev, D. (2022) *How to Write a Press Release*, https://blog.justreachout.io/how-to-write-press-release/, Accessed on 19 September 2022.

Gillmor, D. (2004) *We the Media: Grassroots Journalism by the People, for the People*, Sebastopol, CA: O'Reilly.

The Good Web Guide. (2022) *11 of the Best Alternative News Sites*, www.thegoodwebguide.co.uk/best-sites/best-alternative-news-websites-citizen-journalism/16752, Accessed on 19 September 2022.

Keen, A. (2007) *The Cult of the Amateur: How Today's Internet Is Killing Our Culture*, New York: Doubleday/Currency.

Macquarie University. (2022) *Media and Social Media Guide for Academics*, Sydney, https://staff.mq.edu.au/support/marketing-and-communications/communications/Media-and-Social-Media-Guide_DIGITAL.pdf, Accessed on 19 September 2022.

Mowbray, K. (2022) *How to Write a Viral Press Release on Academic Research*, Bluesky PR, www.bluesky-pr.com/blog/business-education/viral-press-release/, Accessed on 19 September 2022.

NIbusiness. (2022) *Advantages and Disadvantages of Twitter for Business*, www.nibusinessinfo.co.uk/content/advantages-and-disadvantages-twitter-business, Accessed on 19 September 2022.

Oliver, K. and Cairney, P. (2019) The dos and don'ts of influencing policy: A systematic review of advice to academics, *Palgrave Communications*, 5, 21, https://doi.org/10.1057/s41599-019-0232-y, Accessed on 19 September 2022.

Shutterstock. (2022) *Unleash Your Creativity with Unrivalled Images*, www.shutterstock.com/images, Accessed on 19 September 2022.

Simpson, K. (2022) *Engaging with the Media as an Academic*, University Association for Contemporary European Studies, www.uaces.org/resources/articles/engaging-media-academic, Accessed on 19 September 2022.

Chapter 7

Technology tools of the trade

Elizabeth Hidson

Introduction

The visual imagery of this book is strong: journeying along the pathway to professorship. This chapter is about selecting the digital tools for the journey. Various technologies and software applications make the job of building an international research profile possible, from starting out with the nuts and bolts of solo research from your own desktop with little or no funding, through to collaborating with project teams and disseminating internationally. The chapter will be useful not only as a standalone resource but also in support of themes covered in other chapters, such as networking in Chapter 5 and building your media presence in Chapter 6.

The chapter starts off looking at the essential tools for organising your personal research and scholarly activity, digital profile and networks. It then moves on to communicating and collaborating as you expand your focus to the wider academic community. It will look at digital tools for writing and research as well as platforms to disseminate, attract interest in your work and develop your academic profile. The aim is to present and discuss digital tools and how, when and why you might use them as well as reflect on how the investment of time and energy will be useful to your career. Although common software brands or names of applications may be mentioned, this is to help you look at the type of software or technology rather than necessarily personally endorsing specific products.

Objectives

By the end of the chapter you should:

- have reviewed and curated your digital profile;
- have identified online professional networks in your field, ready to join those most relevant;
- have a plan for testing out tools to use for supporting your personal research and scholarly activity, including dissemination, communication and collaboration;
- understand the importance of maintaining a professional presence online.

DOI: 10.4324/9781003217596-7

Getting organised

Access to a personal computer or laptop with reliable internet access is an essential prerequisite for the contemporary academic. You may have your own computer or be provided with a device by your institution. Devices provided for you are likely to have restrictions around administrative rights for installing and updating software, but single sign-on and 'desktop-anywhere' provisions may blur the boundaries between personal and professional technology. Operating both in parallel may be time consuming, so you will need to balance the freedom of a personal device against security and accountability – backups and storage of research material may mean that an institutional device is more efficient for your scholarly life. Updates, device refresh policies and even moving institutions will mean that you need to consider in advance how and where you structure and store your files so that they can be restored as painlessly as possible on a new device. Think ahead when you set up your digital workspace so that you develop routine ways of working that are transferable.

The standard integrated office-type software is probably the most common suite of tools that you will have access to. Productivity software that includes email, word processing and cloud storage is the starting point, so a well-structured email folder and file storage system are vital. Academics who also have student support and assessment responsibilities will know how important time management and working to deadlines is, and this can be vital in making time for scholarly activity and research. Using your calendar to structure your marking schedule, article review and reading and writing 'appointments' allow you maximum control over your academic/research balance. Online calendar management such as Calendly (https://calendly.com/), which integrates with your Outlook calendar, can help you to manage meeting requests and office hours and to protect your valuable research time and respond to unexpected requests. You may also want to consider how you use your email. If all your professional email traffic funnels into just one inbox, it is likely that you will encounter difficulties when trying to set up email cover, or at best, you will need to learn to set up automatic rules within your email system so that you can reduce email time in favour of wider scholarly activity. Something as simple as an automatic email rule that collates all emails that mention the word 'extension' into a folder that you can deal with efficiently at a designated time could be a real time-saver if you are a module leader, for example. These may be issues to resolve at the department or team level. Gaining mutual support to develop a culture of protecting precious time for research and scholarly activity at your institution is important. For many academics, student support is front and central, but academics also need time to research, to write, to network and to engage in peer review in order to sustain their professional development.

The same tools that save you time as a lecturer, such as voice dictation and notes, can be helpful for your research, especially if your software has a mobile or tablet app integration. In educational technology terms, looking at the 'affordances' of the tool is important – its 'potential for action' (Kennewell, 2001, p. 106). The recent improvements in voice recognition and automatic transcription, so helpful in online meetings and video integration for teaching purposes, also have real benefits for transcribing notes for research. We'll look at research methods a little more in the section around digital tools for data collection. It's wise to consider how software developments might have unexpected potential in your scholarly activity.

Your choice of writing tools can also enhance your productivity. We'll see throughout this chapter how software integrations can improve productive use of time. As you write, you'll also need access to your reading, your notes and your referencing system, so it's essential to look at your writing software to make sure it can handle integrations. Although many will stick to standard office software, some like to use (and pay for) dedicated writing software, such as Scrivener (www.literatureandlatte.com/), which incorporates features for planning and structuring as well as writing. A major consideration when adopting any software is the commitment to learning how to use it to get the best out of it, so if you are interested in other writing software, seek out webinars and free trials to assess the software's potential for you.

Organisation of your background notes and materials may well benefit from a similar investment. Microsoft OneNote (part of Office 365), Evernote (www.evernote.com/) and a range of open-source note apps have loyal followings because of the text notes, audio notes, handwriting and OCR (optical character recognition) support, searching and language settings that bring new levels of digital organisation. Apple's notes created on one device are immediately available on your other Apple devices and can be shared with others. Synchronisation, backup and integrations are all aspects that can increase your productivity once you have spent the time setting them up. You need your digital tools to communicate with colleagues as you work.

Having finally carved out time for your writing, it's also worth considering your time protection and anti-distraction tools. The use of 'focus assist' (previously known as quiet hours on Windows) and various do-not-disturb settings built into your device operating system or software may help to prevent interruptions to your thinking and writing time by reducing calls and notifications. Getting involved in writing retreats and groups, even online ones, can give you purpose and accountability for your time. Proponents of the Pomodoro Technique (Cirillo, 2009), which advocates dedicating your time in 25-minute blocks (called 'pomodoros'), can find numerous apps and timers to help maximise your writing efficiency. At their simplest, these tools sit as little timers ticking away while you work and track the time spent. Whether it's a book, a chapter, an article or just a paragraph, your writing project will move ahead when divided into small, manageable chunks. You can reward yourself with a comfort or movement break in the remaining minutes of the half hour.

Reading, curation and reference management

Reference managers such as Mendeley, EndNote and Zotero allow you to organise research sources, which can include books and articles as well as a range of other outputs. Institutions often provide support for at least one of these applications, but it may be that you need to liaise with your IT support to ensure that you can use the full functionality unless you are prepared to change from a preferred application to one that is provided in-house. If you started higher education manually organising your references and can remember scrabbling through books and photocopies to check a reference, you will appreciate the power of a good referencing application. They have a wealth of useful features, of which the referencing is just a small part. A little time capturing the bibliographic details is time well spent.

Referencing software that incorporates web browser and word processing plugins is very helpful. With so many online literature resources available, the digital equivalent of sticky notes can be the web importer plugin or extension, which will allow you to import the publication details and any available PDFs for later review. The details may need some editing, but it certainly removes the issue of forgetting to track useful sources. A bigger danger might be that you import so many interesting articles that you get side-tracked from your main purpose! Figure 7.1 shows the Hidson (2020) paper and its open-access PDF being imported into Mendeley. Mendeley recognises the bibliographic details and creates the reference ready to be imported. You can find quick tutorials for this on YouTube by typing in 'Mendeley web importer'.

The wealth of online journals, repositories, e-books, blogs, free previews in online book sellers and publishers giving free chapters, for example, means that the digital world holds many distractions, but chunking your time effectively should help. One particularly fascinating area is the rise of tools that connect

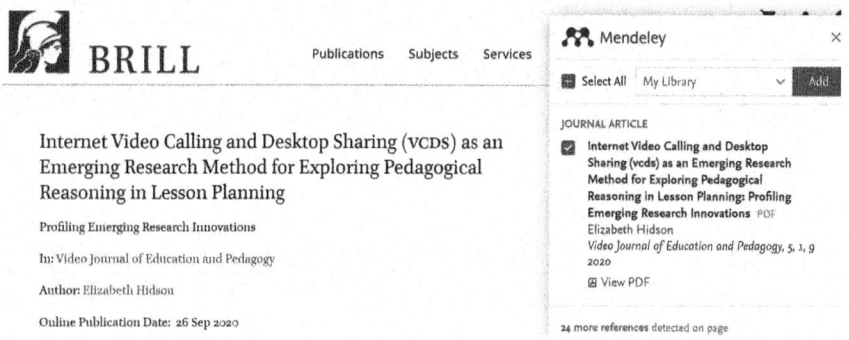

Figure 7.1 Mendeley web importer

Source: Used with permission from Mendeley (Elsevier) and Brill (VJEP)

bibliographic details together and provide interactive visual displays of the research landscape. Some useful examples include Citationtree (https://cita tiontree.org/), Connected Papers (www.connectedpapers.com/) and Research Rabbit (www.researchrabbit.ai/). These also often have public collections, where users can share their curation activity in a particular area. EPPI-Mapper (https:// eppi.ioe.ac.uk/cms/Default.aspx?tabid=3790) research evidence maps provide a similar but more structured visualisation of the work in one area. An example provided on the EPPI website is of an interactive evidence gap map to accompany an article on 'Schools and emergency remote education during the COVID-19 pandemic: a living rapid systematic review' (Bond, 2021).

Systematic review tools are considered later in this chapter.

Taking Research Rabbit, for example, and starting by adding just one paper, it is possible to view all the references in that paper, display connections between them, seek similar, earlier or later work, more work by these authors, dip in and out of abstracts, and develop insights into the trends in your selected field. Figure 7.2 shows a visualisation of one paper – the same Hidson (2020) paper as before, with 27 references. The groupings show connections between the authors, which map onto topics in the literature review, all in a few, quite intuitive mouse clicks. The possibilities for teaching about academic literature, let alone the value

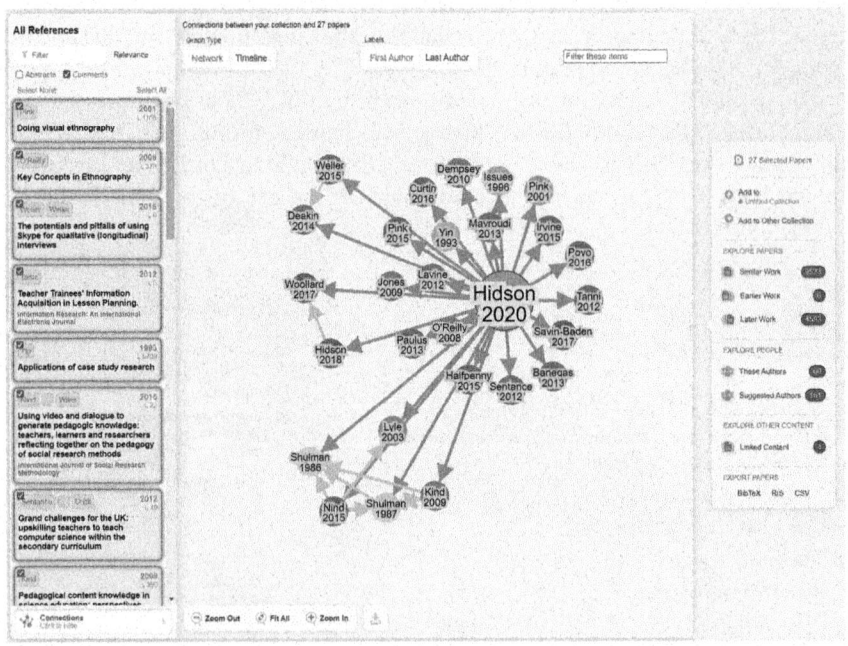

Figure 7.2 Research Rabbit visualisation of Hidson (2020)

Source: Used with permission from Research Rabbit

for an individual researcher, are suddenly very exciting. Again, typing 'Research Rabbit' into YouTube will provide a range of walkthrough videos and tutorials.

Having located your sources and imported your resources and references into your reference manager, it is then possible to categorise them into folders and collections so that you can organise the projects you are working on. You may have a core of papers around the central themes in your area of research interest that you can classify into well-curated lists. You may also have several projects that you are working on, and you can copy references into new collections in order to store all the relevant sources that you will draw from in each project. If you have been able to import a PDF or an article, you can read, search, annotate and make notes from within your reference manager. Even without the PDF, notes can be added to the individual reference. Notebook features allow more general notes to be made while reading, so no moments of inspiration or insight are lost. Where you are working as part of a team, and the whole team has access to the same reference manager, you can share and work directly on documents and references and add notes and highlighting, collaborating seamlessly through the software.

Connecting your reference manager into your writing software is vital. Maintaining momentum as you write is important for productive use of writing time. Having the ability to quickly search for and insert a reference prevents the interruption of your flow or train of thought. Even if you are so engrossed in your writing that you don't want to stop to insert the citation at that moment, typing a quick placeholder in the text and then returning to it at the end of the session to update with correct citations is a good alternative. The added bonus is that if you have set up the end references already, the correct citation is added not only at the point of insertion in the text, but also at the end of the document. Citation formatting can be modified to add in page numbers, suppress the author in favour of the year of publication and group multiple references very easily. The result is a well-formatted, correctly referenced draft that can be shared, as with any other piece of writing. A reader does not need access to the reference manager because the references are now embedded in the written document.

Digital profile tools

The recent pandemic has improved networking opportunities and demonstrated the value of technology for career advancement. Academics who turned to working, teaching and researching from home have been able to find peers to connect with. Even at a time when campus-based seminars were suspended, many academics found themselves receiving unexpected invitations to speak at national or international online events because of the massive expansion in individual and institutional use of online meeting tools.

Institutions usually require staff to maintain an institutional profile, often connected to the institution's research repository. Repositories are important in terms of complying with open access requirements and, in the UK, contributing to the national research assessment exercise that is used to allocate research funds to universities, the Research Excellence Framework (www.ref.ac.uk/). These often encourage links to social media, ORCID profiles and other academic portals.

A little regular time spent curating your digital profile is time well spent. When you need to collate information for author biographies, speaker details, CVs for funding bids, internal research review reports and job applications, it allows a faster and easier turnaround at the point of need. If you have never searched for yourself through Google, it is a useful exercise. One thing you may be able to do through Google is to claim your own Google 'knowledge panel' by confirming your identity, which may give you some control over the automatically generated information derived from internet sources. You will then be able to suggest changes to your featured image, title and social profiles.

Academic portals such as ORCID, ResearchGate, Figshare and Google Scholar draw together your professional interests and outputs, each in slightly different ways. They provide data about your publications drawn from a range of publishers' sites, analytics, statistics and metrics. You can usually amend, claim or reject items that should be in your profile. It can be time consuming to moderate several portals, but once some time has been spent connecting them, usually through your ORCID ID, it requires minimal house-keeping thereafter. There are now ways that even the most 'invisible' academic work such as peer review can receive credit – Publons (http://publons.com/) is one site that allows you to track peer review and journal editing work as well as publications and citation metrics. As an aside, be aware that linking your accounts together will usually require you to have a multi-factor authentication app set up on your phone to verify account activity.

ResearchGate (www.researchgate.net/) has a number of uses. It acts as a social site for researchers to curate a profile, follow others, add freely available research outputs and ask and answer questions. You can set up a 'lab' – a virtual research group – and post project updates. ResearchGate also tracks statistics such as citations and H-index, as well as 'research interest', which they calculate from members reading, recommending or citing a research item (ResearchGate, 2022). The H-index is the number of papers (H) that have been cited at least H times (Spicer, 2015). An H-index of 10 shows that 10 of an author's papers have received at least 10 citations. As with any metric, there are debates about use/misuse and value of metrics in research assessment (see *The Metric Tide* [Wouters et al., 2015]), but there is no doubt that having insight into the impact of your work is important.

Altmetric (www.altmetric.com/) has generated even more attention to a researcher's wider digital profile. The Altmetric score will often be found alongside publications on participating publishers' websites. Altmetric monitors a wide range of sources for mentions of research outputs and provides an 'Attention Score' and details of the output being tweeted, cited and read on Mendeley (a reference manager). It then contextualises that in terms of how much attention the output has received. The aforementioned Hidson (2020) paper had a 'good' attention score, and Altmetric says it has apparently received more attention than most outputs being tracked by Altmetric. Installing a 'bookmarklet' allows you to see the Altmetric data for any publication with a DOI (digital object identifier) – now commonly used for uniquely identifying a document and giving it a unique web address. Researchers can also generate digital Altmetric badges for use on their own websites.

Gaining a better understanding of your own digital academic profile will help you to identify and articulate the reach and influence of your work.

Networks and communities of practice

Monitoring what is happening in your field and the wider academic community is a key skill for researchers. Academics are expected to seek opportunities for external research and funding, as well as avenues for knowledge exchange, publication, dissemination and impact. Institutions have a vested interest in creating a climate that is conducive to research, and it is therefore likely that there are mailing lists and mechanisms for you to be kept up to date with opportunities. You may receive regular institutional mailings from your university's research office where they have collated relevant information for you, or you may have access to external subscriptions such as Research Professional (www.researchprofessional.com/), which sends a weekly funding insight mailing to subscribers and can be tailored to your requirements. Wider professional networks, such as, in the UK, AdvanceHE (www.advance-he.ac.uk/), BERA in education (www.bera.ac.uk/) and specific subject networks, are also useful for making connections with others and keeping abreast of what is happening in your field. Given that academics usually have relatively clearly defined areas of interest, professional associations may offer opportunities for career development and reputational enhancement, especially if they also have in-house publications, journals, editorial or conference organisation opportunities. Different opportunities are available in different countries, so I suggest you speak to your colleagues to find out what networks and research funding opportunities they know about.

A professional Twitter account is very useful for scanning the horizon in your field. You can keep up with calls for papers, conferences, recent publications, opinions and reactions and also develop a professional learning network with others in your field. These may be entirely online communities of practice, or you may encounter your peers at conferences. Twitter has some useful tools for following threads, such as @readwise and @threadreaderapp, where you can request or follow threads as well as bookmarking them. There are also tools for saving, organising and sharing content, such as Wakelet (www.wakelet.com/), especially useful for storing and catching up on Twitter chats. There are many ways that using social media can help you as an academic, which can only be touched on in a chapter like this, or in Chapter 6 – we suggest you follow up with a dedicated book on social media for academics, such as Carrigan (2019).

Collaboration, communication and meeting tools

Although Covid-19 may have spurred far more online collaboration, technology has always helped those who worked at a distance from other team members. Being involved in national or transnational research projects has relied on technology for effective collaboration and project management. Across Europe, Erasmus+ projects (https://erasmus-plus.ec.europa.eu/projects) are good examples of transnational research projects that rely on effective collaboration between partners in different regions. One such project, proPIC Europa (www.propiceuropa.com/), used a range of digital collaboration tools for language teachers' professional development as part of the project focus, with Slack, Padlet, Flipgrid and Google docs amongst the many tools used.

The ability to share working documents is vital when working with others, whether in pairs or larger teams. Setting up a shared Google folder for two collaborators to work on reduces email traffic, allows each partner to see what the other is working on and increases the productivity in the projects. Collaborators can annotate, comment and share links and resources within the shared spaces. This is true of working together on something straightforward like a journal article or funding bid, or of working together to set up the workflow for an edited book. For larger teams, some initial setup and agreement around working practices needs to happen, but then it is about people and time management. Google now has a 'Doc and Meet' feature, where an online meeting can be started from within a Google document or the current tab can be presented to the call.

The process of setting up meetings can be time consuming, but Doodle polls (www.doodle.com/) can speed things up and is much better than a trail of emails backwards and forwards. Shared calendars can help, and online scheduling tools such as Calendly (www.calendly.com/) can take the pain out of setting up meetings, as well as providing confirmation, reminders and protected space in your main online diary.

Microsoft Teams has a similar collaborative structure, meeting feature and built-in file storage to Google Drive, Docs and Meet. When provided by an institution, there may be sharing restrictions so that files and/or meeting access are limited to internal users only. Some institutions may allow externals to be given guest access to Teams, which can facilitate the creation of a shared, multi-institutional group. Once set up, it is possible to move between the accounts provided by the different institutions in a straightforward way. This does place the onus on one partner as the lead partner, willing to provide and administer the space for the others.

Very often, academics will use a range of digital tools for collaboration, depending on their purpose, preference and pragmatism. Some will prefer Zoom over Teams or Google Meet but may have access to all of them, to some degree. Free versions may be time-limited or have a maximum number of attendees. Financial considerations, acceptable use and data protection policies and sometimes even international restrictions may dictate which tools end up being the preferred methods for collaboration. With the ubiquity of online conferencing, you may find that you can also use Zoom, Teams, WebEx or other platforms as part of a wider communication approach, which combined with ticketing options through a platform like EventBrite (www. eventbrite.co.uk/) could bring a whole new level of engagement to your work. The proliferation of webinars has been a real benefit of the pivot online in the wake of Covid-19.

Ethics should also play a large part in choices, especially where research activity is taking place and needs to be covered under one or more institutions' ethical approval for data storage. OneDrive, Box, Dropbox and Google Drive are all providers of file storage and have the ability to integrate with other applications. It is important to consider and, as far as possible, future-proof the tools being selected for research collaboration. An example of good practice is the clear allocation of roles and responsibilities within a team, so that risks are minimised by agreeing working practices and protocols, especially where research data is being collected and will need to be shared for analysis. In order to do justice to this very important aspect of academic life, a dedicated text on managing academic research projects will be helpful, for example, Ewart and Ames (2020), and later in this chapter, we mention project management and publications strategies.

Digital data collection and analysis

Having touched briefly on data collection and ethics, it is worth giving them some individual consideration in relation to digital tools that enable this important aspect of academic work to progress. Most institutions will have some form of online ethical approval in order to submit the research outline, processes and instruments for academic ethical review. This is where an institutional panel reviews the projects that you want to carry out. Part of that process is thinking about the environment in which you carry out your data collection and what the digital implications may be. The idea of doing no harm, ensuring privacy and confidentiality, requires additional consideration if you are using digital and online tools, and ethics must always be a key part of that from the outset. Drawing on the BERA (2018) guidelines as well as research project guidance is a good start, but accessing targeted guidance, for example a BERA case study on using Twitter for data collection case study (Pennacchia, 2019), will help you to reflect on research carried out online.

With the large-scale pivot to research online during Covid-19, the advice and resources of the National Centre for Research Methods (www.ncrm.ac.uk/) were particularly useful, but of course online and digital research methods have

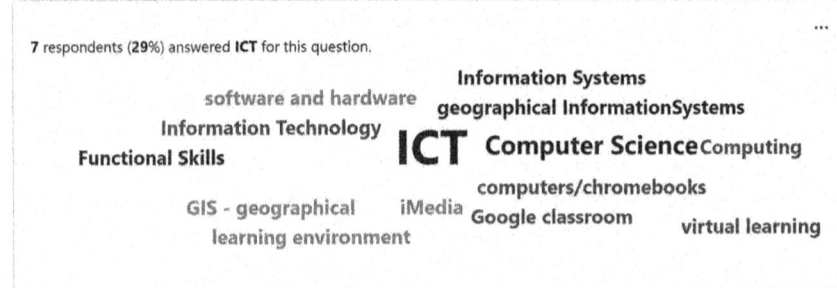

Figure 7.3 Word cloud generated from a meeting poll in Microsoft Teams

Source: Used with permission from Microsoft

a long-established pre-Covid heritage; see for example Hidson (2020), which looks at video-calling and desktop sharing as a purposeful pre-Covid research method.

Survey tools are useful for gathering data sets. You may have heard of SurveyMonkey for online surveys. Microsoft Forms, Qualtrics (www.qualtrics.com/uk/), Jisc (formerly BOS) surveys (www.onlinesurveys.ac.uk/) or REDcap (www.project-redcap.org/) may be provided through your institution, and some may have restrictions on which tools can be used because of information security and data protection requirements. If you are part of an organisation, it is worthwhile to consider running an annual survey in areas of interest to you, so you have data that no one else has that supports you in publishing articles and building your profile as an expert. The students you work with may inspire you to research your practice in education. Education is an area that generates a lot of data, and it may be the case that there are areas of your practice that can be explored with practice evaluation as a starting point but address deeper issues of pedagogy or assessment, for example.

Digital data analysis tools for qualitative and quantitative data may be built into software – for example Qualtrics can do a range of data cleaning, statistical analysis and cross-tabulation as well as text analysis. Microsoft Teams meeting polls have a word cloud feature via Microsoft Forms (see Figure 7.3). This type of feature will be familiar to users of qualitative data analysis software, such as NVIVO (www.qsrinternational.com/nvivo-qualitative-data-analysis-software/home/) and Atlas.ti (https://atlasti.com/). Again, institutions may provide particular software – anecdotally, NVIVO seems to be common in universities, along with quantitative data analysis software like SPSS and RStudio, but other stats software such as Inzight (https://inzight.nz/) and Statscloud (https://statscloud.app/) seem well regarded.

Given the effort involved in learning, using and maintaining skills in a major piece of data analysis software, it is probably worth considering the most common, institutionally provided tools for data analysis unless there are compelling reasons to incur additional expense and learning time.

Systematic review and rapid evidence review tools

Internet access has made it easy to find academic articles, but the volume available can be overwhelming. Systematic review methods have been developed to provide a means for synthesising existing knowledge systematically to give an overview of research findings in a particular area. The methods and digital tools that now exist allow for a systematic review to be extended and built on over time. Systematic reviews can be expensive and slow where there is a considerable volume of material so 'rapid evidence assessment' methods were subsequently developed to provide politicians with an evidence base for practice (Gough et al., 2017).

Two international specialist systematic review centres are the Cochrane Collaboration for medicine (www.cochrane.org) and the Campbell Collaboration for the social sciences (www.campbellcollaboration.org). We suggest you explore their libraries of reviews and the services they offer and consider contributing. Typically, groups of interested academics and practitioners work in teams to undertake reviews. A number of governments use systematic reviews to provide evidence to support decision-making; University College London's Evidence for Policy and Practice (EPPI) centre in the UK has, following many government and EU contracts, developed a software platform facilitating the review process. They also provide training in systematic reviewing, and access to their EPPI reviewer tool may be available if you gain systematic review contracts.

Professor James Thomas is University College London's Director of the EPPI centre's Reviews Facility for the government's Department of Health, England, which undertakes systematic reviews across a range of policy areas to support the department. He provided us with the following description of the EPPI Reviewer tool:

> PPI-Reviewer is a software platform for managing and analysing data for use in all kinds of research synthesis including systematic reviews, rapid reviews, scoping reviews, and traditional literature reviews. Given the particular needs of systematic reviews to ensure rigour in their conduct, as they are frequently used to inform decisions that affect people's lives, the software contains many features specifically to support this type of review. It has recently incorporated new machine learning technologies to make reviewing activities more efficient, including keeping reviews and updates

up to date automatically by finding new research as it is published. It contains a regularly updated copy of the Microsoft Academic dataset, making it even easier to locate relevant research and compile rapid overviews of an area of research very quickly. The software platform is now used by thousands of people internationally to conduct reviews, and is connected via API to other organisations which use its data and machine learning services for their own activities.

See Gough et al. (2017) for more detail as a comprehensive overview of systematic reviews.

Reflection

The professional life of a modern academic is busy and fast-paced. The need to network, collaborate and seek opportunities to engage in the work that you love requires that you can comfortably juggle your time, supported by an array of digital tools. Every element of academic life requires a level of digital literacy, but more than that, an understanding of how they relate to and integrate with each other for maximum efficiency. Your academic literacy, criticality and ethical awareness are essential for navigating the complexity of integrating digital tools into your practice.

It's always important to consider the pros and cons of a task, and Table 7.1 does that with some of the main themes of this chapter. It is expected that you would have your own points to add as things occur to you, and it is important to ensure that you can debate them confidently. Although these are general points, you should revisit them when thinking about any individual digital tool choice that faces you, and then again when you start to work with others. This will help to make sure that you can justify your choices and the implications for you individually or as part of a team. It is often the case that we can spot the problems first, so the Table begins with cons before providing responses in the pros column.

Your checklist and goals: for using technologies effectively

Now use the checklist in Table 7.2 to develop your own training plan.

Table 7.2 Checklist: your digital technology checklist and training plan is freely available for download via the Support Material tab on the Routledge website.

Table 7.1 Analysing the pros and cons of particular digital tools

Cons	Pros
Time and ongoing time management.	Time is always precious for academics, but the gains from efficiency made through software can be significant, or at least reduce the number of smaller drains on your time.
Costs of subscriptions, professional memberships, software purchases. Longevity and lifespan – free versus paid.	These might be offset by using research funding to cover some of the costs or could be covered by your institution. Professional memberships may be covered under job expenses tax relief. Updates and product support may be provided by the institution.
Digital skills need keeping up to date.	Many of these digital skills are integrated with academic practice, so the investment in digital skills is also an investment in academic skills and therefore an investment in your own 'marketability' as you seek promotion.
Horizon scanning – you have to keep up with the direction of digital travel.	Horizon scanning is part of keeping abreast of your field: the digital element is integrated and needed to maintain your capacity to participate in and lead on research.
Resilience – may not be your preferred medium but you still need to join in.	You may prefer the low-tech feel of the printed book or coding by hand, or just feel anxious about the pace at which these practices are becoming digitised: find a peer to support and encourage you if that is the case or look carefully at what the digital tool can do to enhance your insights into your research. Seeing a visualisation of your paper or exploring links that would not occur to you in a low-tech approach may inspire you to embrace digital approaches.
Adopting technology – you have to stick with it because it can be hard to change provider.	It's not impossible, just a little time consuming. People switching phones or getting new laptops manage it relatively swiftly.
What is the currency and discourse of the tool – how popular?	Once you have attained a comfortable level of skill and fluency with one brand of software, you would need to translate the concepts into another brand, e.g., nodes, links and groups in Atlas.ti versus theme nodes and case nodes in NVIVO – similar ideas with different terms. To ensure maximum possible collaboration, it's good to have a spread of knowledge, but as with any negotiation, compromise may be needed if the majority of the colleagues with whom you are working use other tools.

Table 7.2 Checklist: your digital technology checklist and training plan

Technology/software purpose/type and examples	Self-evaluation (level of competence: competent, need more practice, need to test it out)	Notes
Reliable, secure devices for research, writing and collaboration, such as desktop or laptop machine with backups and storage, plus mobile phone and perhaps tablet set up with synchronisation and secure authentication		
Integrated productivity software such as Microsoft Office with email and approved cloud storage (e.g., OneDrive, Dropbox, Google Drive), with word processor connected to reference manager		
Online calendaring system, such as Calendly, integrated into email; Doodle polls or similar for arranging meetings		
Browser set up with reference manager importers and synchronised across devices		
Advanced use of email automation functions, such as rules and mailboxes		
Voice dictation features or apps for automatic transcription		
Dedicated writing software such as Scrivener		
Notes systems such as OneNote or Evernote		
Focus assist and do-not-disturb features in operating system or apps that you use		
Writing time structure features such as Pomodoro timers		
Reference managers such as Mendeley, EndNote or Zotero for organising research sources		
Visualisation tools such as ConnectedPapers, Citationtree, Research Rabbit or EPPI-Mapper for displaying bibliographic connections within papers		
Institutional and social media profiles set up and maintained		

Task						
Academic portals such as ORCID, ResearchGate, Figshare, Google scholar and Google knowledge panel or similar checked						
ResearchGate and Altmetric set up and checked for monitoring profile and statistics						
Investigate networks, such as professional associations, AdvanceHE and own institutional networks						
Twitter account, thread reader and curation apps like Wakelet						
Collaboration tools such as Slack, Padlet, Flipgrid and Google workspace, Microsoft Teams						
Video-calling and desktop sharing platforms such as Microsoft Teams, Zoom or Google Meet for meetings and webinars						
Survey tools such as Microsoft Forms, Qualtrics etc., checking on potential ethics requirements						
Digital data analysis tools for qualitative and quantitative data such as NVIVO, Altas.ti, SPSS and RStudio						
Systematic review and rapid evidence review tools such as Cochrane collection and EPPI reviewer						
Project management tools such as Gantt charts, Microsoft Project, Asana or Trello						
YOUR SPECIFIC GOALS: now record the goals that suit your context and your discipline . . .						

Summary: recognising success and avoiding pitfalls

Hopefully this chapter has allowed you to think about your digital profile and review the way you are represented in the online world. It's important to maintain this professional presence online because we want our profiles to encourage others to engage with our work and consider us as active and impactful in our fields.

You should have identified online professional networks in your field and be ready to join those most relevant to the direction of your work because this will be helpful professionally. Hopefully, the discussion of the range of digital tools will have been useful in showing you how they integrate in a useful way with your academic practice. If any are new to you, we suggest you make a plan to test out some of the tools to support your personal research and scholarly activity, including dissemination, communication and collaboration. In the spirit of mutual support, also consider initiating some discussions about the affordances provided by digital tools and the way that they are used by your colleagues, peers and wider academic field to support their academic, research and scholarly activity.

A good debate between academics is always a useful way to confirm or extend your thinking and learn from others' perspectives.

The consequences of not engaging with technologies will be losing many opportunities to develop your skills and experiences to meet the criteria for professorship.

Note: there are many assistive technologies to help you if you find difficulty in using different technologies, but these are not covered here.

The next chapter introduces you to ways of developing your book publications.

Websites

Altmetric, www.altmetric.com/.
Atlas.ti, https://atlasti.com/.
BERA in Education, www.bera.ac.uk/.
Calendly, https://calendly.com/ – calendar app.
Campbell Collaboration for the Social Sciences, www.campbellcollaboration.org.
Citationtree, https://citationtree.org/.
Cochrane Collaboration for Medicine, www.cochrane.org.
Connected Papers, www.connectedpapers.com/.
Doodle Polls, www.doodle.com/.
EPPI-Mapper, https://eppi.ioe.ac.uk/cms/Default.aspx?tabid=3790.
Erasmus+ Projects, https://erasmus-plus.ec.europa.eu/projects.
Eventbrite, www.eventbrite.co.uk.
Evernote, www.evernote.com/.
Inzight, https://inzight.nz/.
Jisc (Formerly BOS) Surveys, www.onlinesurveys.ac.uk/.
National Centre for Research Methods, www.ncrm.ac.uk/.
NVIVO, www.qsrinternational.com/nvivo-qualitative-data-analysis-software/home/.

Publons, http://publons.com/.
Qualtrics, www.qualtrics.com/uk/.
REDcap Surveys, www.project-redcap.org/.
Research Excellence Framework, www.ref.ac.uk/.
ResearchGate, www.researchgate.net/.
Research Professional, www.researchprofessional.com/.
Research Rabbit, www.researchrabbit.ai/.
Scrivener – Dedicated Writing Software, www.literatureandlatte.com/.
Statscloud, https://statscloud.app/.
SurveyMonkey for online surveys.
UK AdvanceHE, www.advance-he.ac.uk/.

References

BERA [British Educational Research Association]. (2018) *Ethical Guidelines for Educational Research*, 4th edition, www.bera.ac.uk/publication/ethical-guidelines-for-educational-research-2018-online, Accessed on 27 October 2022.

Bond, M. (2021) Schools and emergency remote education during the COVID-19 pandemic: A living rapid systematic review, *Asian Journal of Distance Education*, 15(2), 191–247, https://doi.org/10.5281/ZENODO.4425683, Accessed on 27 October 2022.

Carrigan, M. (2019) *Social Media for Academics*, 2nd edition, London: Sage.

Cirillo, F. (2009) *The Pomodoro Technique*, Vintage edition, Creative Commons, www.pomodorotechnique.com/resources/ThePomodoroTechnique-CHN_v1-3.pdf, Accessed on 27 October 2022.

Ewart, J. and Ames, K. (2020) Managing your academic research project. In: *Managing Your Academic Research Project*, Singapore: Springer, https://doi.org/10.1007/978-981-15-9192-1, Accessed on 27 October 2022.

Gough, D., Oliver, S. and Thomas, J. (Eds.). (2017) *An Introduction to Systematic Reviews*, 2nd edition, London: Sage.

Hidson, E. (2020) Internet video calling and desktop sharing (vcds) as an emerging research method for exploring pedagogical reasoning in lesson planning, *Video Journal of Education and Pedagogy*, 5, 1–14, https://doi.org/10.1163/23644583-00501001, Accessed on 27 October 2022.

Kennewell, S. (2001) Using affordances and constraints to evaluate the use of information and communications technology in teaching and learning, *Journal of Information Technology for Teacher Education*, 10(1–2), 101–116.

Pennacchia, J. (Ed.). (2019) *BERA Research Ethics Case Studies: 1. Twitter, Data Collection and Informed Consent*, www.bera.ac.uk/publication/twitter-data-collection-informed-consent.

ResearchGate. (2022) *Research Interest*, https://explore.researchgate.net/display/support/Research+Interest, Accessed on 27 October 2022.

Spicer, A. (2015) Explainer: What is an H-index and how is it calculated? *The Conversation*, May, https://theconversation.com/explainer-what-is-an-h-index-and-how-is-it-calculated-41162, Accessed on 27 October 2022.

Wouters, P., Thelwall, M., Kousha, K., Waltman, L., de Rijcke, S., Rushforth, A. and Franssen, T. (2015) The metric tide, *Ukri.Org*, https://doi.org/10.13140/RG.2.1.5066.3520, Accessed on 27 October 2022.

Chapter 8

Publishing books

Marilyn Leask with contributions from Routledge colleagues

Introduction

National university student surveys are undertaken in the UK annually. I remember reading this quote from a response from a student at the London School of Economics (LSE): 'One of the best things [about LSE] is that the teachers are the people whose names are on the books'. For me this quotation sums up one of the pleasures of writing a book to be used by one's students: the feedback from those who use and have enjoyed your book. But I find the pleasure is also personal. I write in order to set down what I know and to record what I am learning from the research I undertake. The discipline of writing makes me order my thoughts and helps me identify gaps in my knowledge and in the published knowledge of others. I hope this chapter encourages you to write so that, after the intellectual pain of shaping the written word into a coherent narrative, you experience the pleasure of holding your book in your hand and of your students using and enjoying your work.

Building a career as an author is an essential part of becoming a professor, and this chapter has advice on how to maximise publication opportunities for books from your research. As you read this chapter, bear in mind that academic publishers need authors if they are not to go out of business! So, there is mutual benefit in the shared enterprise of getting a book to publication. This chapter is based on the assumption that you wish to work with a publisher who specialises in publishing books in your field and who is able to reach the intended readership through their marketing and sales channels. Look for those that have display stands promoting books like yours at the main national and international conferences in your field.

Publishing academic journal articles is also expected of professors, as are reviewing journal articles and, in time, having a position on a journal editorial board and taking on editorial responsibilities. The route to editorship and the demands and rewards of journal article publishing are covered in Chapter 9.

You can increase your publication record by linking your academic article publishing and editing roles and your book publishing. This chapter explores how to make the most of both routes to publishing to develop your professional profile and networks.

DOI: 10.4324/9781003217596-8

Objectives

By the end of this chapter you should understand:

- why you might write a book, who the intended audience might be and the options for authorship/editorship;
- how to find a publisher and how to help publishers find you;
- how to plan and structure a book;
- how to construct a book proposal;
- the publishing process;
- contracts;
- how to use your time effectively.

Help! I want to write a book. Where do I start?

Naturally, the prospect of writing your first book is daunting, but if you are driven to write there are a number of simple steps you can work through to reach a successful conclusion. The advice that follows sets out those steps and the decisions you may need to make as they apply to academic books.

Here are two positive things to remember as you embark on this journey:

- Publishers need a constant flow of new manuscripts, so if you can create a book that meets their criteria for inclusion in their lists and has a clear potential market that will cover their costs, then you are on the way to receiving a contract.
- As an academic, you may have written theses at master's and doctoral levels; you may have written research reports; perhaps you have had academic articles published already. These experiences provide a solid foundation for writing a book: you know how to manage your time and to conceptualise the structure for a written report and, as well, you have the personal discipline to complete a writing project.

Decision 1: why write?

This might be an opportune moment for you to pause and consider the question: why do you want to write a book? Your answers will affect the choice of topic and title, the publisher you choose, the numbers of books sold (which affects your royalties – the financial recompense for your efforts). Answering the questions that follow will help you clarify what will become the proposal you put to the publisher.

Decision 2: who are you writing the book for?

Have you a clear audience in mind: the public? students? policymakers? practitioners? your academic peers?

Clearly, different forms of writing and different languages are used for different audiences. If you are writing for students in your discipline, then you will need to include a glossary of key terms, perhaps explaining terms as they are introduced during the book. If you are writing for peers, then you can assume that the reader already has considerable knowledge and you do not have to start with the basics.

The publisher will want to know the audience so they can assess the number of likely sales. This will affect the price of the book and the likelihood that they will recoup their costs in editing, typesetting, designing, publishing, warehousing, marketing and distributing your book. For some subjects, there is a very small market. In England, there are just over 150 university libraries and only 80 or so had teacher education departments in 2021, so the library market for that audience is small (DfE, 2021).

Decision 3: the provisional title

In choosing the title for your book, consider what your potential audience is looking for. Will they be able to find your book easily, or is the title obscure and not likely to be found by any internet search engine?

Will the proposed title convey meaning to the publisher who is making a choice whether your book fits in their list or not?

If a publisher is interested in your ideas for a book, they will ask you for a full book proposal (see below) and will send this out to people in your field for review. Both the publishers and the reviewers are likely to comment on the title, considering whether the title is likely to be attractive to the potential purchasers of the book, including librarians/students/practitioners/policymakers as well as specialists in your field.

Decision 4: what type of book: sole or joint authored, an edited collection?

What your writing experience will have taught you is that good academic writing, drawing on and synthesising research, takes an enormous amount of time. This is one reason why you might decide to co-author with a colleague to produce a jointly authored book rather than a sole authored book. You may decide it is appropriate given the topic to invite different experts to contribute chapters so that your book becomes an edited collection.

The decision about the type of book is yours to make and will depend on the speed with which you want to have the book published and whether you want, for professional reasons perhaps, to be the sole author.

Decision 5: planning the content and structure of your book

Drawing on your existing successful academic writing experience, it may help you to plan the time it will take to produce the manuscript of the proposed book by thinking of your book as

- Equivalent in length to a doctoral thesis or two or three master's theses.

If this feels too daunting, it may help to think of your book as made up of

- Eight or ten articles/chapters that together make a book of 50–70,000 words. So, the task is like writing 8–10 academic articles. If you have written articles already around the theme of the book, you may get permission from the journal publisher to adapt or include these articles as part of your book. There may well be work in any thesis or research reports you have written that can be adapted and included. For example, the literature review part of a thesis may provide a good foundation for a book that builds on the research in the thesis. I started off in academic life thinking once I had published one article from a piece of research I couldn't write additional articles on the topic, but of course with experience I realised that experts in a field steadily build their knowledge, and it is possible to track the development of ideas over decades by reviewing the sequential publications of experts/thought leaders in a field.

If that still feels daunting, perhaps your topic might lend itself to

- An **edited** collection of eight or ten articles/chapters – where, like this book, you invite colleagues in your field to contribute chapters. In my initial proposal to the publisher, I proposed this book as a sole authored book drawing on data from an international survey of professors. However, as I wrote the book, I realised that it would better reflect practice in different countries if I worked closely with such colleagues, asking them to contribute their own chapters and comment on other chapters. This meant I had to renegotiate the contract with the publishers and extend the deadline for publication. Fortunately, the publishers of this book, with whom I have worked for over 30 years, are very understanding of these kinds of deviations from the original contract that occur when a book is actually being written. I suggest you check with the publisher what flexibility there is over deadlines.

If your topic is time critical, then the edited collection approach – working with colleagues to provide a coherent overview of a topic – may enable you to have your ideas published while the topic is still of interest.

In Chapter 4, p. 51, I describe the processes I use from the beginning of some ideas to the submission of the manuscript.

Finding a publisher

As mentioned, publishers are usually keeping a lookout for authors, as without authors they have no business.

To find a publisher for your book, look at which publishers publish in your field by simply looking at the books relevant to your field. Then look at the book lists on their websites and approach the publisher that appears to have a gap in their list when it comes to your topic. In deciding which publisher to approach first, I suggest you approach one that *actively* promotes books published in your field. You may have noticed they send book flyers/emails to lecturers in the field or their flyers are included in conference packs. If you publish with a publisher who is new to your field, then they may not have developed much capacity to market your book themselves. I recall one year where a new publisher approached many academics personally and signed them up to write books. The publisher established an interesting book list very quickly and then was taken over by a much bigger publisher. It is likely the sales of books by those early authors were not high. Some academic authors find that the annual royalty letter from the publisher states there are no royalties because there haven't been sufficient sales. So, it may be worth checking the marketing activities of a potential publisher.

To make contact, they may have an expression of interest form on their website, or an email address.

Helping the publishers find you

Personal contact is to be recommended as it can be quickly established if the potential author and the publisher have mutual interests. There are several ways that you might achieve personal contact with potential publishers:

- a colleague who publishes with your preferred publisher recommends you to their publisher;
- you present your work at a conference; the publisher sees your presentation listed in the conference programme and approaches you;
- you approach the publishers manning the stalls at your professional conference and they put you in touch with the editor who holds the list that your book would appear in;
- your digital profile attracts their interest.

Self-publishing

An alternative route is self-publishing. Amazon has made self-publishing easy. I know colleagues who have gone down this route successfully, but I am not covering that route in this chapter. I mention this option because if you are driven to write and you cannot find a publisher interested in your idea, then you may decide to go down the self-publishing route. See for example Kindle Direct Publishing (https://kdp.amazon.com/en_US/). There are a number of companies supporting self-publishing who will charge you, and an internet search will provide you with options. I mention Amazon because they can offer extensive market access for your book. A word of warning: with self-publishing, do check the quality of the product you are selling carefully as you may not have the support of the high-quality design and editing processes provided by publishers.

If your book is of specialist academic interest, then finding a publisher that specialises in marketing to that market should be your top priority. So, one way or another, you should be able to get your book published. The advice that follows is focused on working with academic publishers. I have had contracts with five different publishers and have contributed chapters to books published by several other publishers over 40 years. Colleagues have shared some of their experiences with publishers. The section on contracts later in this chapter gives you an indication of some of the pitfalls you need to consider.

Time management

Have you got the dedication and drive to write a book? Typically, it takes me 18 months to two years to produce a completed manuscript, depending how much new work is required. Producing a manuscript following the completion of a substantial research project or doctoral thesis may of course be much quicker.

I cannot pretend that pursuing an academic career that involves both teaching and management and research and writing isn't hugely time consuming – it is, hence my inclusion of Decision 1 earlier. You will need to be efficient to manage writing, researching and teaching. Writing has become my hobby. I love the way you can start with an idea and, through either desk research or primary research, you develop your understanding, and the book writing allows me to structure and organise my knowledge. I love the way the mind works to reveal insights based on one's particular experiences and understandings coupled with research findings and the reading of the publications of others.

In the survey of existing professors undertaken for this book, one professor provides the following advice:

> Work collaboratively. Try to ensure that there is a link between your teaching and your research so that you are not pulled into two different directions. Identify a person who inspires you and try to link up or ask to be linked up. Enjoy what you do.

The book proposal: used by the publishers to decide whether to publish your book

The book proposal is the paperwork you prepare and submit to the publishers to enable them to make a decision about whether to publish a book. They will send it to reviewers who are experts in your field as well as to internal reviewers.

The publisher you choose will no doubt have their preferred format. What I cover in this section relates to the proposal I put to the publisher (Routledge) about this book. Obviously, you will need to check what your preferred publisher wants from you. The questions Routledge asks are listed in Table 8.1 and require considerable detail – perhaps in areas you may feel you have no experience in, for example about the potential purchasers and what courses that your text might become recommended reading for. If you put yourself in the publisher's shoes, you'll see it makes sense for them to ask these questions at the beginning of the process.

Table 8.1 The book proposal: a questionnaire filled in by prospective authors at the request of publishers

Below are the main questions that I had to answer in the proposal to Routledge for this book. The full proposal was 6500 words long, excluding the sample chapter requested.

ABOUT THE BOOK: Title, Subtitle: Author(s)/editor(s), Series/discipline

Rationale

1. Why do you think that there is a need for this book?
2. How long would it remain up-to-date?
3. Please provide a brief outline of the current context to your book, explaining – if relevant – how and why recent changes may have taken place to make your book more relevant now than ever before.

Synopsis

4. Please provide a synopsis, stating the mission and scope of the book. This should include: an overview of the book and a statement of its aim, a list of chapter headings, **an abstract of each chapter** – please **do not** provide just a bullet-pointed list of topics covered in each chapter – and a sample chapter, if available.
5. Please indicate the approximate number of words you envisage as well as an approximate number of printed pages (allowing 400 words per printed page) and state the number of line illustrations, photographs and tables that would be included. State if (and why) colour would be required.
6. Please provide a soundbite (around 300 words) about your book, which could be used on the jacket of the book in order to draw the reader in. If you are unsure of the Routledge style, browse similar titles online or in bookshops to get a feel for the way we promote our books.

Readership

7. Who is the readership for this book, and what background do you expect them to have?
8. If you expect your book to be recommended on university or college courses, please provide us with the following additional information: the course titles; an indication of the numbers in which they are run, a selection of the institutions that teach them; at what level; whether your book would be a textbook, essential or recommended reading; if possible, an idea of student numbers.
9. Evidence of a recent increase in the number of courses and/or student numbers is also useful to us, so do provide this if relevant.
10. Does your book have an international appeal? If you think it does, please state why, and in which countries.
11. Are there special professional groups, scholarly societies, or other organisations who would have a particular interest in your book? Please list them.
12. Please provide a list of up to five bullet points of why this book is a 'must-buy' for your target audience.

Competition

13. Please attach a list of competing books, including author(s)/editor(s), publisher, price and year of publication.

14. How will your book differ?

15. If you genuinely feel that your book does not have any competition, please provide us with information about comparable or similar titles in the field.

Your background

17. Please provide a brief paragraph outlining your current job, experience and previous book publications (if relevant).

18. Are you active on social media? If so, please provide details, including for e.g.: number of Twitter followers, blog hits etc.

19. Please let us know if you are writing from first-hand experience in research and teaching.

Timescale

20. Publication to an agreed deadline is fundamental to good publishing. When would you expect to be able to submit a complete manuscript? (Please be realistic.)

Other information

22. Can you suggest three people from whom we might solicit, in confidence, a review of this proposal? Suggested reviewers should be working in this field and able to give an in-depth, unbiased opinion of this proposal. Please do not suggest anyone who is likely to contribute to the proposed book, anyone who teaches at the same institution as yourself or, if your proposal is based upon your PhD or other post-graduate dissertation, anyone involved in its supervision or assessment.

In the rest of this section, I provide advice on possible answers to the questions in the proposal in Table 8.1.

About the book

The title

I have mentioned previously the importance of having a title that has meaning to those who might wish to buy the book i.e. those that you are communicating with.

Authorship

The question of authorship is important as it is linked with recognition about your contribution. Options are covered in Decision 4 previously. It is worthwhile establishing early on the order of names on the book if you are co-authoring or co-editing. Different disciplines have different protocols, so check what is relevant in your field. Chapter 9 provides considerable detail on this matter.

I offer the following guidance: if you are doing most of the work then, at the start of the writing, ask the others being named if you can be acknowledged as the main author/editor. This should indicate to a professorial recruitment panel that you are the initiator and lead contributor. If your name appears last, as may be inevitable if your name begins with letters at the end of the alphabet, then the form of use of 'and' and 'with' in the naming of the contributing authors is significant. The use of 'and' in a list of authors/editors in alphabetical order implies equal contributions. The use of 'with' implies that those whose names follow the 'with' have played a lesser role. See Weber, p. 125 after Chapter 9.

So, do agree on the naming protocols with co-authors/co-editors prior to the submission of the proposal to the publishers.

The rationale

This section is your chance to show how your book will contribute to the field and why it might appeal to potential purchasers. The material you give may be used in marketing, and in addition, editors making a decision about whether to publish it or not may not be aware of the recent developments in your field that make your book essential reading.

The synopsis

The questions in the synopsis section are straightforward, but there are a couple of points to be aware of. If you wish to include colour, this adds to the cost of the book, and you will want to negotiate the inclusion of photographs and colour early on. The publisher will be making a decision about the costs of getting your book to the marketplace and what it is likely to sell for, as clearly, they don't want to publish books that lose them money. If you submit a manuscript that is considerably over the agreed page length, this also may cause the publisher some problems as their financial calculations will be undertaken on the basis of what you submitted in the proposal.

The book series that I have been co-editing for 30 years with invited colleagues started off with a proposal for what we thought might be a fairly small book. This was rejected by a number of publishers initially as they did not want to publish to that market, but one was able to point me in the direction of a publisher who was interested in publishing and we have been partners in an expanding book series for over 30 years. In the end, the first edition of this book weighed a kilo and I had to take three months' unpaid leave to finish it. Why did I do that? Well, self-interest for a start. I wanted the knowledge for myself so that I could teach as well as possible: the book covered the fundamentals for learning to teach in the secondary school, and I was a university-based teacher educator. Following the success of the first book, the publisher asked for a specialist series providing more depth on subject specialist areas than was possible in the first book.

If the field of your university teaching is being stimulated by new developments in the field, then an edited book with chapter contributions from others working in this emerging field might be valuable both to support your teaching and to ensure the latest knowledge is available to students. The thinking behind your decisions may make a conceptual paper of interest to a journal publishing in the field – a book to fit the new programme might help those you teach by providing depth of knowledge to complement your teaching. Writing for a public audience brings extra discipline to your research and construction of new teaching programmes and can give you a number of outputs – academic and professional journal articles and a book.

What makes for a good academic book proposal – a publisher's advice from Taylor and Francis

The mission of a good publisher is to connect authors with readers. The advice here hopefully facilitates that, but a conversation with the relevant editor is often a vital stage to bring together your subject expertise with their publishing expertise. From the perspective of the editor, such conversations can be key to sharpening your proposal in a few key areas:

1. **Title.** We need to ensure that potential readers can find your book easily. The title should give a clear indication of what the book is about.
2. **Include a short CV.** Tell the publisher why you are qualified to write this. This is always important, especially if you are a first-time author.

3. **Readership.** Be specific, detailed and realistic! The clearer you are about who will read your work, the more you'll inspire confidence.
4. **Rationale.** Why are you writing this book? Why is it needed? If research based: what is unique about your research, and how will it help move the field forward?
5. **Contents.** Ensure the content of your book is focused for the readership. Use descriptive chapter headings – a potential reader (and commissioning editor) should know straight away by looking at the contents page what your book is about.
6. **Competition.** Show us you understand the market for your book.
7. **Review process.** Be flexible! Your idea may need tweaking and refashioning to achieve its full potential.

Having provided you with the key tips, it's perhaps useful to reflect on the publisher's perspective when it comes to features of book proposals that tend to sound alarm bells. Here are a few examples:

What authors say	What publishers hear
My book has no competition.	I have not researched the market. There is no market for my book.
My manuscript is complete.	I do not wish to engage with constructive criticism. I want you to read my entire manuscript, but I will not make any changes.
The book will be read by everybody.	The book will be read by nobody.
The book will appeal to students, researchers and practitioners.	The book will disappoint students, researchers and practitioners.

In summary, remember to think about the following areas when you put together your book proposal:

---

4 key tips on how to write a successful book proposal

1. **Topic.** Ensure your book's subject is cutting-edge and important.
2. **Audience.** Know the audience for your book and exactly how your book is relevant to that audience.
3. **Position.** Understand the market, how your book sits alongside existing literature and what makes your book unique.
4. **Structure.** Be clear, concise, and consistent when you present the ideas for your book to your publisher.

If you consider these points, you should be well on your way to writing a successful proposal.

The publishing process

Figure 8.1, which has been kindly supplied by Routledge/Taylor & Francis, outlines the publishing process they use. Other publishing houses' processes are likely to be different, so please use this one as providing general guidance about what happens to your manuscript once you have passed it to your editor.

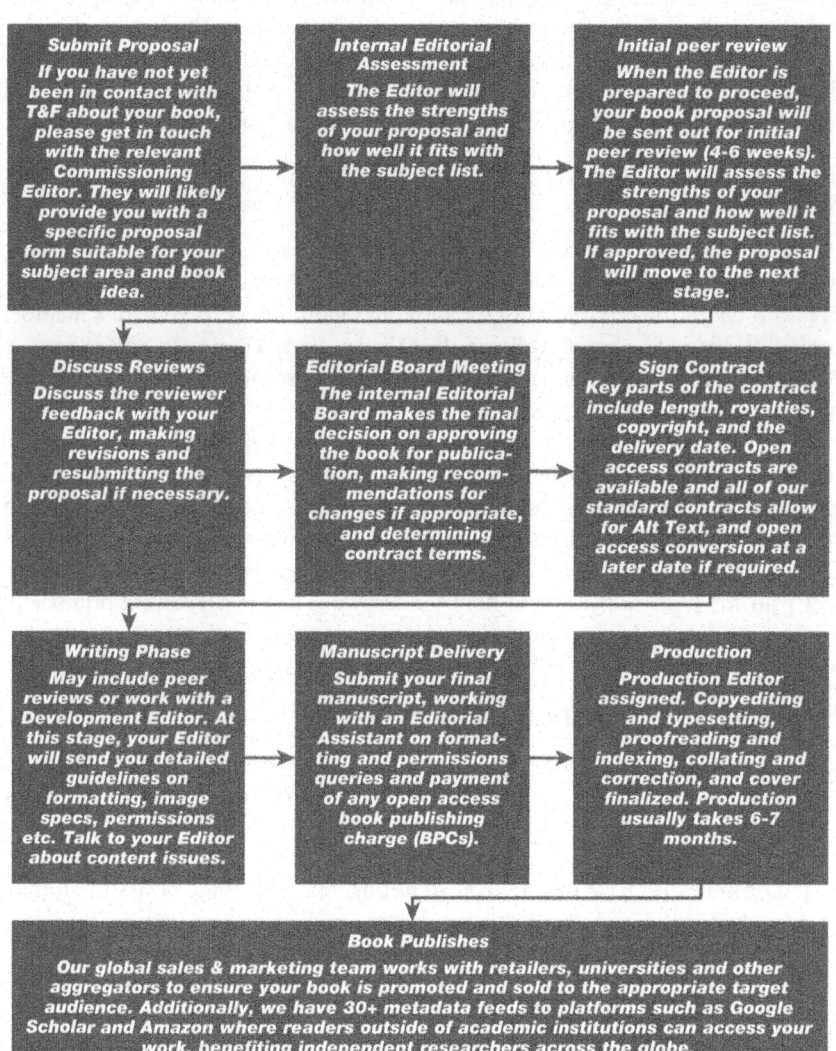

Submit Proposal
If you have not yet been in contact with T&F about your book, please get in touch with the relevant Commissioning Editor. They will likely provide you with a specific proposal form suitable for your subject area and book idea.

Internal Editorial Assessment
The Editor will assess the strengths of your proposal and how well it fits with the subject list.

Initial peer review
When the Editor is prepared to proceed, your book proposal will be sent out for initial peer review (4-6 weeks). The Editor will assess the strengths of your proposal and how well it fits with the subject list. If approved, the proposal will move to the next stage.

Discuss Reviews
Discuss the reviewer feedback with your Editor, making revisions and resubmitting the proposal if necessary.

Editorial Board Meeting
The internal Editorial Board makes the final decision on approving the book for publication, making recommendations for changes if appropriate, and determining contract terms.

Sign Contract
Key parts of the contract include length, royalties, copyright, and the delivery date. Open access contracts are available and all of our standard contracts allow for Alt Text, and open access conversion at a later date if required.

Writing Phase
May include peer reviews or work with a Development Editor. At this stage, your Editor will send you detailed guidelines on formatting, image specs, permissions etc. Talk to your Editor about content issues.

Manuscript Delivery
Submit your final manuscript, working with an Editorial Assistant on formatting and permissions queries and payment of any open access book publishing charge (BPCs).

Production
Production Editor assigned. Copyediting and typesetting, proofreading and indexing, collating and correction, and cover finalized. Production usually takes 6-7 months.

Book Publishes
Our global sales & marketing team works with retailers, universities and other aggregators to ensure your book is promoted and sold to the appropriate target audience. Additionally, we have 30+ metadata feeds to platforms such as Google Scholar and Amazon where readers outside of academic institutions can access your work, benefiting independent researchers across the globe.

Figure 8.1 The publishing process

Source: With thanks to colleagues at Routledge

Contracts

Once you have had your book proposal accepted, you should be sent a contract to sign that specifies date of delivery of manuscript, the length, the royalties, the quality expected and much more. The contract may include penalties for non-delivery or for providing a manuscript that is not of publishable quality. It will normally state that you are responsible for ensuring you have the right to publish all the material in the manuscript and will require you to submit permission letters from those holding the copyright for material published by others that you wish to include. Figures, diagrams and tables must be of high enough quality for print, and the requirements will normally be specified. If figures, diagrams and tables have to be redrawn, then the publisher may ask you to pay for this.

Royalties

Before signing any contract, I suggest you talk to colleagues and take advice. Many elements of the contracts may be negotiable. So, check the small print carefully and check the reputation of the publisher with others. If you are a member of the UK-based Society of Authors, then they provide a contracts advice service. Royalty rates, for example, can vary considerably, and independent advice may help you negotiate a fair agreement.

As well as gaining royalties through your contract, in some countries there are schemes providing an income stream for authors from fees gained from photocopying, online licensing and lending to public libraries. In the UK, authors should register with ALCS (Authors' licensing and collecting service) and the British Library PLR (public lending right) scheme. Both organisations distribute licence fees paid for photocopying and library borrowing in the UK and a number of other countries. I advise you to seek out similar organisations in your own country.

Promising a manuscript submission date

Publishers plan their printing and marketing processes many months ahead of receiving your manuscript, as they have made a commitment to you to have your manuscript published at a particular time.

On a few occasions, I have found that the manuscript simply can't be completed on time and have negotiated extensions, but with some books the timing of the publication is not negotiable because the publishers are targeting a particular market. Academic courses in the northern hemisphere normally start in September or October, and a manuscript may need to be with the publisher in the preceding November/December if the book is to be ready in May for lecturers to decide whether to recommend it to students and to the library for purchase.

A month or two delay might mean you miss the market that year, and in the following year you might find a competitor book has been published that is more up to date than yours.

Correcting the proofs

A month or two after submission of the manuscript, you can expect to get proof copies, which need to be checked carefully and quickly if the production process is not to be held up. At this stage, making changes can be very costly as the book will have been designed and proofread before being returned to you for checking.

Indexing – your responsibilities

You will normally be expected to provide an index, and as page numbers can't be added before you get the proofs, you have to compile the index very close to the publication date. So, best practice is to identify a list of words ahead of time to be included in the index so that this can be completed as quickly as possible. The publisher will normally provide advice about the construction of the index, but for information I include in the references that follow, links to advice about constructing an index.

There are professional indexers who will undertake the job for a fee. I suggest you book them well in advance so that you are not left as I was for my last book, when I was wishing to have a professional indexer but found no one was available. In the UK, the Society of Indexers provides access to a list of trained indexers from whom to choose.

Tax liabilities

Normally you pay tax on your royalties, but you may find that many expenses incurred directly as a result of your writing are tax deductible, such as purchasing academic textbooks, professional association membership fees, conference attendance fees, computers and associated costs. In the UK, membership fees for the Society of Authors are tax deductible, as may be the costs of your home office. Unless there is a large market for your book, the royalties will be very small.

My book publications journey

Since 1984, much of my research has been about the use of digital technologies in the education sector, and this was a significant component of my university teaching. As this was a rapidly expanding field, I was continually involved in research projects and wrote books in order to have a record of the latest research to underpin my teaching. Table 8.2 maps my journey as an author against my academic career. I provide this so that you can see how one thing leads to another. I could not have predicted this journey when I developed my first book proposal more than 30 years ago, but in retrospect it is easy to see how one book proposal led naturally to another.

I have written, as either sole author, editor or co-editor, more than 20 books over the period 1992 to 2022. I am currently working on the tenth edition of one book I co-edit. I have also co-edited a book series leading to 30 or so books produced by authors whom I and my co-editor have invited to contribute.

The point of the anecdote in Table 8.2 is that you cannot predict the outcomes of your book publication. The book above led me to be appointed to a government position tasked with putting online the knowledge base underpinning teacher education. I spent about £20 million worth of taxpayer money on this online resource, only to have it taken offline when there was a change of government in 2010. Educators involved subsequently came together to set up a charity to take forward putting research summaries online for teachers – you can see the result on www.meshguides.org. The resources are freely available and used in all but a few countries in the world.

Table 8.2 My publications pathway

The first book I initiated, in 1990, was with a senior colleague, Del Goddard, in the local education authority I worked for. He was a national thought leader at a time of much investment and development of quality assurance practices in the education system in England. I had been seconded from an advisory role in the local education authority to the University of Cambridge in the UK to work as a researcher on a national research project in school self-evaluation as the local authority was leading in the development of new practices. Several factors influenced my decision to write this book with him:

- The field of work was of national and international interest and I could see he had exceptional knowledge that was only available to people who heard him speak. I felt a moral commitment to my profession to record and share knowledge that can be a benefit to all.
- During my secondment, academic colleagues had asked me, as a practitioner, to review book proposals that they were compiling for submission to publishers. From this work, I learnt how to write a proposal and that publishers' requirements for a book proposal created a solid and clear structure for the book that made it possible to write the book in small sections in the time I had available outside my full-time employment.
- I enjoyed academic writing and research. I had recently completed a number of research reports as well as an 80,000-word MPhil thesis (during maternity leave for my third child). This work, completed over six years, developed my ability to use slivers of time to write carved out of busy family life, to create an extended piece of writing with a coherent narrative and to critique my writing.

Then, following this secondment, I was appointed to a university post in teacher training. I found the thought of training teachers challenging, so I looked for books that would guide my university teaching. I couldn't find the kind of book I wanted, and so I put together a proposal and found colleagues to co-edit the book with me and, in 1994 published a book that at the time of writing is going into the tenth edition. At the time, the national assessment of university staff research did not value the production of books of this sort, and with my co-editors we discussed the likelihood that devoting time to this practice-focused but research-based book would damage our academic careers. We went ahead anyway because we wanted the book to exist.

Your checklist and goals: for book publishing

I find books always take longer than I expect because in undertaking research for the book, new issues and insights arise that need to be included and unexpected events in one's private and professional lives rightly take precedence. Table 8.3 is intended to prompt you to plan your first book.

Table 8.3 Checklist: for use when you are preparing a book proposal is freely available for photocopy or download via the Support Material tab on the Routledge website.

Table 8.3 Checklist: for use when you are preparing a book proposal

ITEM	Achieved?	
	Yes	No
Have you identified a provisional title for your book?		
Have you identified the audience for your book?		
Have you mapped out a structure of your book?		
Have you mapped out each chapter?		
Have you decided what type of book you are proposing: sole authored? co-authored? an edited collection?		
Have you a short list of the publishers who publish in your field?		
Consider the publisher you've chosen: have they a track record of marketing books to the markets you think will be interested in your book?		
Have you a plan for approaching the first publisher in your list?		
Do you have answers to all the questions you are likely to have to answer in a formal book proposal (see book proposal section above)?		
Do you have someone who can advise you on contracts?		
Have you a realistic date in mind for the submission of the manuscript that allows for some slippage to accommodate unexpected interruptions?		
YOUR SPECIFIC GOALS: now record the goals that suit your context and your discipline		

Summary: recognising success and avoiding pitfalls

When choosing areas to research and the titles of the resulting books and articles, ask yourself the question: is this field of study/book/article likely to be of interest to other academics as well as policymakers, industrialists and/or practitioners in your field, and has it the potential to have impact internationally?

Your relationship with your publisher is important not only to make sure that your books are published to high quality but also you may have signed a contract that says you will let them have first option on any subsequent books. In time you may find, as I do, that a good relationship with your publisher means that you are likely to get a speedy response on any ideas you put forward so that before you prepare the proposal, you know they are interested in publishing the book. It also means that you have a direct route for introducing colleagues who are new to publishing to a publisher.

And don't forget when you are published to register with the national agencies in your country who collect and distribute funds from photocopying and borrowing agreements.

Demonstrating that your work has influenced your field is usually a prerequisite to gaining professorial status and to winning research funding. Such recognition can be accelerated by the books you publish. Invitations to give keynotes at conferences on the topics covered by your books may follow and provide clear signs to professorial appointment panels that you are considered by your peers to be making a significant contribution to knowledge in your field. Typically, professorial appointment panels include academic members from your own field as well as those from other disciplines. So, having recognition of your leadership and scholarship from peers makes it easy for colleagues from other disciplines who are on your professorial appointment panel to give you credit for what you have achieved.

The positive consequences of publishing books are many: your name is visible to students on the shelves in the university library, your research is available in hard copy – internet resources can vanish in an instant – and of course the books appear on your CV, showing how your body of published work has developed over time. At the very least, they provide a professional backdrop to your video-conferencing calls and tutorials.

Websites providing further details on the topics covered

ALCS (Authors Licensing and Collecting Service), https://www.alcs.co.uk, Accessed on 23 October 2022.

Routledge Book Editing Services for People with English as a Second Language, https://www.tandfeditingservices.com/services/book-editing-services.html, Accessed on 23 October 2022.

Routledge Support Services for Authors, https://www.routledge.com/our-customers/authors/support-and-services, Accessed on 23 October 2022.
Society of Authors, https://www2.societyofauthors.org, Accessed on 23 October 2022.
Society of Indexers, https://www.indexers.org.uk, Accessed on 23 October 2022.
Wiley Indexing Guidelines for Authors, https://authorservices.wiley.com/author-resources/book-authors/prepare-your-manuscript/indexing.htm, Accessed on 23 October 2022.

Reference

DfE (Department for Education). (2021) *Academic Year 2021/22 Initial Teacher Training Census*, London: DfE, https://explore-education-statistics.service.gov.uk/find-statistics/initial-teacher-training-census#dataBlock-1b0209d7-83c5-49fe-88b0-9f5926ac1969-tables, Accessed on 21 July 2022.

Chapter 9

Writing academic articles for publication and developing your academic profile

Sarah Younie

Introduction

This chapter addresses the writing of academic journal articles or papers for publication, as developing a profile through a body of written work is part of developing a career pathway to professorship. Part of building your profile involves writing different types of publications, from practitioner-informed articles through to double-blind peer-reviewed academic journal papers. The latter maintains the highest academic prestige due to the quality assurance process of having a minimum of two reviewers assess the quality of the paper. The review is undertaken anonymously in order to minimise any bias with respect to reviewers knowing the author. Professors usually are on editorial boards of journals and have experience reviewing papers for publication.

The chapter outlines the different stages of this process and systematically covers designing research for publication, planning the paper, constructing the paper, checking and submitting the paper and revising the paper, each of which forms a separate phase. Each stage requires you to dedicate time to undertake the work, and that can be challenging with respect to your academic workload. Writing will be on top of an academic's day job with respect to planning and delivering teaching, conducting research and completing administration associated with each of these roles.

Given that peer-reviewed journal articles are considered to be the gold standard in academia, this chapter focuses on how to write papers for journal publication; the guidance outlined in this chapter assumes that your writing is for a journal paper based on research, development or evaluation that you are involved in. While material based on undertaking literature reviews or purely theoretical developments does get published in refereed journals, those types of papers are not reporting on original empirical research. That said, it's worth pointing out that such papers, like systematic reviews, can be undertaken without funding and can draw on previous work undertaken for one's doctoral thesis, in particular drawing on the literature review chapter.

DOI: 10.4324/9781003217596-9

Objectives

This chapter introduces you to:

- designing research for publication;
- whose name goes first on a publication;
- planning a paper;
- which journal? choosing where to submit your paper;
- author guidelines;
- constructing a paper;
- checking and submitting a paper;
- the editorial peer-review process;
- revising the paper;
- reviewing journal articles and joining an editorial board;
- starting a new journal.

Designing research for publication

Thinking about publication should start right at the beginning of any research work. Indeed, when identifying opportunities for research, considering outlets for publication may be even as important as finding sources of funding. Many excellent papers have been generated from research with no direct funding at all. It is not necessary to have funding for all research; instead, academic mentors would argue that you actively seek research opportunities for enquiry that will lead to findings of interest to you and others. Remember, you can collaborate with colleagues, teachers and students to address issues worthy of research investigation and seek to find answers to questions that those who are likely to read your research raise.

When designing research for publication, it is also important to consider in advance how to gain impact for your research, as this will affect how you collect and analyse data. In the UK, through the Research Excellence Framework (REF, 2021a, 2021b), university staff research publications are assessed on the quality of their research; this includes not only their research environments, their academic outputs in the form of publications, but also the impact of the research, which is submitted in the form of an impact case study (REF, 2021b). The UK REF defines impact as consisting of 'any effect on, change or benefit to the economy, society, culture, public policy or services, health, the environment, or quality of life, beyond academia' (REF, 2021a, 2021b). Interestingly, impact applies to all academic disciplines and subject areas. Each case study is assessed for its significance, reach and impact of the research. See Appendix 1 for examples of these specific criteria and Grove (2022) for an analysis of the REF exercise.

It is worth reading the REF criteria to gain a deeper understanding of how research is evaluated in the UK. Similarly, if you are working in another country, it is worth consulting your national processes and familiarising yourself with your country's research assessment exercise. See examples through the New Zealand and Australia web-links at the end of the chapter.

When you are developing a body of work as an academic, this is often in a specific field or related fields that have emerged originally from one's doctoral research. Writing a PhD is good preparation for an academic with respect to the rigour involved in the writing process and also honing one's writing skills. However, it is worth bearing in mind that this is only one type of writing, and it is for a very limited audience with respect to the thesis examiners. That said, it is worth 'mining' the PhD for publications after completion, whereby the data can be reconfigured for a journal research paper. Also, as outlined previously, the literature review chapter can be used to develop a systematic review article for a journal. The overall goal is to create a body of work in your field that lays the foundation for your career trajectory to a professor.

When designing research for publication, it is important to remember that there are different types of publication, and targeting different audiences will enable your research to have further reach. Once you've conducted a piece of research that has findings worthy of being shared and published, you would want not only other academics to know of the value of this research but also practitioners in the field, including teachers, teacher educators and students. To this end, one piece of research can have multiple publications coming from it that target different aspects of the education community. This will range from a simple press release to practitioner magazines as well as academic journals. While it is the blind peer-review process that ensures the quality of an academic journal research paper, other types of publication are also subject to Editorial approval, so your writing will still undergo external editing.

So, when building your body of published research, this will involve different types of writing and the identification of specific audiences for the different publishing outlets. Therefore, you need to consider the following: do you want to write 'stories' – case studies for newspapers, practitioner newsletters or professional journals; online blogs for professional bodies such as subject associations; reports for institutional senior leaders or external funders; papers for academic peers? Each of these will require different formats for the results, and if you do not collect appropriate data, your publishing potential is limited. For each audience, consider what aspects of the work will be of interest, and how you can convince the audience to take notice of your findings and ideas. Each of these types of publication can be developed and written from your research project, and each will help to build your wider profile in your discipline; arguably, each has a role to play, while acknowledging that it is the status of the journal articles that carry the most traction with respect to prestige and to being awarded the title of professor.

You will, of course, need to look thoroughly at the relevant literature before making detailed plans for your research. This is particularly important if you are going to write for an academic journal, but in any case, you need to be aware of what is already 'known' about the topic. The literature review you have undertaken for your doctoral studies should provide a firm foundation on which to build. Journal papers require authors to report on original data and what is novel and innovative in the field, which is why it is important not to reinvent the wheel; otherwise, what will you have that is new to say and therefore worthy of publication? So, from your scoping analysis of previously published research in your area of interest, you then need to identify the key issues and findings and ascertain remaining questions; these can be used as headings for notes you make during your research. You can use these notes to reflect on where your data confirms or conflicts with previous work, and in your writing, you seek to explain these features in terms of the different settings – for instance changes in culture, technology or time. This may reveal the need for collecting data in addition to what you had planned in order to ensure that you have sufficient evidence for any claims you might want to make. You can rarely go back to your research setting after you have completed the analysis, so make sure that you gather all the evidence you might need while you have the opportunity.

Methodological issues will not be considered here, but note that the reliability of your research methods is important in ensuring an adequate warrant for your findings. You need to be able to indicate in your writing why your results are credible in terms of the context studied, the appropriateness of your research design/methods, your theoretical framework, the nature of the sample, the rigour of your analysis and the reliability and validity of your findings. Ethical matters are particularly important, and you need to consider what you might want to publish when negotiating access, gaining informed consent from participants, confirming accuracy with respondents and ensuring anonymity. The use of visual material in your publications, while very valuable in helping readers understand the setting, needs particular care in this respect.

Whose name goes first on an academic article?

If you are co-authoring papers or books, then you are advised to agree the order of names on the paper beforehand: preferably before anything is written so that everyone knows the contribution expected of them. In this section, we outline options and refer you to bodies that advise on naming protocols.

Why does this matter? The International Committee on Medical Journal Editors (ICMJE) provides this explanation:

> Authorship confers credit and has important academic, social, and financial implications. Authorship also implies responsibility and accountability for published work.
>
> (ICMJE, 2022, p. 1)

So, your reputation is at stake if you are included in a paper with findings you don't agree with or if you are excluded from a paper with findings from research you have contributed to. See below for further examples.

If you think of how academic articles or books are cited in the body of any text, you will see why this matters. In the body of the text, articles or book citations are by first author surname, et al. (date). The surname that comes first is therefore appearing before the reader more often than the other contributors; it will come up more often in searches, and the implication is that they have been the leader on this contribution.

So, there are potential career and thus financial implications.

If you are working to build a body of publications, every one matters as it takes considerable time to get to publication stage, and you may have nothing to show for the time you put into doing the research in the first place. This will always remain as a gap on your CV. It should be possible to agree with your fellow researchers that the team publishes a range of articles addressing different aspects of the findings from your research with different colleagues being the lead author on different publications.

If there are equivalents to the UK Authors Copyright and Licensing Agency in your country (ALCS, https://www.alcs.co.uk) and public lending right (PLR, https://www.bl.uk/plr), then you can register any papers that you produce and you will receive an annual royalty fee in acknowledgement that your article is likely to have been accessed through libraries and/or photocopied. While this remuneration will be small initially, over a 40-year period these funds will build.

To work out your own stance on authorship, I suggest you consider the extensive guidance of organisations such as the International Committee on Medical Journal Editors (ICMJE) or the Committee on Publication Ethics (COPE, 2022), plus that of journal publishers you are considering submitting to.

COPE provides advice about an extensive range of issues that arise around authorship and intellectual property rights, including the removal of names from articles. One of the contributors to this book reports being a researcher on a government-funded research project for England, which submitted a final report to a government agency only to find that in the drafts for the published version, the government agency had inserted text that was not supported by the data. The whole team then refused to have their names on this report, and the document was published without any acknowledgement of their 18 months of work. Another contributor who was the researcher on a project found that while their name appeared in the inside pages where authorship is registered, their name did not appear on the cover of the book reporting the findings of a research project in which they were involved. I hope these anecdotes empower you to speak up early on in any writing project and establish who is going to lead as a major author.

Another issue you may face is that professors who may have headed up the research proposal, which gained the funding for the project you are on, may in the end be named on publications even though they haven't directly been undertaking this particular research. Here is the ICMJE recommendation on authorship, which you may find helpful to have with you in discussions about authorship. Note the AND in capitals at the end of each line.

The ICMJE recommends that authorship be based on the following four criteria:

- Substantial contributions to the conception or design of the work; or the acquisition, analysis, or interpretation of data for the work; AND
- Drafting the work or revising it critically for important intellectual content; AND
- Final approval of the version to be published; AND
- Agreement to be accountable for all aspects of the work in ensuring that questions related to the accuracy or integrity of any part of the work are appropriately investigated and resolved.
  (International Committee of Medical Journal Editors, ICMJE, 2022, p. 1, www.icmje.org/recommendations/browse/roles-and-responsibilities/ defining-the-role-of-authors-and-contributors.html)

So, I suggest you find out what the naming conventions are for the order of names in your discipline or for the journal you are considering submitting a co-authored paper to. These differ between disciplines, but at the early stage of your career when you are demonstrating that you are able to lead research projects and collaborate with others, it will be important to get this right.

There are different protocols:

- alphabetical order;
- names in order in order of contribution with main contributor first;
- names in order in order of contribution with main contributor last;
- if you are the researcher on a project, you may find your name doesn't appear in any publications except by way of a 'thank you for your work with your name mentioned in the acknowledgements';
- the use of 'and', as in 'Galveston and Murphy', implies equality, whereas the use of 'with', as in 'Galveston with Murphy', implies that Galveston had more of a role than Murphy.

With respect to authorship including a statement about the contribution of each author at the end of the article as requested by some journal publishers, this may indeed be seen as good practice as there is then no ambiguity.

Alphabetical ordering as a matter of course is also to be avoided even if accompanied by such a statement. Weber (2018a, 2018b), from Lithuania, cites research studies that make the case against alphabetical ordering:

there is convincing evidence that ordering alphabetically discriminates against authors whose names appear late in the alphabet . . . the likelihood of gaining tenure at a top-ten economics department is estimated to be about 26 percentage points higher for faculty with an A-surname.

(Weber, 2018a, p. 1)

Weber goes on to suggest alternatives that are worth considering before you make decisions.

Planning a paper

It is worth specifying that a journal article is not a report; it needs to say more than what you did and what you found out. First, consider your work by answering these questions briefly.

- What do you have to say?
- What will your focus be?
- Who will be your audience?

If you are publishing on the basis of research undertaken for a master's or doctoral dissertation, consider how to split it down into separate papers, each one coherent in itself but without repeating too much material.

See the REPOSE Guidelines (Appendix 1, https://eppi.ioe.ac.uk/cms/Portals/0/PDF%20reviews%20and%20summaries/EPPI%20REPOSE%20Guidelines%20A4%202.1.pdf) for advice on structuring papers. This advice was commissioned by Professor Leask in her UK government knowledge management role in order to improve the quality of academic papers so they included the information required if the research was to be included in a systematic review. The Guidelines provide a useful writing frame for authors of academic journal articles.

Which journal? Choosing where to submit your paper

Your second task is to select a target journal. As has been mentioned earlier, in some countries, the government organisation responsible for the research assessment exercise publishes a list of journals that are considered to be of an acceptable quality: check if this applies to your context. The websites list at the end of the chapter gives links to UK, New Zealand, Australian and Polish research assessment websites and the Web of Science Citations Index.

Consider the different types of journals in your field. For example, in the field of education in the UK, there are the following types, which vary by focusing on:

- particular content area e.g. research in mathematics education;
- particular education level e.g. education 3–13;
- general e.g. BERJ (*British Education Research Journal*), learning and instruction;
- technology focus e.g. technology, pedagogy and education;
- purely online journals e.g. *Electronic Journal of E-learning*;
- practitioner journals e.g. enhancing education through technology (Naace).

Selecting journals with the 'best fit' is imperative. It is important that you target those journals that align to the content of your research paper. To this end, start by looking for a wide variety of journals that might be interested in your work. Do not just consider those in your own country. The best-known journals are usually the hardest to get into, primarily because they are higher in the citation indices, which are used to judge research performance in many systems. You can get access to the Social Science Citation Index and see which are less highly ranked, or which are not included at all. These journals may be better while you are getting a feel and developing an understanding for the process involved. Check for special issues that may make your article particularly appealing for selection. Online journals tend to have lower status but may be the most appropriate outlet for work that is better represented in multimedia format, and they should be able to publish your work online more quickly once it is accepted.

Reputable academic journals like those from Taylor & Francis, Elsevier and others do not charge authors for publication. However, do be careful and watch out for journals that will offer to publish for a price, where payment is expected. Be wary as this is not always obvious from a journal's publicity, and sometimes it is only when you are further into the process that this becomes apparent. In fact, there is a growing industry now in this field of journal publication that is purely money making and charging authors, sometimes considerable sums of money, to publish their papers. Also, do be aware that payment can be required for some Open Access routes, too.

Once you have identified those journals that align with your research, the next stage is to get to know a potential target journal thoroughly by reading articles in different volumes/issues and scanning through issues over several recent years. Check the journal's aims and scope as these will clearly outline the academic content areas and types of papers that are acceptable to the journal. You will find the journal aims and scope on their website and also usually on the inside cover or first page of a journal. Bear in mind that there is nothing more annoying for either an editor or a reviewer than to be sent a paper that is not aligned sufficiently closely to that of the journal, and it is only all too obvious that the authors have not taken the time and effort to sufficiently research the journal in which they have targeted. This will lead almost inevitably to an immediate rejection. Therefore, doing your homework on which journals are the most appropriate for your research is essential.

Author guidelines

Next, check the journal's guidelines for authors, which again you will usually be able to find on the website or in a copy of the journal. See for example https://authorservices.taylorandfrancis.com/publishing-your-research/writing-your-paper/writing-a-journal-article/; www.elsevier.com/connect/11-steps-to-structuring-a-science-paper-editors-will-take-seriously.

It may be worth checking on the journal's website or possibly sending an email to the editor letting them know you have done your homework and are interested in submitting an article as you believe it aligns to the journal's aims and scope. You should by way of preparation check the journal's website for:

- aims and scope of academic content;
- turnaround reviewing time;
- turnaround publishing time;
- forthcoming special issues.

Consider what editors are looking for. Many journals, for instance, expect submissions to demonstrate an original, significant and rigorous contribution to the debates in the field, to the archive of research literature, alongside emerging topics of interest and innovation. The reviewers consider how the articles meet the following criteria:

- Does the article address a topic of current concern in relation to the aims of the journal and to what you perceive to be the current state of the field of interest in relation to education? Where relevant, the author might be encouraged to draw out the relation to pedagogy, teacher education and professional development.
- Does the abstract give a clear account of the scope of the paper?
- If the article is concerned with research activity, is the research design sound?
- Does the article distinguish clearly between opinion and empirical evidence?
- Does the article make a contribution to a critical understanding of the issues?
- Does the article alert readers to significant new developments in the subject area?
- Does the article take into account relevant contemporary literature in the area?
- Is the article written in a style that is clear and intelligible to a reasonably well-informed international professional readership?

Constructing a paper

Just as we advise our students to plan and structure their written work, the same advice is relevant to academics when writing their papers. It is vital to have planned in detail the structure of the paper. The following is a sound basis, although of course it may vary according to what you have to say:

1. Set the scene – and engage the reader. So, start by letting the readers know what key issues you are going to cover, why they should be interested, where your ideas fit into existing knowledge and how they extend our knowledge. It is always useful to place the work, whatever the scale of the study, in the wider debates and themes addressed in the journal and associated journals and to consider whether the work contributes a new perspective or extends the evidence base in a new context.

2. Briefly review the recent research literature directly relating to the issues you intend to cover, incorporating older sources where necessary to contextualise the work or make comparative comments. Elaborate critically on aspects of the existing knowledge and research and set up the questions you are going to explore.

3. It is important to ensure that the research focus or question is clear, and that if the work is an empirical study, the rationale for the methodology has been related to the nature of the question.

4. Set out the warrant for the work – why we should believe your findings/claims/recommendations – in terms of:

    •   theoretical base;
    •   engagement with research users;
    •   robustness of research design;
    •   rigour of data collection and analysis;
    •   consideration of alternative interpretations – how do we know that you haven't cherry-picked your results to support a particular belief? How can you assure the reader that researcher bias has been sufficiently dealt with and alleviated?

5. Present the results of your analysis clearly and discuss them critically, making comparisons with previous research where relevant. The presentation of the findings needs to indicate how the data are analysed and used as evidence to support the claims being made from your research study. Develop your argument towards a point and consider carefully how to illustrate your points – diagrams, charts, photos. Most journals are constrained by having to produce a printed version, but if you want readers to access multimedia material, you could provide a link in the text to a website where the material is available. Do ensure though that any visual material has sufficient permissions, including ethical where relevant, for example, if you are using photographs. Publishers will be very mindful of both copyright and permissions with respect to any illustrations, so if a diagram has been adapted from prior research, you must reference the original citation. If you are using any visual material that has been previously published, you will also need the permission of the original publishers, which must be given in writing and presented to the new publishers by way of evidence that you have permission to reuse the image.

6. Argue conclusions and recommendations in relation to the questions set up at the start of your article, with justification in terms of your results and the theoretical base. Consider what insights you can share, and how you can help readers to apply them to their own settings.

A paper does not have to report empirical research, or to be set out in the sequence just detailed, but it needs to be clear about what the reader is going to gain from it, and the key elements of rigour and originality need to be present. In other words, your paper has to contribute something to the field. This is important, as publishers will not be interested in research that simply reproduces findings that are already known. Be clear where your originality lies and what you are contributing in your article that makes it worthy of publication.

With respect to presentation and the use of academic language, be careful that the language you use is sufficiently formal and precise to represent your ideas accurately, but not so complex that readers may not be able to gain the intended meaning. Bear in mind that English will not be the first language of many of the readers, and also avoid making assumptions that readers are familiar with your national education systems and terminology. This is particularly important in international journals where readers will be from different countries, which means it's important to not write in an ethnocentric manner such that only a native audience would understand your paper. It is also worth saying that it is recommended you avoid the use of too many acronyms in your paper or excessive use of jargon.

Checking and submitting a paper

Once you have finished writing your paper, while this is a moment of satisfaction and tempting to submit for review for feedback on it, it's very important to stop and undertake a rigorous process of checking. This is a process of self-editing and its importance cannot be underestimated. The reason for this is that it is very apparent when authors submit papers in which checking has not been undertaken and again, this leads almost inevitably to a decision of 'reject and resubmit'. To prevent against this, undertaking a careful check will help your paper to be more acceptable with respect to meeting academic standards. To this end, a checklist is provided for you later in the chapter that can help guide you.

When you think you have finished:

- Check your introduction, body, and summation. Have you said what you wanted to say and made your points clear?
- Have you provided sufficient context to put the reader into the picture?
- Are your conclusions logical and supported?
- Have you provided signposts and transitions?
- Have you used 'buzzwords' that may not be familiar to all readers, or clichés whose meaning may not be clear?
- Check your data and whether you have provided sufficient detail to support your claims.
- Tables, charts, and illustrations included – are all correct and labelled appropriately?
- Check that you have followed the guidelines provided by the journal concerning length, referencing style, layout, tables, figures, removing author details for blind review, file format etc.
- Is everything relevant? Don't try to make too many points, and cut out anything that doesn't contribute to the points you intend to make.

Next, write the abstract. It is worth doing this at the end, once you have a complete overview of your paper and can effectively summarise your research in a way that captures its aims, research questions, methodology, key findings and conclusion with respect to reporting on its contribution to the field. It should include key terms, too. Be sure that your abstract is accurate and contains a clear and sufficient overview of your research paper. It should not be just a repeat of the first paragraph. This is important because editors traditionally base their choice of reviewers to assign on the basis of the abstract of the paper. It is better to have your paper reviewed by persons who are interested in the topic and have the relevant expertise aligned specifically to your research focus. This allocation of reviewers will be done on the basis of your abstract, which is why it's important to ensure that your abstract does the job of precisely representing your research.

Next is the very careful checking of your references. Be sure the references are accurate, as up to date as possible and correctly formatted in accordance with the journal guidelines. Be sure that the references you cite in the body are listed in the bibliography. And be sure that the references you cite in the bibliography are referred to in the body, too; this is a real danger when you are basing the paper on larger work. Nonetheless, referencing is often a point that is picked up by reviewers with respect to citations not being up to date enough, not extensive enough or inaccurate.

After undertaking your extensive checking, and prior to submitting your paper to a journal, it is recommended that you submit your work for collegial feedback, as a form of informal peer review. It is recommended that you always ask at least two colleagues to act as critical friends – the preceding checklist will be helpful to them, too, by way of guidance.

Also, it is worth thoroughly checking that you have copy-edited the work carefully to ensure that the structure, style of referencing and general accuracy help the reader to engage with the research you are reporting, rather than be irritated by inaccuracies or poor proofreading. This will be done by the publisher, too, before it goes to press, but if you give the reviewers a bad impression, it may not get to that stage. Unfortunately, this can often be the case, and this can be circumvented by authors more rigorously checking their own work before they submit it to the journal. It is always worth, at this stage, going back to the aims and scope of the journal, to check that you meet them explicitly in your paper. It is recommended that this is done alongside checking the journal's technical specifications and that your paper is within the permitted word length and is neither too short nor too long. Also check that your paper strictly adheres to the referencing style specified by the journal and that all other technical requirements are met.

Now you can submit your paper to your selected journal.

The editorial process

Once you have submitted your paper to a journal, the editor will either immediately reject it as unsuitable or will assign it to reviewers, to assess the suitability of your paper for publication in the journal. It is worth stressing that peer review takes time, some months, sometimes many months – reviewers cannot always manage to stick to the timeline that is sought by the journal, as reviewing is dependent upon reviewers' workloads. This can be a frustrating time for authors, who may be tempted to chase the journal editor for updates on their review. However, it is worth remembering that reviewers undertake their work as a voluntary act of academic civic duty, for which they are not paid; they do this work on their own time. To this end, it's important to be patient. Once your paper has been peer reviewed, you will receive a response from the editor. This will either accept the paper as it is (this is extremely rare), accept it subject to minor revisions, require a more major re-work and resubmission or reject it completely (perhaps suggesting a more appropriate journal).

The editor also passes on reviewers' feedback on how the work might need to be revised further.

Revising the paper

Although it can sometimes be uncomfortable to read critical feedback on our own work, it is important to consider it carefully. If the article has not been accepted for the journal, it is useful to incorporate the feedback and revise the work for publication in another journal. But do please remember, you cannot submit work to more than one journal at a time. There are academic protocols that must be adhered to, and this is important for an author's academic integrity.

If your paper is accepted 'with revisions', then it is recommended that you get them done and return them quickly, within the time period specified by the journal, or let the editor know if there will be delays. The editor may ask you to include a commentary on the revisions you have made in response to the reviewers' suggestions – or you provide clear reasons why you have not made the suggested changes, with a justification for your actions. Whenever you make revisions in response to suggestions, it is a good idea to include such a commentary, whether it is required or not – it can save time in what is a lengthy process. Normally, authors will address systematically each comment from each reviewer and make the required changes. Reviewers are very experienced and their suggestions help to improve the quality of the paper and ensure that it is of publishable standard.

Similarly, it is worth bearing in mind that a rejection doesn't necessarily mean it is a bad paper. Consider the feedback, take a new look at the possibilities, make suitable revisions and submit to a different journal. There is something to be said here for developing academic resilience, in which authors learn to tolerate academic criticism in a way that can initially be upsetting or frustrating, even irritating. It is worth holding on to the metaphor that publishing is more of a marathon than a sprint, that there will be injuries and lessons learned on the journey, and one gets tougher with every rejection. This is something that every academic I know has encountered at some point or another in their publishing career. In short, stay strong. Keep writing, and you will get published.

Reviewing journal articles and joining an editorial board

As discussed earlier, your doctoral supervisor and examiners may be able to introduce you to journal editors who are looking for reviewers and possibly new members of editorial boards. Likewise, colleagues in your professional association may also be able to advise you or to facilitate introductions. Professional conferences are another way of making yourself known to editors of journals in your field. The reviews of papers submitted to academic journals are undertaken voluntarily by academics in the field, and in time you'll be expected to demonstrate that you have this status in your field and that you are making this professional contribution. Undertaking peer reviewing as academic citizenship can be seen in part as demonstrating that you are meeting the service element of your professorial application, as it is a voluntary role that academia depends upon to enable the research publication process to be quality assured.

If you do not have such connections, remember there's nothing to stop you from approaching journal editors or editorial board members and offering your services. Normally you would be expected to be a published researcher before taking on such quality assurance roles.

Starting a new journal

Where your field of study is new or it is not covered adequately by existing journals, you may, in time when you have a reputation in your field, consider starting a new journal. One route is to look for a publisher already interested in your field and contact them to see if they would consider a new journal. In the past, journal publication was undertaken by profit-making commercial organisations and learned societies/professional associations. Typically, journal articles can only be accessed through paid subscription or through libraries. The internet does support lower-cost publishing models, and there are initiatives to support open access journals, free at the point of use. However, any publishing has costs, and these have to be covered if a journal is to be maintained long term. With online journals, the production software, design and hosting costs have to be covered, software updates are a regular additional cost and then of course there are editorial costs. Somebody has to undertake the administration of contacts with authors, managing the reviewing processes and then the final copy editor checks on full stops, referencing and so on. The peer-review process is usually undertaken by academics voluntarily.

With respect to the journal industry, Dr Judith Johnson from Leeds University has an interesting blog (https://judithjohnsonphd.com/2019/04/08/how-to-start-a-journal-and-beat-the-academic-publishing-racket/), and you may be interested in her interview with academics who started a journal in musicology. She identifies ten steps in starting a new journal:

Ten steps for starting a journal.

Whatever the focus of your journal, the steps for setting one up are similar.

1. Identify the gap . . .
2. Build a website that will home your journal . . .
3. Set up an editorial board . . .
4. Involve associate editors who can provide support . . .
5. Call for papers . . .
6. Manage your submissions . . .
7. Copy-edit and type-set your articles . . .
8. Apply for an International Standard Serial Number (ISSN) . . .
9. Plan how to give your articles a Digital Object Identifier (DOI) . . .
10. Wider registration. There are a variety of international platforms with which to register journals, including Web of Science, PubMed and SCOPUS . . .

Plus you have to find peer-reviewers.

Your checklist and goals: for publishing academic journal articles

Table 9.1 Checklist: your publication plan for your articles is freely available for download via the Support Material tab on the Routledge website.

Table 9.1 Checklist: your publication plan for your articles

ITEM	Achieved?	
	Yes	No
Have you a plan for your research and publications over the coming years?		
Have you a list of draft titles for articles you might publish from research you have completed or anticipate completing in the near future?		
Have you identified journals that publish articles in your field?		
Have you made a decision about co-authorship, and if so, about the authorship naming convention you will use?		
If you are not already an article reviewer, are there journals you would like to become a peer reviewer for?		
YOUR SPECIFIC GOALS: now record the goals that suit your context and your discipline . . .		

Summary: recognising success and avoiding pitfalls

The intention of this chapter is to help you think clearly about publishing high-quality research papers in academic journals and to alert you to some of the difficulties and challenges that you may need to address specifically about intellectual property rights and authorship of papers.

Junior academic staff may find themselves in uncomfortable positions when it comes to making claims for their research to be adequately recognised under their name. In this book, there is considerable stress on the importance of joining a professional association and contributing to the advancement of knowledge in your discipline. Through such a professional association you should be able to find colleagues who can advise and support you as you deal with the issues outlined in this chapter.

The consequences of not attending to intellectual property rights and authorship of papers are addressed in the chapter.

Acknowledgements

This chapter has been developed from the work of the editors of an international journal published by Taylor & Francis. Having delivered workshops and written guidance to authors submitting to the journal, the editors have presented and outlined these ideas at conferences and in workshops and mentoring sessions previously. I would like to acknowledge the work and insights contained in this chapter that were contributed by Dr Steve Kennewell and Professor Marilyn Leask.

Web sites

Australia, www.arc.gov.au/evaluating-research/excellence-research-australia, Accessed on 29 October 2022.

Authors Copyright and Licensing Agency (ALCS), https://www.alcs.co.uk, Accessed on 29 October 2022.

https://www.gov.pl/web/edukacja-i-nauka/komunikat-ministra-edukacji-i-nauki-z-dnia-1-grudnia-2021-r-w-sprawie-wykazu-czasopism-naukowych-i-recenzow anych-materialow-z-konferencji-miedzynarodowych?fbclid=IwAR0j3O0AbbBQ BZeoltOyl ueEpr_5SPOuZKj8PbiC2k83g4LzL-xs9Momvl0, Accessed on 23 October 2022. Note the column 'Punkty' which lists the points allocated to a specific journal.

International Committee on Medical Journal Editors (ICMJE), https://www.icmje. org/recommendations/browse/roles-and-responsibilities/defining-the-role-of-authors-and-contributors.html, Accessed on 29 October 2022.

Johnson, J., https://judithjohnsonphd.com/2019/04/08/how-to-start-a-journal-and-beat-the-academic-publishing-racket/, Accessed on 29 October 2022.

NZ, www.tec.govt.nz/funding/funding-and-performance/funding/fund-finder/per formance-based-research-fund/and www.tec.govt.nz/funding/funding-and-perfor

mance/funding/fund-finder/performance-based-research-fund/pbrf-2025-qual ity-evaluation/, Accessed on 29 October 2022.

Poland Ministry of Education and Science, Poland.Ministerstwo Edukacji i Nauki. (2022) *List of Disciplines Assigned to Scientific Journals and Conference Materials/ Wykaz dyscyplin przypisanych do czasopism naukowych i materiałów konferencyjnych/*, Accessed on 23 October 2022.

Public Lending Right (PLR), https://www.bl.uk/plr, Accessed on 29 October 2022.

REPOSE Guidelines, https://eppi.ioe.ac.uk/cms/Portals/0/PDF%20reviews%20 and%20summaries/EPPI%20REPOSE%20Guidelines%20A4%202.1.pdf, Accessed on 29 October 2022.

Social Science Citation Index, https://clarivate.com/webofsciencegroup/solutions/ webofscience-ssci/, Accessed on 29 October 2022.

Taylor and Francis, https://authorservices.taylorandfrancis.com/editorial-policies/ defining-authorship-research-paper/, Accessed on 29 October 2022.

References

COPE (Committee on Publication Ethics). (2022) *How to Handle Authorship Disputes: A Guide for New Researchers*, https://publicationethics.org/resources/ guidelines-new/how-handle-authorship-disputesa-guide-new-researchers, https://doi.org/10.24318/cope.2018.1.1, Accessed on 29 October 2022.

Grove, J. (2022) https://www.timeshighereducation.com/features/do-national-research-assessment-exercises-still-pass-peer-review, Accessed on 29 October 2022.

REF (UK). (2021a) *Research Excellence Framework 2021*, Swindon: UK Research and Innovation, www.ref.ac.uk, Accessed on 24 October 2022.

REF (UK). (2021b) *Impact Case Study Database*, https://results2021.ref.ac.uk/ impact, Accessed on 24 October 2022.

Weber, M. (2018a) The effects of listing authors in alphabetical order: A review of the empirical evidence, *Research Evaluation*, 27(3), 238–245, https://doi.org/10.1093/reseval/rvy008, Accessed on 28 October 2022.

Weber, M. (2018b) Alphabetical name ordering is discriminatory and harmful to collaborations, *London School of Economics*, https://blogs.lse.ac.uk/impactofso cialsciences/2018/05/29/alphabetical-name-ordering-is-discriminatory-and-harmful-to-collaborations, Accessed on 28 October 2022.

Chapter 10

Applying for research funding
A vital part of the journey towards professorship

Larissa McLean Davies

Introduction

As you may know already, the main index you can use to measure your academic impact, reputation and significance, the H-index, is located on the 'publish or perish' (PoP) website developed by Anne-Wils Hartzing (2008). When this website and measure were developed in 1999, it took an axiom in common global parlance and made it lore: academics simply must produce to survive. However, as most experienced academics advise, more than 'just' publishing is required. In the modern academy, those seeking robust and sustained academic careers, and working towards professorship, must also show a strong track record of both applying for and receiving research funding. This is not to say that all research requires substantive funding or that one cannot undertake significant, low-cost research, such as implementing large and impactful surveys, without substantive funding. This has become particularly evident through the course of the global pandemic, where survey instruments were used successfully in various national contexts to report on experiences of learning in the pandemic (see, for example, Ziebell et al., 2020), and literature reviews were undertaken to better understand and contextualise these pandemic learning experiences (Carrillo and Flores, 2020). Indeed, in the field of education, this research has enabled us to see how students, parents, teachers and leaders responded to the experiences of home learning, almost, as it appeared, in real time (Morelock et al., 2020). Researchers worldwide were able to pivot quickly to the imperative to give an account of this unprecedented learning challenge and what it meant for children and young people without, in many cases, applying for bespoke grants. Of course, this research, which was successfully undertaken without major grant support, will position those who have undertaken it to be more likely to be successful when applying for funding.

In this chapter, I explore the different research funding opportunities available to academics and discuss approaches and strategies to secure funding from a range of sources. I share my own experiences of applying for and securing funding in an Australian context and offer some advice around building and sustaining a track record of successful bids. While building a publication track

DOI: 10.4324/9781003217596-10

record without external and competitive funding is possible, applying for and receiving funding has become integral to an academic's career. Arguably, it is not possible to make a case for academic promotion, particularly as one becomes more senior, without showing evidence of the ability to convince funders that your research is valuable, necessary and worth directing resources towards. Thus, the basis on which one secures the resources needed to publish (as well as the nature and quality of publications) is an integral part of the academic narrative.

Objectives

In working through this chapter, you will be invited to

- identify different research funding opportunities available to you;
- plan your approaches and strategies to secure funding from a range of sources.

The checklist included at the end of the chapter is designed to help you to plan your strategy for applying for funding for your research.

Who will fund my research? Developing an understanding of grant opportunities

When building an academic career, the imperative seems to be to publish quickly and in the most esteemed journals possible (Aprile et al., 2021; see also Chapter 9). Often this means that an early career academic will repurpose their PhD thesis and focus their attention on conference presentations and other outputs associated with this major work – building networks, reputation and recognition in the field of expertise that they have developed. At this stage, academics fortunate to have strong collegial support may be invited onto bids led by others, which will offer vital experience working in teams (something one doesn't generally experience in doctoral programmes outside of the sciences) and opportunities to co-publish. These are valuable experiences, but it is also important to develop the skills of applying for and leading bids in one's own right.

Before appraising funding opportunities, an initial and core task is to determine what pressing social questions are addressed in one's research. What new knowledge is being developed through this scholarly work? While receiving funding can appear as the goal, it is useful to remember why one is seeking funding in the first place – what questions of significance to governments, industry and philanthropists are being addressed by the stated research programme? A key mechanism for achieving grant or other funding success is pitching the relevance of one's ideas and convincing funders of its likely impact; this task is more achievable if funders can see a clear alignment with their priorities and the vision and commitments of the researcher.

This isn't advice to behave without integrity, but rather to say that our research questions exist within a broader social context and that it is worth spending time identifying these links. For example, a key theme of my research has been understanding barriers to and enablers of teaching Australian literature in schools (a colonised country, Australia has often turned its back on literature written by the inhabitants of this place). Through a partnership with the Stella Prize for women and non-binary Australian writers, this focus has developed into a research concentration on meaningful professional learning for teachers (McLean Davies et al., 2021) and manifested in investigations of the role of Indigenous writers in building English teachers' professional knowledge, and on new methodologies for teacher learning regarding Australian literature (Phillips et al., 2022). So, an initial task for the early career academic is to ascertain what funding sources are available to them and who might be suitable research partners (this includes academic and other possible stakeholder partners), as in many cases, research funding is allocated to teams. It is also useful to consider how one's core research questions might be pursued differently by different funding bodies.

Funding opportunities vary significantly according to context: the national context in which each academic work enables or limits funding sources and possibilities, as does the university context in which one is located. In many national contexts, research is funded through a combination of government, industry and philanthropic means. In my context, Australia, which has a much smaller funding pool to draw on than the UK or the USA, and does not have a strong history of philanthropic funding for research (Department of Education Skills and Employment [Australian Government], 2022), the following categories are used to define research funding:

Category 1: Australian competitive grants, awarded by the federal government. In the Australian context, Category 1 grants are the most competitive, arguably require the most preparation and are assessed according to criteria that are heavily weighted to consider the track record of the applicant/s. ARC grants are the equivalent of SSHRC (Social Sciences and Humanities Research Council Canada). The ARC National Competitive Grants Programme (NCGP) has two main programmes: 'Discovery programme' and the 'Linkage programme'. The Discovery programme comes in various forms, such as the DECRA (Discovery Early Career Researcher) for early career researchers with project costs up to $50,000 for three consecutive years, and the Future Fellowships for mid-career researchers with project costs up to $60,000 for four years. The approval rate for Discovery project applications commencing in 2021 was about 20%. The Linkage programme, on the other hand, has a moderately higher overall approval rate (e.g. 2021 ARC Linkage approval rate 33.3%) and encourages a cooperative approach to research and research outcomes by requiring researchers to attract buy-in from industry partners who can make cash or 'in-kind' contributions.

ARC applications undergo a rigorous multi-part review before a recommendation is made to the education minister for funding. The more funding is open to peer review, the more competitive it will be, and relatedly, the more esteem it is accorded within the academy. While Category 1 grants are desirable and, in my context, considered the equivalent of hitting the research 'jackpot', their rarity means that researchers need to pragmatically consider a range of ways to support their research over the course of a career (I'll discuss this in more detail in the following section).

Category 2: other public sector income. This includes funding for research that has been secured through competitive government tender. For example, in Australia, a State or Territory government might decide that they would like research to improve literacy outcomes and call for interested parties to bid for this research work. In my experience, these grants can be well funded and enable recipients to show, in tangible ways, the impact and translation of their research on end users – in the case of educational research, these are students, teachers, leaders, parents, carers and the community. However, one of the challenges with these grants is that often one may not know about this funding opportunity until the tender is released, and then there is a limited time in which to respond. In this case, a team approach is necessary, and success is more likely if a team is already looking for ways to research the key ideas being prioritised in the tender. For example, in 2019, I led a large multi-disciplinary team in a successful research tender that involved the design of a literacy teaching toolkit for secondary teachers (Victorian Department of Education and Training, 2021). The award of this tender was significantly assisted by the fact that the language and literacy team at my university had identified a gap in the ways that secondary teachers were being supported to develop literacy disciplinary knowledge and had already begun considering ways of addressing this when the tender was released. It is worth working with colleagues to identify research questions you can pursue collectively (what do we have to offer?) and considering how this expertise aligns with the priorities of governments and other stakeholders who will be tendering for research.

Category 3: industry and other income received from the private sector, philanthropic and international sources. Grants secured in this way can be substantial (for example, if supported by a large multi-national company, such as a bank or large corporation, or smaller, if through not-for-profit organisations). In addition, small grants may be available through subject associations (such as the State and National English Teachers' Associations or the geography Teachers' Association) or through not-for-profit organisations. For example, in addition to the aforementioned partnership with the Stella literary prize, I have also received funding from the Australian Copyright Association to undertake research concerned with the ways that teachers were implementing the Australian literature component of the Australian Curriculum (McLean Davies et al., 2018). As noted, these research partnerships are very rewarding; however, it is often the case that they take time to develop. Trust, and a shared agenda, need to be built through conversation. In my experience, small pilot projects (where the partner offers in-kind support through advertising, offering access to networks etc.) are often undertaken before a project that requires partners to provide funding.

In addition to these formal and recognised categories, individual universities, and faculties, may have competitive research funding available for academics at different stages of careers and to advance university priorities. While these small, internal grants are the least competitive and do not carry substantive weight in proportions, they are most helpful, as I will show, in building a track record and the possibility of more substantive funding. I continue to utilise and apply for small seed funding grants, when they are available, through the university, to support the building of a new partnership and the testing of an idea.

Building a track record of funding: making the most of opportunities and diversifying funding sources

I completed my PhD after part-time study in 2007 while working as a senior English teacher in a range of secondary schools, and unlike other colleagues who had published along the doctoral journey, I commenced my post as a Level B lecturer[1] with a range of contributions to professional journals and countless hours of providing CPD, but no refereed publications. With probation criteria concerned with teaching and research looming, my focus was on ensuring timely research outputs. Further, I was facing the additional challenge of entering a field that was aligned with but distinct from my doctoral research. With a PhD in literary studies – specifically in feminist readings of Australian women's writing – I was concerned with establishing myself across the fields of literary studies and education and shifting my identity in the English curriculum field from teacher to researcher. At this time, serendipitously, the Australian government was introducing Australia's first national curriculum and mandating the teaching of Australian literature across the years of schooling (see Doecke et al., 2011, Chapter 1 for commentary about this). Also, and somewhat controversially, this curriculum had returned 'literature' to being a key pillar of the English curriculum (when the more generic term 'text' had become ubiquitous in Australian State and Territory English curricula for over a decade). Although my thesis had not directly addressed these issues, I could see how it could enrich the broader curriculum debate, and therefore my attention was directed towards drawing on my thesis to become part of this major public conversation. Given all of this, research funding wasn't on my career radar as a new academic. Indeed, if I had thought about it at all, it would have been something to consider down the track when I had seen aspects of my thesis successfully in print, and I had established myself as having something of value to offer to the educational/literary/curriculum public and academic discourse.

Fortunately, I had a supportive and experienced mentor who knew that as well as publishing my existing research, it was important to begin building a track record of applying for competitive funding. (Chapter 5 provides examples of the mentoring experienced by the professors who provided data to underpin much of the advice in this book.) I had been employed at a time of major change for my university, a Graduate School of Education had been newly established and pre-service teaching degrees were now only to be offered at a master's level. My mentor encouraged me to apply for one of the small, competitive faculty grants that had become available to undertake research associated with this new initiative. She advised that as an early career academic with a demanding teaching and subject coordination allocation, it was not only valuable to develop the skills of applying for funding but also imperative to develop mechanisms to bring teaching and research activities together. Much time would be spent on teaching-related activities, particularly in the first years of my career, so I needed to make sure my scholarship was drawing on this work.

Preparing the application for this internal application required me to quickly learn the genre of a research proposal and how to pitch an idea that would serve both the intention and needs of those offering the funding. In this case, I was addressing the priorities of faculty leaders who were concerned with the impact and efficacy of these newly recruited pre-service graduate teachers and who were also, more broadly, responding to global debates about teacher quality that were coming to greater attention in the first decade of the new century (see Darling-Hammond, 2008). Within this context, I was bringing to the table my scholarly questions and expertise regarding the teaching of literature and English curriculum. Through this application process, I learned that seeing one's contributions in the context of the needs and imperative being faced by universities, governments and other stakeholders is important in the journey to securing research funding (and, more broadly, as noted, to generative meaningful academic work).

With my mentor's support, I applied for and received a modest sum (about $6K AUS) for a project titled Investigating the 'Making' of Master English Teachers in 2008. This first funded project involved gathering narratives of what had compelled the graduates we were teaching to become English teachers, often changing careers to do so, and interrogating the nature of textual knowledge for 'master' teachers in this discipline area. This project led to publications (McLean Davies, 2011, 2014; Doecke et al., 2011), and through this, I developed a new understanding of a range of methodological research approaches that provided a base from which to apply for further funding. In 2009, I applied for competitive university-wide funding for early career researchers and received $15K AUS to investigate the teaching of Australian literature in a range of secondary schools in light of the new curriculum imperative. This project provided the opportunity to secure the support of a research assistant, who becomes responsible for managing this small project, which included contacting schools, administering the survey I had designed and transcribing interviews. This enabled me to embark on a larger and more comprehensive study.

Early career academics must learn to undertake research using a range of methods and to manage research activities in collaboration with others. Coming from a school environment, where I had been primarily a classroom teacher responsible for myself and answerable to the Head of Department and school leaders, while completing a PhD individually, rather than as part of a research lab, this project afforded me new collaborative research experience, which in turn enabled me to develop a greater network of teachers and academic colleagues working in the field, and some collaborative writing opportunities. In short, these relatively small internal competitive grants gave me a seat at the research table. Through these increased networks, I was invited to contribute to curriculum consultations at other universities and those facilitated by the Australian federal government.

Through the new networks and professional relationships generated by the small, internal grants I received, I was also invited to co-edit a book on the teaching of Australian literature (Doecke et al., 2011). Through this collaboration with my co-editors, who also spanned the fields of literary studies and English education, I was invited to become part of a team intending to bid for highly competitive Category 1 Australian Research Council (ARC) funding. The intention of this grant, drawing on our experience of editing the book and leveraging continued interest in the teaching of literature, was to scale up questions of the ways in which English teachers developed professional and disciplinary knowledge, to undertake a longitudinal, nationwide study and to investigate further the role of literature in a knowledge base for this subject.

Applying for Category 1 funding is, as I suggested earlier, a significant step from the more local schemes, which have a far greater success rate. Our team intended to apply for a Discovery grant, and my co-editors and now research colleagues Brenton Doecke and Philip Mead (who were both at Australian universities other than mine and already professors) encouraged me to lead the project application and saw this as an important way of building the next generation of researchers in our area. In a chapter focusing on strategies for securing research funding, it is essential to underscore the role of mentors in supporting an academic career (this was apparent to me, as I have shown, from the outset). While academics and universities are constantly positioned in competition with one another, vying for funding, opportunities and recognition (Ferguson, 2019; Gardner and Willey, 2018), I am not aware of anyone who has been able to be successful alone, who has not benefited from the sponsorship and support of more experienced colleagues. This then goes to the point of seeking out mentors and colleagues, not simply to advance one's career but to become part of and contribute to a larger conversation and have the opportunity to learn how to help frame and shape the debate.

Our team began working towards this application in 2012 and wrote an article together on literary sociability, a framework we wanted to utilise from literary studies to form a theoretical basis for our work (McLean Davies et al., 2013). We then shared our ideas for this next stage of our work with colleagues and presented them at conferences. Through this, we identified colleagues with interests and expertise that would enhance our bid, and the team, through the addition of Professor Wayne Sawyer, increased (see Sawyer and McLean Davies, 2021). This expanded team then applied for an ARC Discovery grant in 2014. As part of this process, each Chief Investigator for a Category 1 grant must complete a section on 'Research Opportunity and Performance Evidence' (ROPE) (ARC, undated). There are similar expectations for most large-scale grants in other national contexts, such as Canada (see Government of Canada's SSHRC, 2022), the United States (US Department of Education, IES – Institute of Education Sciences, SEER, undated) and the United Kingdom (Besley and Peters, 2006; Wilkinson, 2019). In such sections, researchers explain their impact and, ideally, how this current bid builds on previous scholarship and funding and is part of an intentional programme of significant research. In my case, it was useful to be able to build my narrative on the previous small internal grants.

While we were not successful with this first application, our proposal scored in the top 10% of unsuccessful grants (this almost success was due, in some part, to the many readers who gave us feedback on the text before submission, ensuring its strength and robustness). While failure to receive funding in this context might seem an even greater cause for disappointment – so close and yet so far – at my university, this meant that I was eligible to apply for ARC 'near miss' funding of $30K. The team mobilised this funding to undertake an international pilot, looking at questions of knowledge for English teachers with at least five years of experience in both England and Australia. This pilot became evidence of a track record, project relevance and feasibility in our subsequent application in 2015. For this second attempt, the research team expanded again and included Professor Lyn Yates, who had received sustained ARC funding and international recognition for work concerning questions of knowledge and curricula, and who had previously explored teachers' understandings of knowledge in history and physics. The second application was successful, and the project was funded (for over $800K AUS – the most substantive ARC grant to date for English education) from 2016–2019 inclusive. At the time of writing, this project has produced more than 20 journal articles and a monograph (McLean Davies and Buzacott, 2022). While such effort is taken by applying for a grant, it is easy to forget that it is once the grant has been awarded that the real work begins.

It is generally understood that when one receives ARC funding, it is easier to receive it again: once membership in this exclusive club is achieved, it will be much more straightforward and welcoming at reception. There are many academics whose careers show evidence of this; however, with decreased funding available, this is likely to be less the case in the years ahead. In Australia, government funding for research has dramatically decreased over the past 14 years, from 2.2% GDP in 2008 to 1.7% GDP in 2019 (OECD, 2022). Further, with the funding envelope, some disciplines, such as education, are routinely allocated less research money: over 3000 Discovery project applications were considered for funding in 2021, and of the 603 that were approved for funding, only nine were approved in the field of educational research. This has been met with extreme disappointment by academics in the humanities and social sciences, particularly in education, which receives very limited resources. Indeed, some educational researchers have argued on the public record that the reduced research funding for education in Australia will be the death knell for the discipline itself (Manathunga, 2022), as educational researchers, unlike those in the sciences, often do not have access to substantive philanthropic or industry funding.

I have led or been involved in submissions for projects in four other ARC grant rounds since 2017 – each of these extends or takes up issues raised by the Discovery grant awarded in 2015. One of these applications has been submitted twice, and on the second time, it scored in the top 10% of unsuccessful bids. This resulted, as previously, with the award of university funding, enabling a pilot to be undertaken, papers written and a third application will be submitted in due course. Additionally, the long partnership I have had with not-for-profit organisations has reached a stage where we are ready to apply for an ARC Linkage (industry-based) grant (ARC, 2018). Applying for research funding requires resilience, determination and willingness to play the long game. One very useful piece of advice given to me was to try to turn every unsuccessful application into a journal article – this goes to the philosophy of ensuring that no academic writing is ever wasted and becomes part of scholarly or public discourse.

In a climate where research funding is becoming more difficult to secure, it is vital to explore the different ways research might be funded and to diversify one's funding sources; it is unlikely an academic career will be sustained by one scheme of the funding body. As I indicated earlier, I have experienced success in bidding for Category 2 and 3 grants, and as my career has unfolded, I have recognised the great professional and personal reward I experience in assembling teams, working in partnership with stakeholders and collectively undertaking research that will directly impact on teachers (including the pre-service teacher) and students. To this end, I have led interdisciplinary teams designing a teaching performance assessment for pre-service teachers, a continuity of learning framework for the Northern Territory of Australia and explored the system-level improvements needed to enable teachers and leaders to leverage whole school improvement through rich literacy practices. I have found that research that intersects strongly with what my institution calls 'engagement' suits my academic disposition and aspirations and undoubtedly assisted me on the pathway to professorship.

Developing a digital profile for funders

I was told by an esteemed and successful professor that he made a habit of starting each day on Twitter and would send 'tweets' before he had finished his morning coffee. A few moments on Twitter in the morning reveals that many academics have taken this approach and realised, as scholarship shows, the value of having a social media presence when building and sustaining a career (Britton et al., 2019; Chugh et al., 2021). A social media presence is now part of establishing an academic narrative, and an academic's internet and media presence impact their networking and the dissemination of research and, arguably, future grant funding. Grant assessments, as I have noted, often heavily weigh the track record of the applicants: being known to those assessing the grant bid can therefore be advantageous. In the past two years, my colleague Dr Sarah Truman and I have brought our literary education project together in a virtual 'Literary Education Lab' (https://literaryeducationlab. org). The Lab has been valuable in drawing together like-minded scholars and partners, and the lab's website plays an important role in curating and profiling our research. Potential partners can be directed to the Lab website, which is also used to communicate work in progress and research dissemination events. Much effort goes into funding applications, so it is important, where possible, to raise one's academic profile for potential funders and become recognised for contributing to the areas in which you want to establish your research contribution. Chapter 5 on building your media presence provides more advice.

Your checklist and goals: for bidding for research funding

In this chapter, I have shown how an academic career can be built, step by step; other professors contributing to the research for this book have experienced a similar career path, with mentors and small internal university grants providing initial stepping stones on the pathway to a professorial appointment. In considering the questions in the checklist in Table 10.1, you are providing a foundation for your own career pathway.

Table 10.1 Checklist: building your strategies for applying for research funding is freely available for download via the Support Material tab on the Routledge website.

Table 10.1 Checklist: building your strategies for applying for research funding

ITEM	Achieved?	
	Yes	No
OPPORTUNITIES IN YOUR CONTEXT		
In this chapter, I have outlined the opportunities available particularly to academics in Australia. Have you identified what opportunities are available to you in your own university and within and beyond your own country? Academics in Europe, for example, benefit from being able to apply for European Union research funds that fund research networks across countries.		
AUDIENCES FOR YOUR RESEARCH		
Have you identified potential audiences for your research from those who fund research e.g. industry, government, philanthropists? If not, can you refocus your research to make it more relevant to the challenges these funders highlight through their funding priorities?		
YOUR RESEARCH IMPACT		
References at the end of this chapter include advice about maximising impact. Have you read those relevant to you and made notes for yourself about the areas of development you may need to work on and the preparation you may need to do to maximise the impact of your research?		
RESEARCH FUNDERS		
Have you made a list of potential funders of your research?		
Have you ensured alignment between your research and the funding priorities of the funders you may target first?		
RESEARCH PARTNERS		
Have you taken steps to meet like-minded potential research partners? This might require you to join professional associations or attend conferences. Presenting your work at conferences is one way of finding potential partners.		
YOUR SPECIFIC GOALS: now record the goals that suit your context and your discipline . . .		

Summary: recognising success and managing pitfalls

As I have shown, there is no one way of crafting a successful academic career, and therefore, no correct pathway or approach to securing funding. At a time when academic workloads are more intense than ever (Lee et al., 2022) and the value academics bring to society is under scrutiny (Williams and Grant, 2018), it is important for you to prioritise developing an academic life that is 'valuable' to inhabit (Manathunga et al., 2022), and seek research funding that will enable you to contribute to society in the ways that you have the expertise to make. As I have indicated, for me, one of the greatest joys of being an academic has been the opportunity to work with others – academic colleagues, but also education departments, school leaders and teachers and not-for-profit organisations – undertaking research that has the potential to change practices and embedded notions of what counts as knowledge. I have offered a range of advice in this chapter about approaches to securing funding and building a career. However, I want to emphasise in closing that what will sustain the (often significant) effort required to bid for funding will be the quality of the research questions being asked, the drive to pursue answers and the collaborations and networks that academics are privileged to be part of as they undertake scholarly work.

I have emphasised the importance of ensuring your research is relevant, of finding research partners (whom you may work with over decades) and in developing your personal resilience so that you are able to build on and learn from rejections of your funding proposals.

Note

1 In Australia and New Zealand, teaching and research academics are ranked from A (tutor) to E (professor). Most academics with a PhD undertaking research and teaching duties commence at Level B.

References

Aprile, K.T., Ellem, P. and Lole, L. (2021) Publish, perish, or pursue? Early career academics' perspectives on demands for research productivity in regional universities, *Higher Education Research and Development*, 40(6), 1131–1145.

ARC (Australian Research Council). (2018) *Engagement and Impact Assessment | Home (arc.gov.au)*, https://dataportal.arc.gov.au/EI/NationalReport/2018/, Accessed on 4 October 2022.

ARC (Australian Research Council). (undated) *Research Opportunity and Performance Evidence (ROPE) Statement | Australian Research Council*, https://www.arc.gov.au/about-arc/program-policies/research-opportunity-and-performance-evidence-rope-statement, Accessed on 4 October 2022.

Besley, A. and Peters, M. (2006) Neoliberalism, performance and the assessment of research quality, *South African Journal of Higher Education*, 20(6), 814–832.

Britton, B., Jackson, C. and Wade, J. (2019) The reward and risk of social media for academics, *Nature Reviews Chemistry*, 3, 459–461, https://doi.org/10.1038/s41570-019-0121-3, Accessed on 14 October 2022.

Carrillo, C. and Flores, M.A. (2020) COVID-19 and teacher education: A literature review of online teaching and learning practices, *European Journal of Teacher Education*, 43(4), 466–487. DOI: 10.1080/02619768.2020.1821184

Chugh, R., Grose, R. and Macht, S.A. (2021) Social media usage by higher education academics: A scoping review of the literature, *Education and Information Technologies*, 26, 983–999, https://doi.org/10.1007/s10639-020-10288-z, Accessed on 14 October 2022.

Darling-Hammond, L. (2008) A future worthy of teaching for America, *Phi Delta Kappan*, 89(10), 730–736.

Department of Education Skills and Employment (Australian Government). (2022) HERDC Specifications for the collection of 2022 data – Department of Education, *Australian Government*, https://www.education.gov.au/research-block-grants/resources/herdc-specifications-collection-2022-data, Accessed on 16 October 2022.

Doecke, B., McLean Davies, L. and Mead, P. (Eds.). (2011) *Teaching Australian Literature: From Classroom Conversations to National Imaginings*, Kent Town, Australia: Wakefield Press, 1–14.

Ferguson, H. (2019) *University Research Funding: A Quick Guide*, https://www.aph.gov.au/About_Parliament/Parliamentary_Departments/Parliamentary_Library/pubs/rp/rp1819/Quick_Guides/UniversityResearchFunding, Accessed on 14 October 2022.

Gardner, A. and Willey, K. (2018) Academic identity reconstruction: The transition of engineering academics to engineering education researchers, *Studies in Higher Education*, 43(2), 234–250, https://doi.org/10.1080/03075079.2016.1162779, Accessed on 14 October 2022.

Government of Canada, Social Sciences and Humanities Research Council (SSHRC). (2022) https://www.sshrc-crsh.gc.ca/funding-financement/merit_review-evaluation_du_merite/index-eng.aspx, Accessed on 4 October 2022.

Hartzing, A. (2008) *Publish or Perish*, https://harzing.com/home, Accessed on 4 October 2022.

Lee, M., Coutts, R., Fielden, J., Hutchinson, M., Lakeman, R., Mathisen, B. and Phillips, N. (2022) Occupational stress in university academics in Australia and New Zealand, *Journal of Higher Education Policy and Management*, 44(1), 57–71.

Manathunga, C. (2022) *Why we must take the pulse of education research in Australia now | EduResearch Matters (aare.edu.au)*, https://www.aare.edu.au/blog/?p=13652, Accessed on 4 October 2022.

Manathunga, C., Black, A.L. and Davidow, S. (2022) Walking: Towards a valuable academic life, *Discourse: Studies in the Cultural Politics of Education*, 43(2), 231–250.

McLean Davies, L.J. (2011) Magwitch madness: Archive fever and the teaching of Australian literature. In: Doecke, B., McLean-Davies, L. and Mead, P. (eds.) *Teaching Australian Literature: From Classroom Conversations to National Imaginings*, Kent Town, Australia: Wakefield Press, 129–152.

McLean Davies, L.J. (2014) You are what you read: Text selection and cultural capital in the (globalising) English classroom. In: Goodwyn, A., Reid, L. and Durrant, C. (eds.) *International Perspectives on Teaching English in a Globalized World*, New York: Routledge US, 235–244.

McLean Davies, L.J. and Buzacott, L. (2022) Rethinking literature, knowledge and justice: Selecting 'difficult' stories for study in school English, *Pedagogy, Culture and Society*, 30(3), 367–381.

McLean Davies, L.J., Buzacott, L., and Martin, S.K. (2018) Growing the nation: The influence of Dartmouth on the teaching of literature in subject English in Australia. In: *The Future of English Teaching Worldwide*, Abingdon: Routledge, 146–158.

McLean Davies, L.J., Doecke, B. and Mead, P. (2013) Reading the local and global: Teaching literature in secondary schools in Australia, *Changing English: Studies in Culture and Education*, 20(3), 224–240, https://doi.org/10.1080/13586 84X.2013.816529, Accessed on 14 October 2022.

McLean Davies, L.J., Truman, S. and Buzacott, L. (2021) Teacher-researchers: A pilot project for unsettling the secondary Australian literary canon, *Gender and Education*, 33(7), 814–829, https://doi.org/10.1080/09540253.2020.173531 3, Accessed on 04 October 2022.

Morelock, J.R., Sochacka, N.W., Lewis, R.S., Walther, J., Culloty, C.M., Hopkins, J.S. and Offune, C.K. (2020) Using a novel research methodology to study and respond to faculty and student experiences with COVID-19 in real time, *Advances in Engineering Education*, 8(4).

OECD. (2022) *Gross Domestic Spending on RandD (Indicator)*, doi: 10.1787/ d8b068b4-en, https://data.oecd.org/rd/gross-domestic-spending-on-r-d.htm, Accessed on 04 October 2022.

Phillips, S., McLean Davies, L. and Truman, S.E. (2022) Power of country: Indigenous relationality and reading Indigenous climate fiction in Australia, *Curriculum Inquiry*, 52(2), 171–186.

Sawyer, W. and McLean Davies, L. (2021) What do we want students to know from being taught a poem? Knowing in English special issue, *Changing English*, 28(1), 103–117, Accessed on 04 October 2022.

US Department of Education, Institute of Education Sciences (IES). (Undated) *SEER Standards for Excellence in Education Research – Standards for Excellence in Education Research*, https://ies.ed.gov/seer/index.asp, Accessed on 14 October 2022.

Victorian Department of Education and Training. (2021) *Literacy Teaching Toolkit Level 7 to 10*, https://www.education.vic.gov.au/school/teachers/teachingre sources/discipline/english/literacy/Pages/default.aspx#empty, Accessed on 14 October 2022.

Wilkinson, C. (2019) Evidencing impact: A case study of UK academic perspectives on evidencing research impact, *Studies in Higher Education*, 44(1), 72–85.

Williams, K. and Grant, J. (2018) A comparative review of how the policy and procedures to assess research impact evolved in Australia and the UK, *Research Evaluation*, 27(2), 93–105.

Ziebell, N., Acquaro, D., Pearn, C. and Seah, W.T. (2020) *Examining the Impact of COVID-19: Report Summary*, University of Melbourne: Australian Education Survey.

Chapter 11

Leadership, mentoring and paying forward

Marilyn Leask and Irma Eloff with Professors
Ling Siew Eng, Jan Fazlagić and Nabi Bux Jumani

Introduction

In the previous chapters, you have been presented with ideas about how to develop your academic profile through your research, your publications and the media. This final chapter discusses how you might build your profile as a leader so as to meet the expectations placed on professors to be leaders: in their discipline, their university, their mentoring, their research, their publishing, their income generation and their professional conduct.

Mentoring, actively supporting junior staff in developing their academic profiles, is a way of paying forward your debts to your mentors so that junior colleagues can themselves develop rewarding academic careers and contribute new knowledge to your discipline.

Professors from different countries have contributed to this chapter, giving you an insight into the expectations of professors in different contexts. I am grateful to them and to the other contributors to this book for their friendship and professional collaboration over decades.

Objectives

By the end of this chapter you should have:

- identified the leadership demands on professors in the country/countries in which you would like to work as a professor;
- identified a range of leadership opportunities available to you in your context;
- decided whether to join or build international and national collaborative networks in your field;
- articulated your personal values with respect to service to your country, your peers and your community;
- planned how to manage your well-being;
- assessed the physical, social and psychological risks you may face;
- sketched out your plans for developing and then implementing your leadership skills in the areas relevant to your context.

DOI: 10.4324/9781003217596-11

Leadership demands and opportunities

There are many theories about leadership, and it is worth spending some time reviewing these and thinking through how, given your personal characteristics, you might become an effective leader. See for example the Simplilearn (2022) overview of forms of leadership: which ones suit your personality and your context?

The University of Adelaide has a statement about the expectations of professors as leaders. The quotes below are taken from their 2018 document:

> a professor is someone whose performance and pre-eminence as a scholar of international standing has been recognised by the academy, and . . . maintaining the standing of the professoriate is dependent on professors continuing to be exemplary in their conduct and output. . . . Our professors' academic expertise is widely acknowledged. The new [Professors as Leaders] statement also emphasises their role in upholding the University's values and exemplifying the highest standard of ethical practice and integrity at all times.
>
> (University of Adelaide, 2018, p. 1)

> Professors communicate, educate, challenge, and motivate others. While conducting research, your task focuses on your relationships with other colleagues in your discipline around the world. Through service your focus is with local and state professionals in your area. In teaching, your focus is on your students. But the core challenge is the same – getting others to grow, learn, and develop based on your contributions to their lives in and out of the classroom.
>
> (University of Adelaide, 2018, p. 2)

Your university will have various expectations of professors, written or unwritten; for example, you may be expected to demonstrate leadership through engagement in university-run open lecture programmes or conferences. If you engage with/contribute to/develop your department's/university's conference programme, not only will you be demonstrating leadership within the university but you will also have the opportunity to identify and contact leading researchers to invite them to give keynotes at conferences. This engagement gives you the chance to expand your network and find other academics with interests similar to your own, and so provides a way to develop future research and publishing collaborations.

You may be expected to give an inaugural lecture, and you may wish to review examples of these, which are available on YouTube as well as on university websites, and plan for yours. See for example the University of Birmingham website listing their inaugural lecture series (University of Birmingham, 2022).

> An inaugural lecture is a key milestone in any academic's career, signifying their promotion to 'Professor'. It is an opportunity for our new professorial colleagues to present their innovative research first-hand.
>
> (University of Birmingham, 2022, p. 1)

You may also have the opportunity to nominate leaders in your field as honorary or visiting professors to your institution. Your institution will have protocols about these appointments, which may not require funding to be available. Likewise, typically universities annually recognise the achievements of people in fields associated with the university through the granting of honorary degrees. Again, engaging in this work gives you the opportunity to speak with, learn from and network with people who normally you may not come across.

Typically, professors will be involved in or lead a research group/centre. However, to become a leader you need to have followers, who will normally include:

- colleagues including other professors with similar interests: cross-disciplinary collaboration is usually encouraged;
- early career academics who are developing their knowledge and expertise in your field and with whom you are taking a mentoring role (either through explicit agreement or implicitly through how you work together);
- PhD/master's students who are deeply interested in your main research areas;
- your ex-students (alumni) who do not work in academia but have taken jobs in the wider world can provide you with up-to-the-minute case studies and examples of what is happening in your field, perhaps contributing to webinars in order to ground what you are teaching in up-to-the-minute practice (see Chapter 4 on working with alumni).

In time, a professor's research profile will attract applications from doctoral students to study with them (or the professor may bid for internal/external funding for others to work with them), thus building what can become a collaborative research network. The research group provides a framework for a professor's mentoring role, inducting staff into research and publication processes and so providing a foundation for staff in the research group to become the next generation of professors. Professors typically can offer opportunities to their mentees to become involved in collaborative research and writing, to review journal articles, to edit professional journals, to write book proposals, to write research bids, to undertake research for sponsors and to manage research projects.

Collaborative working with peers with similar interests can be tremendously rewarding as you advance knowledge together. Professors Leask and Younie first saw the power of this way of working in the mid-1990s when leading a project funded by the European Union on how we might use the internet to support teaching and learning. There was no existing knowledge to draw on, and so together they developed and tested ideas across several countries. They developed a new term for this way of working – we called it 'communal constructivism' (Leask and Younie, 2001). They saw this way that colleagues were working and learning together to push the boundaries of knowledge as being different to Vygotsky's social constructivist theory of learning, which describes how individuals learn from a more knowledgeable other. When you are creating new knowledge, there are no knowledgeable others, only colleagues who, like yourself, are creating new knowledge in the field.

Your personal professional standards and accountabilities

As well as the university-wide accountability measures governing your work, as set out in Chapter 3, as a professional you are expected to have a set of personal values around service and personal standards. In your promotion to professor, an assessment was been made about your integrity and personal professional standards. Hutchin (2008), among others, sees these personal professional standards as being expressed as three forms of accountability that govern the work of professionals: contractual, moral and professional accountability. The sections that follow outline what this might mean for those in professorial roles as they take on leadership roles.

Within your university: your contractual accountability

Your contract with your employer will specify expectations the university has on you for leadership. For example, the University of Adelaide's formal document (2018) *Professors as Leaders* sets out very clearly how professors are expected to lead. The data from the survey underpinning this book shows that, in some settings, the professorial contract is standard with the salary being set and with levels of progression formally identified. In other settings, the professorial contract is negotiated on an individual basis along with the salary, with all this information being confidential.

The discussion that follows provides further explanation of what might be meant by professional and moral accountability.

Within your profession: your professional accountability

Professional accountability is defined as your accountability to your profession and to your peers to uphold the highest standards. Accountability procedures operated by national professional bodies offer opportunities within your professional group to take on leadership roles. Professional bodies/associations may permit or prevent registration as a professional, thus having the authority to prevent members working in their chosen profession. They may hold enquiries into poor practice. 'Fitness to practice' assessments are also a form of professional accountability:

> Fitness to practise is the ability to meet professional standards; it is about character, professional competence and health. According to the [UK] Health and Care Professions Council (HCPC), someone is fit to practise if they have 'the skills, knowledge, character and health to practise their profession safely and effectively'.
>
> (Office of the Independent Adjudicator, 2023)

Typically, professional bodies/associations have a set of requirements for the recognition of individuals as professionals in the field, such as qualifications and demonstrable effective practice. In addition, they normally publish a code of ethics that governs the professional practice of members and provides a framework for holding members of the professional group to account. (See for example New Zealand College of Clinical Psychologists, 2012; National Association of Professional Social Workers in India, 2015.)

> The American Nursing Association's Code of Ethics defines professional accountability as being 'answerable to oneself and others for one's own actions.' Not only do we hold high clinical practice and ethical standards for ourselves, but we must also be willing to accept professional responsibility when or if deviations from care standards occur.
>
> (Davis, 2017, p. 1)

Your personal values: your moral accountability

Your personal values will shape the leadership you show as a professor: how you act is influenced by your moral compass. Caldwell and Anderson (2021) define several types of leadership, and you may find it helpful to read this article and think about what characteristics you would like to describe your leadership. Your personal values will guide your decisions about how you allocate your time and with whom you work, particularly with respect to service to your country, your peers and your community.

Typically, professorial contracts specify research and/or teaching responsibilities, including the raising of research funding. Some, however, specify engagement with the community beyond the university – as a form of public service linked with the role. This public service could be at local, regional, national or international levels. It could be service to your professional associations or to community organisations. Again, this is an area to explore in your conversations with professors already working in the institutions you would wish to work in yourself as a professor.

Leadership well-being

Current elevated societal awareness of well-being has catapulted psychological sciences across various scientific fields into the forefront of public debate. Whereas any reference to 'well-being' in the committee rooms of academia would have been frowned upon as recently as two decades ago, it is now on the agendas of strategy meetings at universities around the world. The well-being of students, the well-being of academic staff, the well-being of administrative and support staff and environmental well-being are being prioritised. It stands to reason that leadership well-being is pivotal in this regard.

Leadership well-being affects multiple layers of staffing within university systems. At the macrosystemic level, the Special Initiative for Mental Health

(2019–2023) from the World Health Organisation (2019, p. 1) has indicated that 'Mental health conditions contribute to poor health outcomes, premature death, human rights violations, and global and national economic loss'. It can be argued that some similar outcomes could potentially be detected at the level of universities. In taking a broad perspective of professors as intellectual leaders, investments in leadership well-being may therefore yield systemic benefits.

Perspectives From Malaysia, Pakistan and Poland

In this section, three professors provide an overview of the pathway to becoming a professor in their respective countries. If you have read the previous chapters, you should now be in a position to plot your own pathway to professorship in such a way that you meet criteria for appointment in a number of countries. Indeed, many professors do move between countries for permanent or visiting roles. Academics who are deeply expert in a field of knowledge and who have built the sort of academic profiles proposed in this book should find they have opportunities to travel and work across the world: sharing and creating new knowledge with peers and mentoring the next generation of knowledge leaders in their field.

Overview 1: the pathway to professorship: a Malaysian perspective

Overview 1 comes from Professor Ling Siew Eng, Professor in Mathematics at Universiti Teknologi MARA (UiTM), Sarawak branch.

The journey to becoming a professor covers the first two phases of academic life, which are 'taking' i.e. learning from peers and mentors, and 'making' i.e. your personal pathway. The professorial role is the third phase, which is 'paying back'.

In the 'taking' phase, academicians need to search for the requirements to be awarded a professorship in their university and learn the skills to achieve the requirements. Generally, there are seven assessed areas in which you need to excel before you, as an academician, can be awarded the title 'Professor'.

The first area is *teaching and supervising*, which are the main tasks of academicians. Beside lecturing and tutoring, academicians need to supervise undergraduate students' projects and the dissertations or theses of post-graduate students.

The second area is *research, publication, and conference contributions*. All academicians need to be involved in research and publication at local, national or international levels. This area includes their role in journal editorial work. The role of academicians in national and international conferences is included in this area. These roles include being part of a conference organising committee, being a keynote or plenary speaker, a session chair or as a presenter.

The third area is *consultation and/or expertise*. Academicians need to be involved in consultancy projects and serve as an expert in their field such as an expert panel member, as an evaluator, reviewer and as an invited speaker. Other roles include drafters of policy, standards, guidelines, procedures or parliamentary acts.

The fourth area is *innovation, commercialisation, and entrepreneurship*. Academicians need to show their innovative skills via winning awards, product copyright or patent or through an excellence, innovation and creative group lead by the academician with members from their organisation. Commercialisation of innovative products is also one of the key indicators. Involvement of academicians in entrepreneurial projects and raising funds from entrepreneurial programmes will add value to an academician's claims to satisfy the criteria for achievements in this area.

The fifth area is *service to the university and society*. Service to the university includes service in the university's management team, or on activity organising committees of the university or faculty and representing the university, including in sporting and other non-academic activities. Other indicators of service to the university include membership of associations or organisations of professional bodies within the field of expertise or a non-professional body, recognised at the national or international level. Besides this, contributions to students' development are also indicators of service to the university. Involvement in community or NGO(s) activities indicates the academician's contribution to society.

The sixth area is *academic honours and awards*. Academic awards include prizes, excellent service, and scholarship awards, while academic honours include appreciation within and beyond the university for the academician's charitable contributions.

The last area is *quality of leadership and personality*. Academicians need to show their quality of leadership via their driving force on academic excellence or leadership of their profession through activities such as contributions to faculty academic leadership, a centre of excellence, research and development, entrepreneurship etc. The quality of personality assessment includes characteristics or special qualities possessed by the staff: integrity, teamwork, authoritative leadership etc. The last but not least activity in this last area is networking. Academicians need to network with experts within faculties and universities at national and international levels for more collaboration in writing and research to gain wider knowledge and skills and, at the same time, to contribute to the new knowledge in their discipline.

After understanding the criteria to be a professor, academicians need to self-access their abilities and skills to achieve the criteria. Next, they need to plan to learn the skills they are lacking and, at the same time, plan a series of milestones to achieve all requirements. A practical milestone is to start with the criteria they can achieve now, where they have the skills to carry on, and then at the same time, acquire the new skills to fulfil all requirements. At this point, the academician has already entered the second phase: making (a contribution). In this phase, they will be carrying out their plan, raising their achievements and finally hitting all targets. At this point in time, the academician should submit their application to be awarded a professorial title.

After winning the professorial award, the third phase of the professional journey begins. Facilitating, mentoring and contributing to society, the nation and the world are the expectations of a professor. At this stage, a systematic facilitating or mentoring plan will guide the direction of a professor's work. To be an effective mentor, identify the mentees that you can work with. Prepare, plan and carry on your role as a facilitator in your field at local, national and international levels. Besides this, the most significant contributions may be with local communities, as working with professors with the same background and knowledge of the environment will enable you to identify the issues within the society, then remedies and improvements, and will enable you to solve these issues using scientific methods, tools and measurements. This improvement role can be extended to national and international levels with similar issues. In addition, joining an international level special interest group will pull existing resources and leading thinkers together and enable you to contribute towards new knowledge.

Overview 2: the pathway to professorship: a perspective from Pakistan

Overview 2 comes from Professor Nabi Bux Jumani, Vice President (Administration and Finance), International Islamic University, Islamabad, Pakistan. Previously a dean and director of the Directorate of Distance Education at IIUI, he has also worked in the Federal Ministry of Education.

Teaching is considered one of the most prestigious and challenging careers that an individual can pursue in Pakistan. You have to work long hours in a stressful and disciplined environment. The universities are meant to be knowledge creators and bring innovative ideas to the field. The path to professorship in Pakistan is a long journey requiring multitasking, including teaching, research, administration and community service. The primary duties of faculty include effective classroom teaching, academic advising and counselling of students, participation in departmental committee work, continuous development of the curriculum through assessment, applied research or scholarly activity and service such as assisting in recruitment of students and initiatives designed to help students succeed academically, as well as other assigned duties.

The respective faculty chairpersons review the performance of the faculty members on a semester and annual basis for their assigned tasks. The faculty members in the universities of Pakistan may be assigned other administrative responsibilities like hostels management, academic advisors, the controller of examinations etc., and from mid-career onwards they are members of various academic and administrative committees within and outside their departments and faculties. The most senior professor in the faculty would be the dean of the faculty, who takes on the role for a tenure of three years; as the most senior faculty member in the department, they would chair the departmental meetings and so on.

In Pakistan, to be a lecturer, the minimum requirement is 18 years of education in the relevant field; for assistant professor, in most fields a PhD is required; to qualify for associate professor status, a minimum of ten years of teaching experience at higher education, along with ten research publications in journals recognised by the national government body, the Higher Education Commission, are required. To be eligible to apply for professorship, one needs to have at least

15 years of teaching experience in higher education and 15 research publications in national or international journals recognised by the Higher Education Commission, of which four must be from the last five years. That means the faculty members are required to update their research on a regular basis.

In higher education, recruitment is done for each post separately, and the applicants have to go through a selection process each time they want to apply for the next post, unlike school educators, who are promoted to the next grade/position with experience. Selection is done on open merit, and the faculty members need to prove their knowledge, skills and competencies for being selected for the higher position. For professorship, selection is even tougher as the cases are evaluated by international and national experts in the field before the selection interview panel. The criteria for selection include contribution to teaching, supervision of MS/PhD students, relevance and impact of research projects on development of the country, publications, contributions to the profession, such as through membership of professional bodies, editors of research journals, reviewer for journals/conferences and contributions to society.

The journey doesn't stop here; professors can then apply for the status of meritorious professor, to which the syndicate of the Higher Education Institution would appoint only a few retired professors of top rank upon qualifying and applying, and this status is for life.

Overview 3: the pathway to professorship today: a Polish perspective

Overview 3 comes from Professor Jan Fazlagić, Professor in Management at the Poznan University of Economics and Business Poznan, Poland.

Today in Poland, the path to professorship starts, as in many other countries, with the position of assistant professor. A university may hire a person with an MA, but such a newly hired researcher is expected to complete his or her PhD within a certain time, usually four years. (See Appendix 2 for an introduction to the complex political background to academic life in Poland.)

After obtaining the PhD title, most frequently universities promote the researcher to 'adjunkt' (adjunct) professor and sign a new work contract expecting the newly fledged PhD to obtain another post-PhD degree called 'habilitation' (Polish National Agency for Academic Exchange, 2022). The criteria for obtaining a habilitation degree are usually higher than those of its lower rank counterpart – the PhD. You are expected to obtain your habilitation degree in nine years. Once you get your habilitation degree, you are usually promoted to 'nadzwyczajny' (professor – this translates as 'extraordinary professor', but this is a junior professor role).

The habilitation degree candidate has to:

- write a book;
- demonstrate experience in conducting research studies;
- have a track record in peer-reviewed international journals.

Academics who do not obtain their hab. degree in nine years may be sacked or, more frequently, offered a chance to get their hab. degree in the following few years: in this 'second chance' period, they become 'senior lecturer', with their teaching load increased from 240 hrs per year to roughly 360 hrs.

The Polish ministry of science and education developed a system of ranking for most of the peer-reviewed journals in the world, and an extensive list of journals shows the appropriate number of points for the publication (Ministry of Education and Science, Poland/Ministerstwo Edukacji i Nauki, 2022). Polish researchers are evaluated based on the number of points they gather and also the value of publications in points (one cannot compensate for the higher number of points from many low-ranking publications with a lack of high-ranking publications in his or her track record).

The habilitation degree usually increases job security at universities in Poland, especially due to the demographic crisis, which means that the number of students who are taught at universities has dropped dramatically over the last 15 years in Poland. One could say that the habilitation degree is the equivalent of the full professor role in other countries because universities in other countries do not require professors to obtain the hab. degree on the path to full professorship ('Profesor Belwederski' or 'profesor zwyczajny' – 'ordinary professor').

Poland is one of the few countries in the world where the full professorship is awarded by the head of state.

In other words, each professor with the habilitation degree may continue his research in such a way that his or her further achievements can be encapsulated in the application – to the government – for the full professorship. This prestigious title is given by a special commission situated at the ministry level. The application is reviewed by over five experts in the field, and it is a three-stage process.

Each applicant for the full professorship title is expected to publish an original book containing their research results. The book is reviewed and submitted as a part of the application for the full professorship. The criteria are very strict, and it is customary that applications are turned down. The decision of whether an applicant is going to receive or not that full professorship is made by a committee of 12 experts from the scientific disciplines represented by the applicant. The process of application may last several years from the moment the applicant submits his or her application.

The criteria under which the application for full professorship is evaluated include:

- the quality of the book itself;
- the engagement project;
- research project management achievements in the field of academic education;
- internationalisation of research activities;
- the number and the quality of peer-reviewed articles;
- cooperation with the external environment etc.

There is some element of subjectivity, and it is up to the applicant to demonstrate and highlight which of their achievements are worth evaluating by the committee. The applicant is expected to provide the full list of publications, certificates, selected books and full versions of articles to be reviewed by the committee. Every professor applying for full professorship is required to write an extensive description of his or her achievements divided into three periods: before obtaining the PhD title, before obtaining the habilitation title and after obtaining the habilitation title. Thus, the full professorship application form encapsulates the full academic life of the applicant.

These examples, from three quite different countries, coupled with the other examples given throughout the book, show that the criteria to be met are very similar between countries: good teaching, impactful research, service, a substantial publication record and recognition that you are held in esteem by peers. A major difference between countries, which is one of the findings underpinning the ideas in this book, is that in some countries, the knowledge of academics is valued by those making decisions e.g. government ministers and policy officers, and in other countries the knowledge of academics is considered irrelevant or even threatening, as the following section on risks outlines.

Risks

Academic freedom of expression

A wide range of literature on the matter of academic freedom was reviewed for this section, and it seems that maintaining the freedom for academics to research and publish their findings if they are critical of established ideas in society is challenging even for societies that consider themselves democracies.

Chapter 6 introduces you to different ways of thinking about your online and offline media presence, which then allows you to demonstrate your thought leadership in your discipline. However, you need to consider the personal risks you take in speaking out as an academic, in leading new thinking and undertaking research that yields findings uncomfortable to those in power. Your assessment of the risks in your context may outweigh what you consider to be your moral and professional responsibilities to speak out.

The University of Nottingham, which has campuses in China, the UK, and Malaysia, makes this statement:

> Freedom of speech and the free exchange of ideas, in pursuit of truth and knowledge, are central to the University of Nottingham's mission to enable students and staff to collaborate in learning, scholarship, and discovery. In all the University does, it values inclusivity, ambition, openness, fairness, and respect. . . . The University commits to promoting these freedoms so that students and staff can become acquainted with new information and ideas and with diverse viewpoints; the University will foster its students' and staff's

wellbeing by providing them with a supportive environment which encourages civil and peaceful debate and in which they can challenge their own and others' beliefs and opinions and can scrutinise these on their merits. . . . The freedom of expression applies not only to information or ideas that are favourably received, but also to those that offend, shock or disturb. It applies to all who wish to seek, receive or impart information and ideas of all kinds, and includes the right to protest peacefully. The University will actively promote and facilitate freedom of speech and allow for robust and civil debate. By helping students develop the skills to engage critically with new ideas, the University seeks to prepare them for the challenges they will face once they graduate. At the same time we will continue to engage with and provide an environment and infrastructure to support the wellbeing of both speakers and those who may object to a speaker or are for whatever reason concerned or offended by them. . . . In seeking to protect the freedom of speech of its staff and students, the University will take appropriate measures, in accordance with the terms of this statement, to assist staff and students whose freedom of speech is threatened by third parties.

Physical risks

While academics may understand the value to a society's development of the academic role and freedom to undertake research that might challenge existing practices, ways of thinking and doing things, there is ample evidence from many societies that government ministers may not accept this role.

Shamoo (2011), an Iraqi heritage academic living in the USA, documents the murders of hundreds of Iraqi academics in the early 2000s, events that had considerable news coverage. Careful research shows that over decades, the killing, imprisonment or restrictions on employment of researchers/academics from different countries (see for example Cambodia – the Killing Fields: Center for Holocaust and Genocide Studies, undated; China – the Cultural Revolution: Ramzy, 2016).

Political risks and equitable access to academic jobs

While the killing of academics to suppress independent thought is a risk in some countries, more common is the restricting of access to jobs and research funds to those whose work is considered favourably by those in power.

There are plenty of examples of countries switching from a liberal regime to an intolerant regime within a short period, and vice versa, with the ideologies behind the political parties impacting on the freedom of speech of university staff. In the USA, for example, the McCarthy era in the 1950s resulted in academics suspected of being communist sympathisers being removed from their posts (Dwight D Eisenhower Document Archive, 2022). At the same time, the opposite was happening in other countries. Professor Fazlagić (Appendix 2) reports that in Poland from 1945 to 1989, academics who were not communist sympathisers were prevented from working in universities. In Appendix 2, Professor Fazlagić provides a brief history of the influence of the state on professorial appointments following Poland's loss of independence after the Second World War and the impact on the professoriat of being brought under the Soviet Union's control 1945–1989: the impact of the period on academic life and thought, he argues, continues to influence the appointment of professors in Poland today.

As a university leader, you will have a role in deciding whether the appointment processes in the university are open and transparent and equitable or not. Professors responding to the survey indicated that there are many instances where appointments to professorships are made that seem to be justified by the evidence of academic achievement. Putting in place protections to ensure equitable access to academic jobs and research funds as well as protecting freedom of speech is not uncommon. See for example the staff appointment policies of Oxford and Cambridge Universities in the UK, which express the university's desire for a diverse workforce rather than one where those on appointment panels just appoint people like them (University of Cambridge, 2022; University of Oxford, 2022). You may wish to check if anti-discrimination policies are in place in the universities in which you work or wish to work.

If you work in a country where there is strong political influence on universities and the freedom of academics to report their research and indeed to apply for academic posts, then it may help you to see how your country can change by reading about the Polish experience in Appendix 2.

Government ministers in democracies are not immune to the desire to crush criticism. The so-called post-truth era established during Trump's US presidency (2016–2021) and the UK's Brexit campaign was a period where politicians from the parties in power appealed to the public's emotions and fears and rejected logic and research (see for example: the videos of UK Secretary of State for Education, Gove, 2016; and the Institute of Government [UK], 2016). In 2010, Gove, the newly elected secretary of state for education for England, called academics who challenged his policies 'the blob'; he said 'the public have had enough of experts' (Gove, 2016; Institute of Government, 2016; Robinson, 2014). Evans (2018) and Macfarlane (2011) report research undertaken with UK professors on their role, with Macfarlane describing the UK professorial role as being 'an intellectual leader: role model, mentor, advocate, guardian, acquisitor and ambassador' (p. 1) – yet, in a government minister's eyes, these same people are 'the blob'.

Using emotive language to put down opponents became a characteristic of UK and US government leaders' language at this time (Trump regularly used the term 'fake news' to decry those challenging him). In recognition of this challenge to previously held notions of truth, the Oxford dictionary declared 'post-truth' as the Word of the Year in 2016, with the definition being: '*post-truth* is an adjective defined as "relating to or denoting circumstances in which objective facts are less influential in shaping public opinion than appeals to emotion and personal belief'" (Oxford University Press, 2016). Academics search for ways to reduce uncertainty about the world through their research, so the rejection of the possibility of 'truthfulness' by these politicians at this time allowed them to reduce public discourse to a free for all battleground of ideas without reference to history or evidence.

So, you may find your academic career is subject to political ideology beyond your control. In the UK, the 'Brexit decision' to leave the EU put at risk academics' engagement with the European community of scholars, with academics finding already-agreed funding for their projects might be withdrawn if UK academics were project leaders (British Heart Foundation, 2022). Prior to Brexit, UK academics had been disproportionately successful in bidding for European-funded research (Royal Society, 2022). Russia's invasion of the Ukraine in 2022 brought to an end decades of collaboration between scientists in different countries (Plackett, 2022).

Psychological and social risks

There are also psychological and social risks in the pathway to professorship. Academic advancement is often uneven and dependent on the decision-makers of the time. In the internal university environment, academic career trajectories are tied to the terms of appointment of vice-chancellors, rectors, deans, deputy-deans and academic heads of department – all of whom might have various levels of influence on promotions and appointments. In addition, the variance between scientific disciplines may mean that promotion criteria can be interpreted differently in different faculties and schools, resulting in internal tensions. This shifting landscape necessitates reflexive acuity and continued adjustment to changing institutional priorities. In the external environment, professors may also come under pressure to either continue to retain the status quo in their field or alternatively to radicalise theoretical developments, instead of crafting research priorities according to their own empirical investigations. The personal psychological distress that these dynamics may create is evident.

You will need to make an assessment of the risks you face in your own context, being aware that risks change with political administration, current thinking in your discipline and, to some, extent media preoccupations.

Your checklist and goals: for developing your leadership skills

Now fill in Table 11.1. As you make notes in this, your last checklist, look back at the lists you have created from previous chapters. Taken together, these lists provide you with a toolkit to create your pathway to professorship.

The Checklist in Table 11.1 on 'looking forward to taking a leadership role in your discipline and in your university', is freely available for download via the Support Material tab on the Routledge website.

Table 11.1 Checklist: looking forward to taking a leadership role in your discipline and your university

ITEM	Achieved?	
	Yes	No
YOUR LEADERSHIP STYLE		
Have you considered which leadership theories might be useful in guiding your development as a leader given your personal characteristics and the context in which you are working?		
LEADERSHIP: DEMANDS AND OPPORTUNITIES		
Do you understand how the different forms of accountability – moral, professional and contractual – are likely to impact on you if you gain a professorial post in your current institution and country?		
Have you identified which leadership opportunities are likely to be available to you within your context, and have you got plans to take advantage of these opportunities?		
Are you aware of how your personal values and ways of working might support or hinder you in mentoring staff who will be the professors of tomorrow?		
INTERNATIONAL COLLABORATION		
Have you identified how you are going to build your international network of fellow academics interested in similar areas of research?		
SERVICE: LOCAL, REGIONAL, NATIONAL, INTERNATIONAL		
Have you identified how you might build a profile that demonstrates you are providing a service to the local, regional, national and international community based on your research and expertise?		
RISK ANALYSIS		
Have you analysed the risk factors to you and your family if you become a thought leader in your country?		
Are you working in an environment where academic freedom of expression is protected? Are you free to push the boundaries of knowledge and to engage in debate? If not, then you may need to make a decision to avoid research on topics that can be seen as political.		
YOUR SPECIFIC GOALS: now record the goals that suit your context and your discipline . . .		

Summary: recognising success and avoiding pitfalls

Demands on professors vary between countries and settings, so you will need to do your own research about what is expected in the country/countries in which you would like to work as a professor.

At this point, at the end of this book, you might take a moment to think about what you would like your legacy to be of your academic career: How would you like to be judged for your contribution to academic life: contractually, professionally, morally? In different places in the book, we talk about the three phases of your academic life – learn/earn/return. Initially, you take from your community – learning from your study and your mentors. During the early stages of your academic life, you are making your career, and at the latter stage of your career, you are paying back your academic community's investment in you. What are your plans for this last stage of your career – once you become a professor?

You are likely to find parts of the academic world to be hugely competitive. Many universities are in one type of club or another to enable them to make claims about their unique contribution to their communities. In some countries, elitism is used as a non-rational way to distribute scarce resources, but what national research exercises find is that ground-breaking research can be found in any type of university. What we have found over our decades of working with students as well as working nationally and internationally with thought leaders is that human beings have phenomenal capacity to learn, to solve problems and to contribute to the well-being of their own communities. These capacities can be released or suppressed by the teachers who shape their education and the knowledge they have.

We hope you find your university teaching and your engagement with students' minds as well as your research provides you with a fulfilling life in the way it has done so for us.

References

British Heart Foundation. (2022) *Government Announces Plan b for European Research Funding*, https://www.bhf.org.uk/what-we-do/news-from-the-bhf/news-archive/2022/july/government-announces-plan-b-for-european-research-funding, Accessed on 23 October 2022.

Caldwell, C. and Anderson, V. (2021) University professors as 'transformative leaders', *The Journal of Values-Based Leadership*, 14(1), 1–12, https://scholar.valpo.edu/cgi/viewcontent.cgi?article=1349&context=jvbl, Accessed on 23 October 2022.

Center for Holocaust and Genocide Studies. (undated) *Cambodia 1975–79 University of Minnesota*, https://cla.umn.edu/chgs/holocaust-genocide-education/resource-guides/cambodia, Accessed on 23 October 2022.

Davis, C. (2017) The importance of professional accountability, *Nursing Made Incredibly Easy!* November/December, 15(6), 4, doi: 10.1097/01.NME.0000525557.44656.04.

Dwight D Eisenhower Document Archive. (2022) *McCarthyism/The 'Red Scare'*, https://www.eisenhowerlibrary.gov/research/online-documents/mccarthyism-red-scare, Accessed on 23 October 2022.

Flinders University. (2019) *Academics Must 'Trump' Fake News*, https://news.flin ders.edu.au/blog/2019/02/02/academics-must-trump-fake-news/, Accessed on 23 October 2022.

Gove, M. (2016) Britons have had enough of experts, *Sky News Interview*, 25 June, https://www.youtube.com/watch?v=GGgiGtJk7MA, Accessed on 23 October 2022.

Hutchin, R. (2008) *Teachers' Perceptions of Accountability and Professionalism in Newly Created Specialist Schools*, EdD thesis The Open University, https://oro.open.ac.uk/64842/1/13890024.pdf, Accessed on 23 October 2022.

Institute of Government. (2016) *Has the Public Really Had Enough of Experts?* 14 September https://www.youtube.com/watch?v=_5lF6ReLLIc, Accessed on 23 October 2022.

Leask, M. and Younie, S. (2001) Communal constructivist theory: Information and communications technology pedagogy and internationalisation of the curriculum, *Journal of Information Technology for Teacher Education*, 10(1–2), 117–134, http://dx.doi.org/10.1080/14759390100200106, Accessed on 23 October 2022.

Macfarlane, B. (2011) Professors as intellectual leaders: Formation, identity and role, *Studies in Higher Education*, 36, 57–73, doi: 10.1080/03075070903443734.

Ministry of Education and Science, Poland. Ministerstwo Edukacji i Nauki. (2022) *List of Disciplines Assigned to Scientific Journals and Conference Materials/Wykaz dyscyplin przypisanych do czasopism naukowych i materiałów konferencyjnych/*, Accessed on 23 October 2022, https://www.gov.pl/web/edukacja-i-nauka/komunikat-min istra-edukacji-i-nauki-z-dnia-1-grudnia-2021-r-w-sprawie-wykazu-czasopism-nau kowych-i-recenzowanych-materialow-z-konferencji-miedzynarodowych?fbclid=I wAR0j3O0AbbBQBZeoltOy1ueEpr_5SPOuZKj8PbiC2k83g4LzL-xs9Momv10, Accessed on 23 October 2022. *Note the Column 'Punkty' Which Lists the Points Allocated to a Specific Journal.*

National Association of Professional Social Workers in India. (2015) *Code of Ethics for Professional Social Workers in India*, https://www.napswi.org/pdf/NAPSWI_Code_of_Ethics), Accessed on 23 October 2022.

New Zealand College of Clinical Psychologists. (2012) *Code of Ethics for Psychologists Working in Aotearoa/New Zealand*, https://www.nzccp.co.nz/assets/Uploads/Code-of-Ethics-English.pdf, Accessed on 23 October 2022.

Office of the Independent Adjudicator. (2023) *Fitness to Practice*, https://www.oiahe.org.uk/resources-and-publications/good-practice-framework/fitness-to-practise/what-is-fitness-to-practise/, Accessed on 23 October 2022.

Oxford University Press. (2016) *Word of the Year*, https://languages.oup.com/word-of-the-year/2016/, Accessed on 23 October 2022.

Plackett, B. (2022) *The Future of Research Collaborations with Russia*, https://www.nature.com/articles/d41586-022-00761-9, Accessed on 23 October 2022.

Polish National Agency for Academic Exchange. (2022) *Initiating the Habilitation Proceedings*, https://nawa.gov.pl/en/recognition/recognition-for-academic-pur poses/initiating-the-habilitation-proceedings, Accessed on 23 October 2022.

Ramzy, A. (2016) *What Was the Cultural Revolution?* https://www.nytimes.com/2016/05/15/world/asia/china-cultural-revolution-explainer.html, Accessed on 23 October 2022.

Robinson, N. (2014) Michael Gove battling 'the blob'. *BBC News*, https://www.bbc.co.uk/news/uk-politics-26008962, Accessed on 23 October 2022.

Royal Society. (2022) *How Much Funding Does the UK Get in Comparison with Other Countries*, https://royalsociety.org/topics-policy/projects/uk-research-and-european-union/role-of-EU-in-funding-UK-research/how-much-funding-does-uk-get-in-comparison-with-other-countries/, Accessed on 23 October 2022.

Shamoo, A. (2011) *Who Assassinated Iraqi Academics?* Foreign Policy in Focus, https://fpif.org/who_assassinated_iraqi_academics/, Accessed on 23 October 2022.

Simplilearn. (2022) *10 Major Leadership Theories Every Manager Should Master in 2023, UK: Simplilearn*, https://www.simplilearn.com/top-leadership-theories-every-manager-should-know-article, Accessed on 23 October 2022.

University of Adelaide. (2018) *Professors as Leaders*, https://www.adelaide.edu.au/hr/organisational-development/performance/professors-as-leaders, Accessed on 23 October 2022.

University of Birmingham. (2022) *Inaugural Lecture Series 2022–2023*, https://www.birmingham.ac.uk/university/colleges/socsci/events/inaugural-lectures/index.aspx, Accessed on 23 October 2022.

University of Cambridge. (2022) *Welcome to Equality, Diversity & Inclusion*, www.equality.admin.cam.ac.uk, Accessed on 23 October 2022.

University of Oxford. (2022) *Equality Policy*, https://edu.admin.ox.ac.uk/equality-policy, Accessed on 23 October 2022.

World Health Organisation Special Initiative for Mental Health (2019–2023), https://apps.who.int/iris/handle/10665/310981, Accessed on 23 October 2022.

Assessing research environment, research income and institutional and departmental research strategies

A framework for self-assessment by university faculties in the UK

Prepared by Prof. Marilyn Leask, University of Bedfordshire, October 2010

The purpose of this framework is to provide details of characteristics of high-quality research environments for departments to use in reviewing their provision and in planning and articulating their improvement journey. The evidence base for the framework is provided by an analysis of one-third of the institutional submissions to the UK research assessment exercise (RAE, 2008). The framework builds on these data and the professional knowledge of the author having spent 18 months engaging with the RAE 2008 as an education panel member and the criteria for judging quality.

- Part 1 Criteria for assessing the research environment **provided for students**;
- Part 2 Criteria for assessing the research environment **provided for staff**;
- Part 3 Indicators of excellence from research income data;
- Part 4 Assessing published outputs;
- Part 5 Institutional/departmental research strategy.

Part 1: Criteria for assessing the research environment *provided for students*

Student data

- doctoral degree numbers are sufficient to create a supportive environment;
- completion rate is close to or higher than the national average (the relevant national higher education funding body may be able to provide these averages);
- the student body is diverse and adds an international dimension to the research environment

Resources

- if necessary, a recruitment strategy is employed to try to ensure an intake of sufficient students to provide a vibrant culture – note circumstances of institutions with significant numbers of part-time students or in remote locations should be considered;
- student bursaries are available from internal or external sources e.g. to ensure an international student body;
- library and online services are available similar to those available to staff, as below;
- a designated research resource room for academics and/or students exists and is well equipped;
- post-doctoral fellowships are available for national and international students funded by internal or external sources.

Training programme

- systematic programme exists;
- team supervision used to give good support to students;
- collaboration across faculties.

Courses

- MRes and research methods training available;
- generic skills: academic writing, using sources, online services;
- specialist training e.g. qualitative analysis;
- post-grad summer schools/weekends for all on courses requiring dissertations with visiting speakers and seminars.

Seminars

- regularity and frequency e.g. 10 events per year or more;
- formal and informal;
- range of external/international speakers, including research users from time to time;
- range of topic and interdisciplinary;
- speaker expertise.

Support for transition to academic world

- are students supported to attend national and international conferences?
- is there support for student publishing: refereed journals; books/chapters; web; other print media?
- students are entered for awards e.g. best dissertation etc.;
- doctoral-level students have a chance to be engaged in funded research;
- annual student conference occurs with all students presenting – format as for proper conferences.

Part 2: Criteria for assessing the research environment *provided for staff*

Research groupings

- groups and staffing of groups appears to be logical;
- professorial staff head up research areas;
- journals are based with research groups;
- research group meetings are regular and develop the research culture.

Staff support and development

- staff are allocated research mentors;
- staff undertaking their own doctoral studies have fees remission;
- staff undertaking their own doctoral studies have timetable relief;
- a research development fund is available for pump priming new areas of work;
- access is provided to successful bids and specialised support for bid writing;
- appraisals of research and writing plans are undertaken by professors;
- study leave, sabbaticals, protected time: amount and frequency are in line with norms for the subject; the process for access to research leave is clear;
- workshops are held for staff capacity building e.g. on submission of bids, theorising applications, developing methodologies, introduction to new methods such as systematic reviews; methodological expertise is built: qualitative and quantitative;
- new supervisors are paired with experienced supervisors.

New staff

- support is provided for teaching fellows to become research fellows;
- systematic induction is given into research and the academic role;
- probation requirements are supported e.g. the organisation provides mentoring, a structured induction programme, an analysis of needs with development then of an individualised support programme;
- first grant support for new staff e.g. internal or through support for application to providers of support for new researchers.

Part 3: Indicators of excellence from research income data

- range of funders: charities, government agencies; ESRC, regions/local authority, international;
- externally funded post-doctoral fellowships for home and international students;
- average research income per member of staff: is around or higher than the national average (the relevant national higher education funding body may be able to provide these averages).

Part 4: Assessing the quality of research outputs

The criteria for judging the excellence of outputs used in the 2008 RAE were originality, significance and rigour.

Originality: original research

- grapples with new or complex problems (what are the core problems in our disciplines – is there research we could do collectively to bring new insights to these);
- is not a replication of other work;
- does not just apply well-used methods to straightforward problems;
- tackles existing problems in new ways;
- literature reviews e.g. from PhD/EdD theses can demonstrate originality if they analyse the field in new ways, or provide new conceptualisations;
- methods used for PhD/EdD work could be published and count where the methods are original.

Significance: the work

- addresses important practical current problems and provides trustworthy results;
- may be empirical or may be theoretical;
- may provide new conceptualisations for either the policy or practice audience;
- is impactful on policymakers or practitioners;
- provides value for use/impact over time;
- affect the thinking of others: theoreticians, practitioners and policymakers.

Rigour may be demonstrated through

- methodological rigour; theoretical robustness; reliability and validity, integrity, consistency and ethical considerations;
- 4*: quality that is world leading in terms of originality, significance and rigour, reaching high standards, providing new directions to thinking;
- 3*: quality that is internationally excellent in terms of originality, significance and rigour, but which nonetheless falls short of the highest standards of excellence – the work might be well regarded internationally (or of a standard equivalent to internationally influential work);
- 2*: quality that is recognised internationally in terms of originality, significance and rigour; of sufficient quality to have been published in an international leading journals, although not necessarily published there;
- 1*: quality that is recognised nationally in terms of originality, significance and rigour, acceptable for publication in a national peer-reviewed journal;
- ungraded: quality that falls below the standard of nationally recognised work or work that does not meet the published definition of research for the purposes of this assessment e.g. teaching materials.

Part 5: Institutional/departmental research strategy

Mission statement and research strategy

- mission statement sets out vision to be world class e.g. supporting research of national and international excellence, ensuring link between research and teaching, engaging in applied/cross-disciplinary research linked with strategies for user consultation/informing research users;
- research strategy demonstrates a planned and resourced improvement journey.

Institutional investment

- library: holdings – books, journals, interlibrary loan, advice from librarians;
- online services: desktop the staff and students; 24-hour of IT access;

- funding:
  - o devolved to research groups;
  - o financial support to new researchers and for the development of small-scale projects; dedicated research administrator;
  - o research leave (competitive basis).
- seminars/conference programme:
  - o regular internal research-based conferences;
  - o annual research days/research staff conference – perhaps with students, international and national speakers;
  - o focused on capacity building – perhaps run by students as part of induction into academic life.
- research support unit:
  - o full-time specialist staff;
  - o supports dissemination, knowledge transfer, user engagement and monitoring e.g. checking publishing happens and that academics are supported in press releases and gaining media coverage in press as well as practitioner and professional journals to reach relevant user groups;
  - o internal research newsletters;
  - o supports bid process: costing, managing, archiving, IP management;
  - o monitors outputs and activity year on year e.g. records of authored books, edited books, book chapters, peer-reviewed papers, funds for research and consultancy, publications in other media, number of research projects, influence on practice, % engagement of staff in research – is it growing?

Institutional/departmental structures and processes

- partnerships, networking and collaboration:
  - o international:
  - o visiting professors national and international provide input to staff and student seminars/training days;
  - o links with international universities/collaborative research/teaching;
  - o international staff exchanges;
  - o strategy for ensuring student cohort is international;
  - o formal collaborations.
  - o interdisciplinarity:
  - o collaboration across the university in research, methodologies, and theoretical work;

○ graduate school exists with shared teaching across the university;
○ research and capacity building takes place between faculties;
○ formal collaborations.
○ research community: clear sense of purpose and good foundations on which to build? collegiality, departments have designated research coordinators.
• quality assurance:
○ research board/committee operates effectively;
○ peer review of research applications before submissions;
○ monitoring quality and progress of funded projects;
○ research strategy;
○ research ethics.

Reference

RAE. (2008) *Research Assessment Exercise Panels of Assessment*, Cheltenham: HESA, https://www.hesa.ac.uk/support/documentation/research-framework/rae-2008.

Political impact on the professoriat and freedom of speech for academics

An example from Poland

Professor Jan Fazlagić, Professor in Management at the Poznan University of Economics and Business Poznan, Poland

Poland has a long-established university system with one of the oldest universities in the world, established in the 14th century. However, Poland's loss of independence when it became part of the Soviet Union Bloc in 1945, after the Yalta Conference (where Polish people had no say over what happened to their country), was to have a profound effect on the professoriat that lasts to this day.

The Soviet system favoured the working class as leaders in creating a socialist society. Members of the intelligentsia were treated with suspicion, a situation exacerbated by the fact that pre-war Polish intelligentsia were also known for their predominantly anti-communist stance. The introduction of the new political system by the communists in post-1945 Poland also included a plan to create a 'new' socialist intelligentsia; professors with a pre-war academic track record, or even students entering universities after WWII with a pre-war intelligentsia family background, were discriminated against unless they openly admitted their loyalty to the new system and denounced their pre-war Polish patriotic values.

To further break up the pre-war academic culture and traditions, many universities in Poland were broken up into specialised higher education institutions. For example, medical science, agriculture and economics were separated from the traditional universal universities.

It is worth mentioning that pre-war professors in Poland represented world-class standards in many scientific disciplines, including STEAM. Polish mathematicians from the University of Lwów (now Lviv in Ukraine) created the world famous Lwów School of Mathematics. Young Polish researchers from the University of Poznan broke the German codes of Enigma, which paved the way for Alan Turing and the teams at Bletchley Park in the UK to decrypt German messages in the Second World War.[1] Another example of the high quality of education in Polish universities before WWII is the story of Stanislaw Ulam,[2] who received a master's and a PhD from the Lvov Polytechnic Institute. In 1939, Ulam fled Poland, shortly before the German invasion in September. In 1943, he was invited to work on the Manhattan Project at Los Alamos, which produced the atom bomb, and subsequently worked on thermo-nuclear reactions.

In the Soviet period, Poland, as with all countries of the Eastern Bloc, became a partly militarised society that manifested itself in high government expenditure on the defence budget and those segments of the education system that might have a positive impact on the military performance in an anticipated war with the West. Specifically, physics and mathematics were promoted as the means to supply the socialist economy with highly skilled labour for the defence industry. It should not be surprising that much effort was made to support the development of physical education, both at K–12 education and so-called academies of physical education – also with the intention to provide the socialist society with fit and healthy future soldiers. On the other hand, social science research, especially sociology, was considered to be suspicious as part of 'bourgeois science'. Research in economics and management also suffered from strong political influence. In order to make an academic career in the field of economics and management, a professor had to distinctly promote and provide scientific evidence on the superiority of the socialist economy and the socialist enterprise over their Western counterparts. Only the most ardent followers of the systems were allowed to maintain research contacts with Western universities. Not surprisingly, many research fellows, including those participating in the Fulbright programme, were members of, or recommended by, the Communist Party (see for example: Onet, 2008; Wieczorek, 2020, 2022).

One aspect of the academic life during communist times that there is not space here to discuss in detail was the infiltration of academic circles by the communist Secret Service. At the same universities, according to some accounts, up to 50% of all professors were secret agents of the Polish or Russian intelligence.

These various mechanisms produced professors with dubious academic skills but loyal to the Polish government. A term was coined, BMW (*bierny-mierny-ale-wierny* – Eng. *passive-mediocre but loyal*) to describe their academic prowess.

Post-1989 – the year Poland re-gained independence

Post-1989, there was no all-out retribution on these professors in the Polish universities. On the contrary, many professors who had been the proponents of the previous system continued their academic careers in the free Poland, to the dismay of others who had suffered under the communist system. For example, pre-1989, many universities took very seriously the education in the field of propagating socialist ideas in the society. Post-1989, professors who specialised in this field simply changed the label into . . . *public relations* or started to teach marketing according to American textbooks hastily translated from English.

Post-1989, a short path to full professorship was provided to those academics who were not active in the Polish Communist Party or known to be the all-out supporters of the regime. The idea was to open up the professoriate to new ideas, but many of those professors promoted in the early 1990s would not qualify for the full professorship now.

These historical appointments of professors are relevant to the prospects of academics' careers today in many Polish universities, especially public ones. These professors were responsible for selecting and training newer generations of researchers in Poland, passing on many of their values and work habits. Therefore, the historical background of the Polish professorship is still of high relevance today, allowing academics to understand the current state of the matters in the Polish academic world. That the cultural legacy of the previous decades may remain in the hearts and souls of many Polish professors means younger generation professors may find they face invisible barriers to promotion.

To recapitulate, paths to professorship in Poland have been subject to many changes over the last decades. It is worth noting that many of the points made about the background of the Polish professorship are relevant to other socialist countries in the Eastern Bloc, including former Yugoslavia and Soviet Union countries.

Notes

1 *Forgotten heroes of the Enigma story*, www.nature.com/articles/d41586-018-06149-y.
2 www.atomicheritage.org/profile/stanislaw-ulam.

References

Onet. (2008) *Entuzjastyczny Pomocnik Rotfeld*, https://wiadomosci.onet.pl/kiosk/entuzjastyczny-pomocnik-rotfeld/v8kp4, Accessed on 23 October 2022.
Wieczorek, J. (2020) *Plagi Akademickie[Academic Plagues]*, Kraków: Wydawnictwo Gazety Polskiej.
Wieczorek, J. (2022) *Trąd W Pałacu Nauki. Ku Jakiej Cywilizacji Zmierza Świat AkademickI*, Kraków: Wydawnictwo Gazety Polskiej.

The REPOSE guidelines

Guidelines for the REPOrting of primary empirical research Studies in Education

Mark Newman and Diane Elbourne
(https://eppi.ioe.ac.uk/cms/Resources/Tools/
TheREPOSEGuidelines/tabid/759/Default.aspx)

What follows is background about the purpose of these guidelines and why are you might use them when you are writing academic articles. Please refer to the full document, which can be found on the University College London Institute of Education EPPI Centre's website, as above.

The guidelines provide a framework for academic articles, which mean your articles include all the information needed if they are to be referenced in a systematic review. Below I give you the background to the development of these guidelines, and I urge you to use them. When I'm writing an academic article I have them in front of me, and I use voice dictation to draft the article as I go through the suggested headings. I find it saves me a massive amount of time.

Background to the REPOSE guidelines: knowledge management using the internet

The REPOSE Guidelines were created in response to a need identified as the internet made the finding of academic papers easy.

The UK Labour government (1997–2010) put considerable funding into building the evidence base for policy. There were a number of national and international initiatives at this time, including OECD-coordinated initiatives, to develop knowledge management and information management strategies to take advantage of the opportunities that were emerging as the internet started to become widely used.

It is easy to forget how recent an innovation the internet is and how protocols for the use of digital technologies are still developing.

In 1995, following an educational visit to Australia where I saw what academics in teacher education were doing to explore the use of the internet to support teacher professional development, I had a meeting with the lead computing curriculum inspector for schools and teacher training in England. He knew of no one who was taking forward these ideas. I then had a meeting with an education minister about the possible uses of the internet to support teacher professional development, and it turned out that he had no idea what the internet was.

Ten years later, I had a knowledge management role in the government agency – the Teacher Training Agency for schools.

When ministers were looking at introducing primary modern foreign languages into the primary school, I was required to provide a briefing about what the evidence base was for effective pedagogical practices. I let a government contract for a systematic review and those undertaking it found 5000 relevant articles. However, many of the articles could not be included in any systematic review because they did not have sufficient information, for example about ethical approaches, sample sizes, whether the respondents were volunteers or not and so on.

The intention behind the REPOSE Guidelines was to improve the quality of articles so as to provide a foundation for the undertaking of systematic reviews.

I hope you enjoy using them as much as I do.

Marilyn Leask
January 2023.

Website

The REPOSE Guidelines: Guidelines for the REPOrting of Primary Empirical Research Studies in Education Mark Newman and Diane Elbourne, https://eppi.ioe. ac.uk/cms/Resources/Tools/TheREPOSEGuidelines/tabid/759/Default.aspx, Accessed on 30 October 2023.

Index